Books by William Ashworth

Hell's Canyon: The Deepest Gorge on Earth
The Wallowas: Coming of Age in the Wilderness
The Carson Factor
Under the Influence: Congress, Lobbies and the American
    Pork Barrel System
Nor Any Drop to Drink

NOR ANY DROP TO DRINK

by William Ashworth

SUMMIT BOOKS
New York

SUMMIT BOOKS and colophon are trademarks of Simon & Schuster
Designed by Irving Perkins Associates
Manufactured in the United States of America
1 2 3 4 5 6 7 8 9 10

Library of Congress Cataloging in Publication Data

Ashworth, William, date.
Nor any drop to drink.

Bibliography: p.
Includes index.
1. Water supply—United States.   2. Water—
Pollution—United States.   I. Title.
TD223.A83   1982   333.91′00973   82-10453

ISBN 0-671-43551-5
ISBN 0-671-45950-3 (pbk.)

FOR JOHN WESLEY POWELL (1834–1902),

geologist, explorer, and water crusader,
who told the Los Angeles International Irrigation
Congress of 1893: "I tell you, gentlemen, you are
piling up a heritage of conflict and litigation over
water rights, for there is not sufficient water to
supply the land."

CONTENTS

INTRODUCTION

IT WAS A good place to grow up in. There was a park with a tall slide, and a little river with minnows in it that you could catch in coffee cans if you were careful, and a college campus with old brick buildings and broad tree-shaded lawns and a clock in a tower with deep bells that boomed the hour and, at seven o'clock every evening, played a half-hour concert. This was Pullman, Washington, in the early 1950s. In the spring, there were butterflies on the lilac bush in our front yard; in the autumn, the leaves turned in the schoolyard, and the wheat-covered hills around town were golden with the weight of harvest. In the winter, snows came for sledding and building igloos and making snowballs to throw at my sister; icicles hung from the eaves to be broken off and delicately nibbled, and snowmen sprouted from every lawn in our neighborhood. And in the summer, there was the fountain on Main Street.

The fountain on Main Street was a public drinking fountain, a little stub of quarter-inch steel pipe sticking up in the middle of a small concrete basin on the side of the old City Ice Company plant, across the street from the J. C. Penney's building and next to the Washington Hotel. On the long, lazy summer afternoons, homeward bound from the swimming pool or the park or wherever it was we had happened to be going that day, my friend Andy Harris and I would ride our bikes through town and pause in the shade of the ice plant, the fan of cool air from the open doors washing over us, for a long, cold drink of that water. The water was passed through the plant's ice-making apparatus before bubbling out into the basin, and that made it a wonderful spot to come to on a hot day. The ice company, however, wasted no energy pumping it: it pumped itself. The plant was built over the site of the city's first deep-drilled well. When M. C. True had brought that well in, in 1890, the gusher had shot nearly ten feet high: Pullman's groundwater was under artesian pressure, and though you had to go down 150 feet or so to reach the stuff, when your drill finally bit into the aquifer you would be rewarded with a flow of such force that one early entrepreneur harnessed the upward-driving jet from his well to power the machinery in his meat-packing plant. In 1911 there were eighteen of these wells in operation, and Pullman was booming itself proudly as the Artesian City. By the time I was growing up there the luster of this label had been diminished somewhat, but the water still flowed; that fountain on the side of the ice plant was pure artesian water, bubbling from old man True's original well, supplying the ice company with its raw material, and then flowing under its own pressure to that cement-lined basin by the sidewalk where a couple of kids with bikes could stop and slake their thirsts in the heat of a 1950s summer afternoon.

I still have relatives in Pullman, and though I now live nearly seven hundred miles away I usually manage to get back for a visit at least once a year. In many ways, the town has changed very little. The same two-story brick buildings still line the old business district along Main Street; the clock tower with its singing bells still sprouts among green lawns on the college campus—now Washington State University—and small boys with bicycles still roam the city streets on hot summer afternoons. But they no longer stop in the shade of the old City Ice Company to quench their August thirsts with the icy water from Old Man True's original well. They can't: the ice plant is gone. A branch of one of the major Washington state banks occupies that lot now; it offers no public drinking fountain to passersby on the sidewalk, and if it did, the water would have to be pumped. Pullman's wells are still technically artesian, but they are no longer flowing. The static level in the wells now sits fifty to sixty feet below the surface, and the waters are declining at the rate of a foot and a half during an average year.

Pullman, the Artesian City, is going dry.

What has happened to Pullman's water supply? What has happened to the water supplies of Leoti, Kansas, and Trenton, New Jersey, and San Diego, California? What has happened in Elmhurst, Illinois, where the wells have declined an average of fourteen feet each year since 1960, forcing the inauguration of a massive water-conservation program to stretch available supplies until rights could be established and pipelines laid to import drinking water from Lake Michigan? What has happened in New York City, where the water department has run newspaper ads requesting children to rat on the water-use habits of their parents and the mayor's office has prepared serious contingency plans for distributing emergency supplies of bottled water to city residents in the increasingly likely event that the taps run dry? Why should water—the stuff of life—be suddenly in such overwhelmingly short supply around the country that one water expert refers to it, not jokingly, as "an endangered species" and another finds it necessary to publish a gloomy warning in a national magazine of large circulation that "there is no synwater industry to bail us out"? Where have we gone wrong?

This book is an attempt to explain.

...I

Paupers in the Midst of Plenty

LIFE ON EARTH is bound inextricably to the presence of water. It is the one unvarying necessity for all living things. There are life forms—the anaerobic bacteria—which can do very well without oxygen, and in fact are destroyed by exposure to it. There are creatures deep in caverns which can live without light; there are plants that can survive indefinitely without any food but sunlight and air. There is nothing that can live without water. Water is the basic material of protoplasm, the life stuff of the living cell. Stained red with iron and other necessary impurities, it becomes blood, to transport the body's nutrients and wash away its wastes. Sticky with sugar in the stem of plants, it becomes sap. We drink it; we grow our crops with it; we use it for a multitude of industrial purposes, for transport and for cooling, as a solvent and as a raw material, for food, for furniture, for books, for automobiles, for jewelry, for gasoline, and for everything else under the sun. "Noblest of the elements," sang the poet Pindar some twenty-five centuries ago, and for all the generations from that time down to this that truth has been constantly reaffirmed.

We Americans are the inheritors of a continent once richly endowed with this most precious of all natural resources. Early settlers found this land an Eden, laced with great rivers, bubbling with springs, bathed by sweet rains, and cupping some of the world's most magnificent freshwater lakes. William Bradford of the Plymouth Colony wrote of enjoying "the best water that ever we drank" out of the stream the Pilgrims had named, with marvelous creativity, Town Brook; settlers on the Connecticut were so enamored of its waters that they first named it the Fresh River, and the Dutch on Manhattan wrote home ecstatically of brooks "pleasant and proper for man and beast to drink, as well as agreeable to behold, affording cool and pleasant resting places." The Mohawk was "as clear as crystal and as fresh as milk." Farther west there was the Sangamon, with its "pure and transparent waters," and the Mississippi, "Father of Waters," and the Ohio, that "clear majestic tide" which the French knew as La Belle Rivière and whose "limpid waters" inspired the early traveler and historian Charles Fenno Hoffman to write effusively that the stream and its lush valley made "a moral picture whose colours are laid in the heart, never to be effaced."

Such was the wealth the colonists found—and proceeded to squander like spendthrift schoolboys. Today the Eden has vanished; the "limpid waters" and the "cool and pleasant resting places" are virtually gone. Large cities, farming regions, and even whole states report water shortages. Throughout the length and breadth of the continent, wells are running dry, pollutants are pouring into streams and seeping into aquifers, and once-sweet waters are turning saltier than the sea. Great cities, their own waters long since overcommitted or fouled beyond human use, reach hollow tentacles hundreds of miles into the surrounding countryside, sucking up whole rivers and diverting them across mountains and deserts and sprawling farmlands to the taps and toilets of their citizens. Farmers too move water about on a massive scale, bleeding rivers into tens of thousands of miles of irrigation ditches which finger out across the nation's croplands like the circulatory system of a gargantuan and bloated starfish. Increasingly, these water-transfer systems interlock, the intake pipes of one region creeping like furtive fingers into the water supply of another. New York City, Trenton, and Philadelphia jockey over the Delaware River; the state of Nebraska sues upstream interests in Wyoming for diverting too much water from the North Platte; west Texas casts covetous eyes on Louisiana's section of the Mississippi; and Denver, Phoenix, and Los Angeles, separated from each other by distances approaching a thousand miles, battle with escalating rancor over the limited resources of a single stream, the increasingly saline Colorado.

Even with these massive transfusion systems in place, there is seldom enough. New York City water—imports and all—is being used at a rate sixteen percent higher than engineers say the water system can safely supply, a water shortfall of some 200 million gallons per day. For Tucson, the figures are sixty-two percent and 37 million gallons. New Jersey's water demand outstrips its supply by 90 million gallons a day; California's daily deficit is 2.6 *billion* gallons. Long Island's three million residents draw their water from an underground reservoir that has become, in the words of one report, a "severely contaminated industrial sewer"; the water in the island's wells has turned into a witch's caldron of toxic chemicals, and many of them have had to be closed. On the Great Plains, the nation's breadbasket, groundwater supplies are expected to be exhausted in many areas by the year 2000, leaving farmers without enough water to grow crops.

Civil engineers and other professionals who work with water supply have a useful concept known as "safe yield," which may be described in simple terms as the amount of water a given supply system can dependably produce year after year, no matter what the weather does. A water system is said to be operating "within safe yield" if the demands for water deliveries from the system are less than the amount it will always be able to deliver even in the driest of years. This is, of course, the situation that all water systems would prefer to be in. Fewer and fewer are. All across the country, demand is growing while supply is shrinking, and in an alarming number of places the rising demand curve has crossed the falling supply curve and now runs above it. We are, in fact, perilously close to overtaxing our water supplies on a nationwide basis—to exceeding safe yield for the continent itself.

We thought the resource was limitless, but we were wrong. There are limits, and those limits have arrived. Our land still seems a land of plenty: but we have become paupers in the midst of it.

To understand how it is that here on our water planet we can come so close to running out of water, we must first understand a few things about the resource itself, and about the many ways in which we use it and—all too often—abuse it.

The earth contains enormous amounts of water. More than seventy percent of the planet's surface is covered with it, to depths that approach seven miles. There are 315 million cubic miles of it in the ocean basins, and 7 million cubic miles locked in the polar ice caps, and 53,000 cubic miles spangled out over the surface of the continents in the form of lakes, and ponds, and rivers, and sparkling mountain brooks. Nineteen million cubic miles interlace the solid ground beneath our feet; nearly 4,000 cubic miles float through the air over our heads. All in all, we have a planetary resource—conservatively estimated—of some 344 million cubic miles of water: about 379 quintillion gallons, enough to form a sphere nearly half the diameter of the moon. Enough to provide more than 88 trillion gallons for each man, woman, and child on the face of the earth.

Not all of this vast resource is available for our use, of course. More than ninety percent of it is ocean water, too salty for drinking or growing crops or even for most industrial purposes. Another six percent lies so deep in the earth —two miles and more—that no practical well can reach it. Thirty-four hundred cubic miles are locked up in the bodies of living things or tied into the soil in the form of "bound water," giving the soil its characteristic texture but unavailable for use by plants or for extraction by wells. More than seven million cubic miles are ice. When all these things are subtracted, barely 0.05 percent of the world's total water budget remains available for human use.

But even that tiny percentage works out to be an enormous amount. Our planetary freshwater resource—excluding the polar ice caps and the mountain glaciers—is some 162,000 cubic miles, enough to provide every person on earth with 42 million gallons. And this resource is constantly renewing itself. More than four trillion gallons of rain fall each day on the continental United States alone, approximately eighteen thousand gallons apiece for each of our 230 million citizens. By contrast, our daily bodily requirement—the amount of water we need to consume each day to stay alive—is only a little under two quarts apiece, or about thirteen thousand gallons in an average lifetime. We receive as a daily gift, free from the skies, nearly half again as much water as all of us will ever drink in our entire tenancy on this planet.

Given figures on this order of magnitude, it may be difficult to see where the crisis lies. If our drinking water is being replaced at a rate 36,000 times faster than we can drink it, why do we worry about running out? Where is the shortage? Is there a shortage at all?

When questioned directly in this manner, most water-supply experts would have to answer no. We have, and always will have, all the water we will ever need to live on. Nevertheless—and at the same time—we are experiencing severe water-resource problems, including problems of supply, in virtually every section of the country. We have no shortage, but we are running out of water just the same.

There are several reasons for this apparent paradox. To begin with, we use water for many things besides drinking; those two quarts we consume each day are only a tiny fraction of the amount we actually require. We use water to wash our hands, and wash our dishes, and flush our toilets, and cook our morning oatmeal and our evening vegetables. A five-minute shower with a conventional shower head takes twelve gallons; five minutes of watering the lawn or the garden consumes fifty gallons. All in all, the average American puts to direct use, running through the faucets of his home, not just two quarts but closer to ninety gallons of water every day. And that is barely the beginning. The same group of unusual characteristics—high specific heat, extreme fluidity, and unparalleled dissolving power—that make water indispensable to life also make it invaluable for industry, and as a consequence it is the most heavily used of our natural economic resources; there is not a single manufactured item in your house which did not require water for its production. The steel in your washing machine took roughly 4,500 gallons to produce; the rayon in your living-room carpet, about 50,000 gallons. The car in your driveway represents a water investment of about 100,000 gallons, plus another 200 or so every time you fill the gas tank. Mining the few grams of gold in your wedding ring may have taken as much as 2,500 gallons. A sugar-processing plant uses roughly four million gallons per day; a plastics plant, 180,000; a large brewery, as much as fifteen million. A coal-fired power plant uses about 900 gallons of water for every kilowatt-hour of electricity produced—not counting the water used to mine and process the coal and transport it to the plant in the first place. All in all, manufacturing and energy production in this country use a total of 140 billion gallons of water every day, or about 600 gallons per person.

Added to our 90-gallon individual allotments, that makes 690 gallons.

Then there is food production, and that—thanks largely to irrigated agriculture—takes even more. A bushel of wheat represents a water investment of 15,000 gallons; a thousand-pound steer, some 3.5 million. A single egg on your breakfast table took the equivalent of nearly 2,000 glasses of water to get there. All told, the water required to put an average day's food on the table for a family of four works out to about 3,200 gallons, or enough to fill a small swimming pool. The weight of the food consumed is about twenty-four pounds; the weight of the water behind it, just under thirteen tons.

When agricultural, industrial, energy, and domestic needs are added together, our per-capita water use as a nation turns out to be not the survival level of two quarts, but approximately 1,500 gallons per day. We use not one thirty-six-thousandth part of our daily gift from the skies, but closer to one tenth.

Adding to the difficulties posed by the fact that our use of the resource is so enormous are the difficulties posed by another and more ominous fact: the resource itself is shrinking.

To be sure, this is not a literal shrinkage. Water is among the most difficult of substances to destroy, and the small amounts we do manage to break up—for instance, in the production of hydrogen by means of electrolysis—are more than offset by the amounts we create by burning hydrocarbon fuels such as gasoline and natural gas. (There are also, many geologists believe, small amounts of water—called "juvenile water"—constantly being created deep in the earth and finding their way to the surface through cracks in the deep ocean floor.) Nevertheless, the amount we have available for most uses is constantly and alarmingly decreasing. The reason is pollution. We are not destroying our water; but we are rendering it unusable, and that amounts to the same thing.

The scope of this problem is immense, and we are nearly all affected by it. Its ubiquitousness is probably best shown by a 1978 government report, *The Nation's Water Resources 1975–2000*, which listed only eight states as having no serious occurrences of groundwater pollution, and only two—Montana and Kansas—as having no serious occurrences of surface water pollution. Little water escapes this invasion. In some places, even the rain is polluted—and since the rain is the ultimate source of all freshwater on earth, this pollution has extremely serious consequences, even though it is (so far) very minor.

Finally—and perhaps most important of all—there is the question of distribution. Despite the pollution, despite the huge amounts we use, there is really no serious threat that we will run out of water in this country. We have enough, and we will continue to have enough for the foreseeable future. The problem is not that it is inadequate. The problem is that it is not in the right places.

About 1.6 quadrillion gallons of rain fall on the United States each year—enough so that, if it were evenly distributed, it would cover the entire country to a depth of more than two and a half feet. But it is far from evenly distributed. More than forty percent of the nation's rain falls east of the Mississippi, on just twenty-four percent of the land. Little South Carolina (31,000 square miles) receives more than 26 trillion gallons of rain a year; giant Nevada (110,000 square miles) receives barely half of that. Annual rainfall at Baltimore, Maryland, is more than five feet; at Yuma, Arizona, it is less than three inches. The upshot of these discrepancies is that some places get ample rainfall; some places get adequate rainfall; and some places do not get nearly enough. Generally speaking, the ample lands are in the East; the adequate lands, in the Midwest. The arid lands are in the West.

The eastern border of the arid lands can be defined with some precision. John Wesley Powell, the one-armed Civil War veteran, water activist, and Grand Canyon explorer, pointed that border out more than a hundred years ago: it is that line to the east of which the land receives more than twenty inches of rain per year. With more than twenty, you can grow crops unirrigated; with less than twenty, you cannot. Because this twenty-inch rainfall contour, or isohyet, is located on the Great Plains, far from the influence of mountain ranges or ocean air masses, it is almost perfectly north–south; and because of a lucky accident of the early mapmakers' art, it is easy to spot. As Powell wrote in his *Report on the Arid Lands of the United States*, the first document to realistically assess the problems and potentials of the American West:

> The eastern boundary of the Arid Region . . . is doubtless more or less meandering in its course throughout its whole

extent from south to north, being affected by local conditions of rainfall . . . but in a general way it may be represented by the one hundredth meridian, in some places passing to the east, in others to the west, but in the main to the east.

Get out a map of the United States and locate the hundredth meridian on it, tracing it from Canada to Mexico on its thousand-mile journey down the Great Plains. Beginning near the small town of Carpenter, on the Canadian border, it sweeps down through North Dakota and South Dakota, bisects Nebraska, plunges on into Kansas. Dodge City sits directly on it. It slices the panhandle neatly off Oklahoma, runs the border between Oklahoma and Texas for 130 miles, and slices southward into the Texas heartland, nicking Sagerton, separating Sweetwater from Abeline, and running down the valley of the upper Nueces River. Two dozen miles above Laredo, it fords the Rio Grande and disappears into Mexico. East of this line, generally speaking, there is enough water for most purposes; west of it, there is not.

Perhaps this would not be a problem, but for two reasons. The first is that this nation grew up on the Eastern Seaboard and formed its water-use practices there, where there is always plenty of rainfall. And the second is that the historic tendency in this country has always been to move westward. Landing from the Atlantic, the early European settlers moved up the coastal valleys toward the setting sun, pooled briefly behind the Alleghenies and then breeched them, flooded the Midwest, fingered out across the Great American Desert like the edge of a rising tide. By the middle of the nineteenth century, the wave of advancement had reached the Pacific. Here, because there was no place further to go, it stopped. The energy behind it, however, remained; people from the East continued to move westward, filling in the gaps in California and Oregon and Washington, spilling over backward into Idaho and Arizona and the Rocky Mountain states. This movement is still going on today. Between the 1970 and 1980 censuses, for example, the population of New York State declined by about 1.6 percent; at the same time,

AVERAGE ANNUAL PRECIPITATION INCHES

the population of Oregon climbed by nearly seventeen percent. The population of North Carolina grew modestly, from
5.1 to 5.6 million, or approximately ten percent; the population of Arizona exploded from less than 1.8 million to more
than 2.4 million, a growth of better than thirty-six percent.
Overall, those states west of the hundredth meridian grew at
a rate two and one half times faster than their Eastern cousins. And since the West is so much drier than the East, this
means that the actual per-capita amount of rain which fell in
the vicinity of each U.S. citizen decreased over this period
at a rate far faster than the population increase alone would
indicate. We have water; but we are rapidly and methodi-
cally moving ourselves away from it. And in the process, we
are creating severe and sometimes unsolvable problems.
Our Sun Belt cities grow; but it is rain, not sun, that we must
have in order to provide water.

As the population has shifted westward, so has the agriculture that supports it. As late as 1920, a full fifty percent of all
U.S. crops were grown east of the tier of states—North Dakota to Texas—that contains the hundredth meridian. Today,
that amount has shrunk to less than thirty-four percent. But
because crops cannot grow on the West's tiny rainfall, this
westward shift in agriculture has led to a veritable explosion
in irrigation. Between 1940 and 1980, irrigated acreage in
the West more than doubled, with some areas—western
Kansas, for example—showing increases of as much as three
thousand percent.

All this, of course, has put a tremendous overburden on
the West's scanty water resources. But not all water distribution problems are found in the West; even the rain-rich
East is showing signs of the kinds of stress caused by not
having enough water in the right places. The reason, here,
is not too little water for a given locality, but too many people.

Despite the westward movement, most of our population
still lives in the East, clumped into cities that have simply
outgrown their ability to efficiently supply water at the rates
their citizens demand it. New York City's use figure, for ex-

ample, is 190 gallons per person per day; with a population of 7.4 million and a rainfall of forty-two inches a year, this means that even if the city could collect and utilize every drop that fell—instead of the one drop in three that is closer to reality—it would still need a catchment basin ten miles wide and nearly one hundred miles long merely to keep up with daily demand. Other cities in the East and the South—Boston, Philadelphia, Washington, Atlanta—are experiencing similar difficulties. The problems caused by the concentration of water demand can lead to other problems, many of them severe. New York's financial crisis has been caused at least partially by the capital demands made on the city's government by the need to maintain and expand the water system. Groundwater withdrawal from beneath Orlando, Florida, has opened great caverns in the earth, and Orlando has begun collapsing in upon itself; Houston, with the same problem but different underlying geology, is slowly sinking into the sea.

Limits are limits, and even when those limits seem very high indeed, it is still possible to bump up against them. And when those limits are imposed, not by humans, but by nature—in this case, by the finite size of this round wet ball we call the earth—there is no way that bumping up against them is not going to hurt.

Perhaps the real problem is one of attitudes. Children of a culture born in a water-rich environment, we have never really learned how important water is to us. We understand it, but we do not respect it; we have learned to manipulate it, but we have never really learned to handle it. Where it has been cheap and plentiful, we have ignored it; where it has been rare and precious, we have spent it with shameful and unbecoming haste. We have shunted it from place to place across the landscape with reckless abandon; we have pried open great natural storehouses of it, and spent millions of years' accumulation in a few short decades. Everywhere, we have poured filth into it. We have done these things purposefully; we have not done them maliciously; but we have done them. And in the long run, that is all that really counts.

Turn the tap; water runs out of it. Pull the plug; water runs away down the drain. We all do these things perhaps a dozen times a day, and we never pay too much attention to them. Water is something we take for granted, like breathing in and out or watching the sun come up. But we cannot afford to take it for granted much longer. For many years, knowingly or unknowingly, we have been deferring the costs of our water-use practices into the future. Now the future has arrived, and the bill is about to come due.

CHAPTER **2**

Circles of Mist and Storm

OVER THE LONG centuries since our birth as a species, we humans have increasingly managed to divorce ourselves from the natural world. We have created clothing to protect our bodies from the elements, and tamed fire to warm ourselves in the winter, and built houses to keep the rain and the snow and the wind from invading our territorial space. In our cities we are insulated from the touch of earth by pavement, and closed away from all but a sliver of sky by the walls of tall buildings, and protected from the sight of all green and growing things except those we have tamed and placed there on purpose—usually not for their naturalness, but for their ability to function as decorations. Locked behind windows of glass that frame the world like a picture, breathing filtered air whose temperature has been determined by the flick of a dial, we can be forgiven for assuming that what the natural world does is no longer of concern to us. But we make this assumption at our own peril.

Water generally fits into the category of things which we presume we have tamed. Reservoirs and pumps collect our water for us; pipes deliver it, and gleaming faucets, designed by decorators, present it to us prettily cleaned and sterilized and adjusted to the temperature we personally ordain from moment to moment. But the illusion of control is just that: an illusion. The water in our reservoirs and pipes and faucets remains water, and as water is still part of the hydrologic cycle, the great planetary water engine that drives all life on this green and rolling earth. The rivers still gather the rain; the seas gather the rivers, and the sun gathers the seas, lifting them skyward in the form of clouds to drift over the land and fall as rain once more. It is these agelong and endless chains of evaporation and precipitation—these circles of mist rising and storm falling—that set the limits within which we exist; and as we approach those limits, it becomes increasingly necessary for us to understand what they are, and to realize, as we unfortunately still have not done, that we cannot eliminate them, or even alter them by more than the smallest of transient amounts.

The hydrologic cycle has its roots in the special and unique properties of this commonplace but altogether remarkable substance we call water.

Some of these properties can only be described as miraculous. Water is, for example, among the least viscous of fluids; it flows easily and rapidly from the moment it thaws, moving downhill in obedience to gravity over even the slightest of imperceptible slopes. This extreme fluidity also makes it easy to pump, a fact which renders it ideal for use as a transportation medium in a complex circulatory system such as a human bloodstream. Water has an extremely high surface tension and an even higher wetting ability, factors which together are responsible for the phenomenon of capillarity—the ability of water to creep upward, in apparent defiance of gravity, through the tiny pores of the soil and the thin, hollow filaments in the stems of plants. It is the closest thing we have to a universal solvent: given enough time, it can dissolve nearly anything. A glass of water sitting on your table is slowly becoming a very dilute solution of glass molecules, rivers running to the sea are dissolving their beds as well as wearing them away, and the sea itself has accumulated so many dissolved solids over the long millimillennia of its existence that out of each cubic yard of ocean water nearly a full cubic foot will be composed of ions of any of several thousand different substances, ranging from common salt to silver, platinum, and gold.

When water doesn't dissolve a solid, it often interacts in other interesting ways with it. It may form a suspension, breaking the material down into small enough particles so that they spread evenly through it and do not readily settle out. A suspension retains the chemical properties of the solid and adds to them the fluidity of a liquid. In extreme cases, the suspended material will break down into small enough units that it will *never* settle out, forming a "colloid"—such as milk—with some of the properties of a suspension and some of a solution. Or the water may invade a substance on an even more intimate level, entering into its molecular structure as so-called "water of crystallization" and causing it to become more rigid and more tightly organized than it was by itself. The sugar on your breakfast table, the washing soda in your laundry, the plaster on your walls, and the concrete in your driveway all contain large amounts of water, chemically unchanged but bound into the structure of the host molecules and responsible for most of the physical qualities we have come to associate with the resulting material—the crystals of the sugar and the washing soda, the hardness of the plaster, the strength and durability of the concrete.

Of all the unusual properties of water, however, none is more unusual—or more vitally important—than its behavior in relation to heat and cold. Water has a higher specific heat than virtually any other substance on earth, which means that it can absorb proportionately enormous amounts of energy without appreciably changing its own temperature. This helps to temper the climate of our water planet, keeping the temperature extremes within limits that life can tolerate. For a small molecule, water has an extremely high boiling point; fluorine, for example, which has a molecule almost precisely the same size as water, boils at minus 306 degrees

Fahrenheit, more than 500 degrees lower than water's 212. Water is the only substance known which exists, under normal earth-surface conditions of temperature and pressure, in all three states of matter—solid (ice), liquid (water), and gas (water vapor). Perhaps most peculiar of all, water is the only common substance that expands rather than contracts when it freezes. Ice at 32 degrees Fahrenheit is nine to eleven percent larger than water at the same temperature. Because of this, ice floats—an extremely important fact without which the seas would have long since frozen solid from the bottom up, locking the planet in a perpetual winter in which no life stirred.

It is this remarkable set of relationships between water and heat which gives birth to the hydrologic cycle. In its basic form, the cycle is quite simple. Sunlight falling on those great planetary solar-energy collectors, the seas, raises the energy level of the molecules in the surface layers of the water. Some of these molecules convert to their gaseous form, water vapor. Water vapor is lighter than air; it rises quickly through the atmosphere until it reaches the cool upper levels, where it condenses back into liquid in the form of tiny droplets, still light enough to float on the wind but heavy enough to rise no further. Clouds of these droplets gather together and are blown over the land. In the clouds, the droplets find each other and begin accreting into larger and larger drops. Eventually, these drops become big enough that the winds can no longer support them. They fall as rain. The rain runs into the rivers; the rivers run into the sea, and the process begins all over, as it has for the last several billion years, as it will continue as long as the sun and the waters exist.

Because this basic process is so simple, there is a temptation to dismiss it as something thoroughly understood and therefore irrelevant. This would be a grievous error, for two reasons. The first is that the hydrologic cycle is a dynamic phenomenon, not a static one, and as such is under the control of a subtle and constantly shifting array of forces—wind speed, air temperature, variations in land surface and tem-

perature, and the like—which make predicting its operation
in any but the most general terms a very chancy business at
best. And the second is that the basic hydrologic cycle is not
the only one that exists. There are cycles within the cycle,
and cycles within those, and crossover loops between cycles,
and the upshot of it all is that once a water molecule lifts out
of the sea on its sun-given wings, the possible pathways
looming before it are so multitudinous and so tangled that
no one could possibly foresee where—or when—it will
eventually come back home.

Our ignorance of this maze of potentialities is one of the
major reasons our water supply is currently in trouble, and it
would be well for us to examine a few of them now.

The North American continent is approximately three
thousand miles wide, with the United States stretching across it, as the song says, from sea to shining sea. East to west,
the nation is divided into three roughly equal parts by two
prominent north–south lines, the Mississippi River and the
eastern escarpment of the Rocky Mountains. The eastern and
western thirds are mountainous; the central third is flat and
relatively featureless. A great arm of the Atlantic, the Gulf of
Mexico, cuts inward along the southern border of the country, through the eastern and halfway through the central portions, providing a maritime climatic influence clear to the
center of the continent. In the Northeast, a series of large
freshwater seas, the Great Lakes, serves the same maritime
function. Thus the eastern portion of the continent is dominated by water-related features to a far greater extent than is
the West.

Weather patterns move over this huge and varied landscape in a generally west-to-east pattern, fed by the hydrologic cycle and driven by an Earth trying constantly to turn
out from under its mantle of air. Born in the cold crucible of
the Gulf of Alaska, moisture-laden winds sweep inland over
western Canada and are deflected south by the Coriolis Effect, the drag of the earth's rotation which causes whirlpools
to circle clockwise in the Northern Hemisphere, counter-
clockwise in the Southern. On their curving course east and
then south, these winds strike the mountains of the West,

losing their moisture to the wet Pacific Northwest, and by the time they have crossed the Rockies to the Great Plains they are mostly dry. Here they encounter winds moving north from the Gulf of Mexico, the western limb of a Coriolis-induced swirl centered on the North Atlantic. The gulf winds are wet. The two air masses mingle, forming an unstable mixture which moves northward over the Ohio Valley and the Alleghenies, raining as it goes. Evaporation from the Great Lakes replaces the moisture lost to rain over the Midwest, and the air is still wet and unstable as it hits the great mountain masses of the Northeast, rains its heart out, and exits eastward over the Atlantic toward Europe.

It is this great sweep of weather that determines our general rainfall patterns: wet in the East and the Pacific Northwest, semiarid over the Great Plains, bone dry in the Southwest. It is not the sole determinant, however; local conditions can alter things drastically.

One of the first detours faced by a raindrop in its trip through the hydrologic cycle is caused when it runs up against the continental coastline. Land gains and loses heat much more rapidly than water, and as a consequence where the two come together there is always a zone of fluctuating and battling air masses. If the land is colder than the water, air from the sea will cool as it approaches the shore; the cooler air can hold less moisture, and rain results, pulling the water out of the clouds before it has gotten more than a mile or two inland. This is why coastal areas, particularly in the cooler latitudes, tend to have so much rain—and why inland areas, as a consequence, have so much less: the rain has dropped out of the air before it gets there.

If the land is warmer than the water, the air heats up instead of cooling as it passes over the coast, and unless rain is already pouring out of an incoming cloud there will be no rain at all: in fact, the cloud is as likely as not to disappear. In the warmer latitudes, the land is always warmer than the water. It is this that accounts for the sunny climates—and chronic water shortages—of such places as Florida and southern California.

If a cloud manages to carry its water past the barrier of a

cool coastline, the next hazard it meets is likely to be the so-called adiabatic phenomenon, caused by fetching up against a coast-paralleling chain of mountains. The word "adiabatic" technically means occurring without loss or gain of heat, which can get confusing because although adiabatic-caused rainfall does not involve a change of heat, it does involve a change of temperature. This seemingly impossible condition is the result of variations in air pressure. Air currents hitting mountains are deflected upward; they carry their water vapor with them. The higher they go, the less pressure there is on them from layers of air above; the less pressure there is, the farther apart the molecules of the air spread. The air mass becomes larger, and the same amount of heat must spread over a greater amount of territory. A temperature drop results. The water vapor, of course, responds to this temperature drop as it does to any other: it condenses out into rain. As a result, the windward side of a mountain chain is always wetter than the leeward side.

The differences can be immense. The north side of Mount Waialeale, on the Hawaiian island of Kauai, is the world's wettest place, with an average annual rainfall of more than 450 inches; a few miles to the southwest, on the Na Pali coast, near-desert conditions exist. In the Pacific Northwest, the Puget Sound and Willamette Valley areas of Washington and Oregon are wet, with forty inches and more of rain each year; beyond the Cascade Mountains to the east, rainfall drops to little more than nine inches.

The dry leeward side of a mountain range is known as its "rain shadow." One such shadow extends eastward from the Rocky Mountains in Colorado. The city of Denver sits in it —which is one reason the Denver water department has had to burrow through the Front Range, to the wet west side of the mountains, to gather water to satisfy the city's immense and growing thirst.

More detours await a drop of water after it hits the ground. The ground-based portion of the hydrologic cycle is largely determined by the continental drainage pattern—the course and shape of rivers, the channels that rainfall takes as it runs off the land and back to the waiting sea. In the United States, this drainage pattern is dominated by two great watershed divides: the crest of the Alleghenies, separating the waters of the Atlantic from the waters of the Gulf of Mexico, and the crest of the Rockies—the so-called Continental Divide—which separates the waters of the Pacific from the waters of the Gulf. Thus the continental United States is divided into three drainage areas, just as it is divided into three topographical regions.

The drainage-area boundaries, however, do not follow those of the topographic regions.

The Atlantic drainage area is small, with short, powerful rivers fed by the heavy rainfall of the East. Only one of these, the St. Lawrence, is large enough to class with the world's great rivers; only a few others, the Hudson, the Delaware, the Potomac, perhaps the Susquehanna and the Savannah, can really be called major watercourses.

The Pacific drainage area is not much larger; it has numerous small coastal streams and two large interior river systems, the Columbia and the Colorado, draining the northern and southern sections of the Rocky Mountains. Between these two great rivers lies an enormous area, the Great Basin, with no drainage at all; the little rivers fed by its tiny rainfall run down from the hills, pool on the flats, and evaporate back into the sky. The Great Basin covers most of Nevada, half of Utah, and parts of Idaho, Oregon, and California.

The central drainage area is, by contrast to the Atlantic and Pacific drainage areas, immense. It covers the entire central topographic tier plus large sections to the east and west. Branches of it reach as far toward the Atlantic as the states of Virginia and New York; as far toward the Pacific as New Mexico and the Montana/Idaho border. Virtually all of this great region is drained by a single stream, the Mississippi, and its two great tributaries, the Missouri and the Ohio; in all of the central drainage region, only the short streams of the Gulf Coast and the arid Rio Grande Basin of west Texas and central New Mexico do not empty to the sea through the great maw of the Father of Waters.

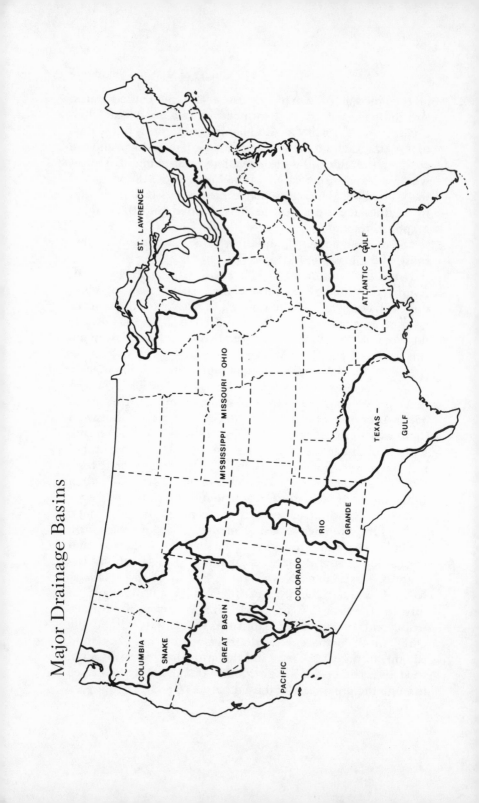

Major Drainage Basins

An understanding of surface drainage patterns is critical to an understanding of water-resource problems, not only because they are a major factor in water availability—it is easier to get water from a running stream than from any other potential source—but also because they define water-resource-planning regions, tying seemingly distant areas together in a web of interconnected influence. It is important to realize, for example, that water-resource decisions in Montana will affect water-resource decisions in Louisiana, because both states draw their water supplies principally from the Mississippi-Missouri river system. Important as they are, though, these surface drainage patterns are only part of the story. Under natural conditions, only an average of one drop of precipitation in three will reach a stream or a river—and because of this, it is only one third of our water resources that are affected by surface drainage patterns.

What happens to the other two thirds of the rainfall? The answer to that question varies greatly from situation to situation. Some drops will fall as snow in the mountains, where they may wait for the melting heat of spring to be released— or may be locked into glaciers for several thousand years. Some will enter the soil, either to become part of its composition—as "bound water"—or to be sucked up by the roots of plants and exhaled as vapor from their leaves back into the waiting air. (In well-vegetated areas, this process, called evaporation/transpiration or "evapotranspiration," may provide significant amounts of the moisture in nearby air masses.) Some drops may fall on the leaves of plants and never make it to the earth at all. Others may pool on flat, impermeable surfaces and, when the sun comes out, simply evaporate back into the air. But most will just sink slowly into the ground until they reach the zone of saturation, or water table—and at that point a whole new series of events, the groundwater cycle, comes into play.

We Americans are heavy users of groundwater. Of the 61,000 municipal water systems in this nation, 50,000—more than eighty percent—obtain water for their customers at least partially from underground sources. About fifty percent of the water we drink—and about twenty-five percent of the water we use for all purposes—comes from beneath the ground. The amounts represented by those percentages are huge: 57 million gallons a minute, 3.4 billion gallons an hour, a staggering 82 billion gallons a day sucked out of the earth to wash our cars and flush our toilets and water our crops and pour down our parched throats as everything from beer to instant breakfast. And yet, of all the forms in which we use water, groundwater is probably the least understood. Our national groundwater knowledge is buried under generations of encrusted myth: water witching, and "underground rivers," and spontaneous generation, and a whole host of other once-credible but now long-disproved beliefs which have somehow managed, despite our national worship of science, to hang on to their following long past the time they should have been gracefully retired. The persistence of these beliefs vastly complicates the job of groundwater management. They offer false hopes in place of realistic assessments; they suggest "solutions" which, because they are based on faulty premises, immediately become part of the problem.

And, needless to say, they drive water experts absolutely nuts.

"When you talk about groundwater," sighs geologist Doug Shakel, "the first thing you have to do is to convince people that there isn't a big underground lake down there, with little men in boats paddling back and forth checking the water supply." Shakel teaches geology at Pima College in Tucson, Arizona. A big man with a dark beard, he dresses like an undergraduate—a common trait among geology teachers. We are stretched out on the grass of the courtyard outside his office in the bright March sun, discussing Arizona's water problems. These are severe. Parts of the state are using water at a rate nearly five times as fast as rainfall can replenish it. To maintain this massive imbalance, Arizonans use groundwater on a huge scale. More than sixty percent of all water consumed in the state comes from beneath the ground. Very little trickles back in. Every year, Arizona's groundwater reserves shrink by more than 800 billion gallons.

"People believe in water behind dams," says Shakel, eyeing the crowds of passing students. "They don't believe in water in the ground, even though they use a lot of it. The mentality of water under the ground is just not understood. The trouble is, you're talking about wet dirt—and wet dirt does not appeal to people. They want water in a ditch, where they can see it. Water in the ground, as far as most people are concerned, just doesn't exist.

"You know, you see Jack and Jill run up the hill to fetch a pail of water, and the well is there, and nobody ever asks why it's full of water. I asked my aunt that when I was a kid, and she said, 'Well, the rain falls into the well.' And I was just a little kid, but I was smart enough to know that Jack and Jill's well *always* has a roof over it. If the well has a roof over it, how the hell does the rain get into the well? And yet, nobody takes it the next step, and says, 'The water's in the ground, and it leaks into the well.' "

Shakel is exaggerating a bit—a vice he admits to being prone to—but he is basically correct. Few people do understand what we might refer to as the Jack-and-Jill model of groundwater geology: that the water is in the ground, and it leaks into the well. And this is somewhat strange, because most of us have seen this principle in action at one time or another.

As any child knows who's ever been given a shovel and bucket to play with on the beach, when you dig a hole in the dry sand beside the ocean nothing happens; but if you keep on going down until you get into the wet sand, the hole fills up with water. The reason is simple and obvious. Sand grains are angular, and when they rest on one another they leave little gaps. Water droplets can flow through the little gaps. The ocean is right there, just a few feet away, and the water from it flows into the gaps, filling them up. That's what makes the sand wet in the first place. When you dig a hole into that sand, you are merely replacing a lot of the little gaps with one gigantic one—and the water can fill your gigantic gap just as easily as it can fill the little ones the sand makes. It proceeds to do so. The hole turns into a pool.

Essentially this same thing is going on any time you have an underground water supply. Someplace down there, there is a layer of material—fractured rock, dirt, sand, volcanic cinders, or what have you—that is full of little gaps. Somewhere—perhaps directly under your feet, perhaps down by the creek, perhaps over in the next county—that material with all the little gaps in it intersects the surface so that water can get in. The water trickles down through the little gaps, filling them up. When it reaches a well, which is a big gap, it fills that up, too. That is all. No underground rivers or lakes, none of the water witcher's so-called "veins," none of Doug Shakel's little men in boats. Just a lot of little, tiny, interconnected gaps with water filling them. A layer of material that fits this description is known as an aquifer, and unless you punch your well down through the roof of a limestone cave—which may, indeed, have an "underground river" in it—intersecting an aquifer is the only way you will ever get water into it.

Aquifers come in various types, with various characteristics. If the gaps are big and well connected, the water will flow easily from one to the next; if they are small and poorly connected, the flow will be restricted. If there are plenty of gaps, there will be room for a lot of water; if there are only a few gaps, the amount of water the aquifer can hold will be limited. Hydrologists refer to the rate of flow in an aquifer as its "permeability" and the amount of water it can hold as its "porosity." The two are not necessarily related. Basalt, for instance—a product of volcanic eruptions—is notorious for having plenty of big gaps, but next to no connections. It is porous but not permeable, and it makes a lousy aquifer. On the other hand, a block of granite with a single long crack through it may be permeable but not porous; water can flow easily through the crack, but there is very little storage capacity. Thus granite too makes a singularly poor aquifer. The best aquifers are both porous and permeable—buried beds of sand and gravel, for instance, or volcanic cinders, or heavily fractured bodies of sandstone or limestone.

Whatever the type of aquifer, whatever its flow and storage characteristics, one thing must be kept in mind: the aquifer, and the water within it, represent a detour, not a dead end. Even in an aquifer, water remains under the control of the hydrologic cycle. It flows downhill like any other water; at the end of its journey, it will trickle into the sea and enter the evaporation phase of the cycle once more. It may take generations, in human terms, for this to happen; it may have to wait for the upheavals of geologic time; but it will happen. The hydrologic cycle is complex, but it is closed, and water always remains part of it, wherever it is.

The fact that the hydrologic cycle is closed also means this: the things that we do to one part of the cycle may affect other parts that we do not intend to change. These changes are, by their nature, unexpected. It is the need to learn to expect these unexpected changes that makes knowledge of the hydrologic cycle so important.

Over the past several hundred years—and especially over the past fifty—there has been a considerable amount of human interference with the hydrologic and groundwater cycles. Most of this interference has been unintentional, but the fact that we didn't originally plan to do it doesn't make its effects any less severe. The clearing of forests has reduced evapotranspiration; this means that there is more water available for runoff, but it also means that there is less water vapor in the air, and some scientists believe that this has caused a slow drying of the world climate. Parking lots, streets, and buildings prevent the infiltration of rainwater into the earth, cutting off aquifers from their source of supply and causing them to run out of water. The reflective surfaces and lack of evapotranspiration in a city also causes a significant increase in temperature, altering the city air's water-carrying ability. Particulates poured into city air by stationary power plants and internal-combustion engines create "seeds" for raindrops and hailstones to form around. High-speed-transportation corridors create winds which may alter the movement of weather patterns. In upstate New York, for instance, old-timers insist that the completion of

Interstate 90 through the Mohawk Valley south of the Adirondacks caused storm centers to move twenty miles to the north.

These are some of the deep underlying problems that plague us as we muddle toward the limits of our once-vast stores of the fluid of life. Clearly, we cannot simply go on assuming that we have tamed our water and it will always be there at our command. For despite all we can do with water, despite all the pipes with which to move it and the chemicals with which to sterilize it and the filters with which to filter it and all the various and sundry hoops we are able to make it jump through, there is one thing we cannot do: we cannot make it. Thus the hydrologic cycle—and its offspring, the groundwater cycle—will always remain the true ruling factor. And to deny these plain and incontrovertible facts—to insist, as a spokesman for one of our major Western city water departments did to me not long ago, that the city was entitled to a certain amount of water *because it had bought and paid for it*—is to suffer a delusion that offers nothing but disaster down the long afternoon of the future. The hydrologic cycle, to put it bluntly, does not care much about who buys and pays for what, and this gentleman's city cannot buy what is not there. It and other cities must grasp this fact: the water is limited. Otherwise, today's shortages will simply grow worse tomorrow, and all the taxes, all the engineering skill, and all the laws in the world will not be able to prevent the fact that our children, and their children, and their children after them, will be going to bed thirsty.

CHAPTER 3

Cities in the Sun

THERE HAVE BEEN cities on earth for at least twelve millennia. Never before, however, have those cities put the terrible burden on their water supplies that ours do today.

We live in a city-dominated culture, one which has no real counterpart at any other time in history. Early cities, with few exceptions, were small. Ebla, one of the greatest metropolises in the world at the time of David and Solomon, had scarcely 30,000 residents; Jerusalem in its prime at the time of Christ had about the same number, Athens of the Golden Age perhaps 10,000 more. Rome, bloated and unstable at 800,000, was overthrown by the barbarian hordes and had shriveled back to under 20,000 by the Dark Ages. In 1500, at the beginning of the Renaissance, there were in all of the Western world only six cities—Paris, Lisbon, Naples, Milan, Venice, and Constantinople—with populations in excess of 100,000. London at that time was little better than an overgrown village; it didn't break into the six-figure population ranks for another hundred years.

In America, there was really no significant city growth until well into the nineteenth century. As late as 1850 only New York, Boston, and Philadelphia had populations in excess of 100,000, and more than eighty-five percent of the

American people lived on farms or in villages of fewer than 8,000 residents. But the winds of change were beginning to blow: prodded by the Civil War, the next few decades would see massive alterations in American population patterns. By 1910, the number of cities whose populations had passed the magic six-figure mark had reached fifty; three (New York, Philadelphia, and Johnny-come-lately Chicago) had passed one million; and the proportion of the country's population residing in towns of more than 8,000 had climbed to better than one third.

This explosion of cities has continued, and even escalated, through the twentieth century. Today, three out of every four of us are classified as urban dwellers. More than fifteen million people live in New York and Los Angeles alone. Five other cities have passed the one-million mark, and several more are close; nearly seventy have populations in excess of 250,000, and the number with more than 100,000 residents is almost literally beyond count. City boundaries have reached out to touch one another, creating megalopolises; more than half of us live in just thirteen of these supercities, which may incorporate several thousand separate communities and stretch for more than a hundred miles. We are, like it or not, an urban culture, and we have urban problems. Central among these is water.

Water has always been an overriding concern for those who would found cities or promote their growth. The rivers that thread their way through the hearts of nearly all the cities in the world are no accident; the cities were placed there, in virtually every case, because the rivers offered the promise of adequate water supplies. The souls of European cities are tied intimately to their rivers: Paris to the Seine, Rome to the Tiber, London to the Thames, Moscow to the Volga. Each of these rivers once provided all of the water for its city, and most still supply a portion, though they have long since become inadequate to the full task. Paris went looking for water from the Alps during the Second Empire, London was digging wells by Shakespeare's time, and Rome —as every schoolboy knows—abandoned the filthy and overtaxed Tiber at the time of the Caesars, laying aqueducts to the mountain streams of the distant Apennines. (The Romans, as always, did their work well. Some of those aqueducts are still in use today.)

American cities, with rare exceptions, have also been founded near rivers, and have usually depended on them for much or all of their water supplies. Corridors of cities thread the American landscape wherever there are corridors of water. New York, Poughkeepsie, Kingston, and Albany bead the Hudson; Wilmington, Philadelphia, and Trenton cling to the Delaware, Washington shoulders the Potomac, Akron and Cleveland bridge the Cuyahoga. The Ohio has given birth to Pittsburgh, and Cincinnati, and Louisville, and numberless smaller cities. New Orleans has the Mississippi, St. Louis the Missouri, Denver the South Platte, Portland the Columbia. Even Phoenix and Tucson originally had rivers flowing through them, the Salt and the Santa Cruz, though both of these are now totally dry.

All—or nearly all—of these cities once depended on their accompanying rivers for their total municipal water supplies. Some still do: Louisville draws its water entirely from the Ohio, and New Orleans from the Mississippi, to this day. In most cases, however, it became apparent quite early in the life of each city that the river it stood upon was not going to be able to satisfy the demands of the population that the city fathers hoped to attract. This led to searches for new supplies. Other rivers nearby would be tapped; wells would be dug. But all too often, as the cities prospered and their water demands grew, not even the wells and the nearby rivers could keep pace.

By the beginning of the twentieth century, signs of stress were already appearing in the water supplies of many American cities. Artesian pressure had been lost at Savannah, Montgomery, Des Moines, Atlantic City, and many other places; Baltimore and Brooklyn were pumping salt water from previously fresh wells; San Francisco and Los Angeles, their local sources severely overtaxed, were reaching tentatively toward the streams of the distant Sierra; and New

York—which had long since outgrown the brooks of Manhattan, polluted the Hudson beyond use, and sucked the Croton dry—was hard at work on a tunnel designed to bring water from the Catskills, more than one hundred miles away. These, however, were bush-league compared to the water problems that our cities face today. Some examples follow.

Wichita, Kansas: This city of 300,000 on the south-central Kansas plains straddles the Arkansas River but draws most of its water from wells punched into a thick deposit of Pleistocene-era gravels, called the Equus Beds, some twenty-five miles to the north. The Equus Beds are what geologists call a "recharge system," which is to say that they are open to the surface of the ground and are able to soak up virtually all the rain that falls upon them. Unfortunately, this is not enough. The recharge amounts to perhaps 120,000 acre-feet —39 billion gallons—per year. Wichita and other communities in the surrounding four-county area which draw from the Equus Beds take nearly all of that now, and expect to need almost twice as much within the next twenty years. Even now in a year of low rainfall wells will be drawn down significantly—a serious proposition, because the freshwater resources of the beds are abutted by a huge underground store of saltwater called the Hutchinson Salt Member. If too much freshwater is drawn out of the Equus Beds, the saltwater will move in, contaminating the beds and rendering much of their water undrinkable. Wichita has no other potential source of water. "We've got a reservoir out here that's umpteen square miles wide and fifteen feet deep," says one local water activist, "and there's talk of another, but it's probably years off." Even if the new reservoir goes in, there will be trouble, because the Arkansas doesn't have enough flow to supply a city the size of Wichita. Wichita, apparently, is going to have to gird itself for a long thirst.

Washington, D.C.: The nation's capital depends on the Potomac River for its water supply, diverting some 300 million gallons a day into intakes at Little Falls, a mile upstream from the District of Columbia boundary, and Great Falls, some ten miles farther up. There is no municipal water-supply company, as such: the system was built and is operated by the Army Corps of Engineers under the terms of a law passed by Congress in 1859.

Following the great Eastern Seaboard drought of the mid-1960s, Congress asked the Corps to initiate a study of future supply and demand for Washington. The results, published in the form of numerous ponderous volumes in 1973 and then modified and slimmed down into a one-volume *Washington Metropolitan Area Supply Study* two years later, were more than a little disheartening. Although the yearly flow of the river averages out to more than five billion gallons per day, the Corps found that during the summer, when demand is highest, it could get down to as low as 390 million. This was dangerously close to current demand levels, and far below projected demand, which was estimated to reach better than 700 million gallons per day before the year 2000. Solutions to this dilemma were—and are—virtually nonexistent. The Corps has proposed a complicated series of dams, pumped-storage projects, and regulating basins for the Potomac and its tributaries to even out the flow through the year, but these would drown numerous historic and recreation sites, a number of major transportation corridors, and parts or all of several thriving communities, and they have been thoroughly rejected by an aroused public. There are no dependable groundwater reserves, and all nearby rivers have been completely appropriated by other communities in the Washington metropolitan area. Currently, Washington residents are practicing aggressive conservation techniques —and keeping their fingers crossed.

San Diego, California: Located in a sunny coastal basin one hundred miles south of Los Angeles and just a few miles from Mexico, California's second largest city boasts a population of just under one million and a rainfall of scarcely ten inches per year. With local surface supplies next to nonexistent, and underground supplies scarce, the city must import virtually all of its water. For years, this has meant lifting part of the Colorado River over the San Bernardino Mountains and piping it south via the twin branches of the San Diego Aqueduct. But Colorado River supplies will soon be drastically cut due to the demands of the Central Arizona Project, which the Supreme Court has ruled is entitled to part of San Diego's share. Theoretically, this deficit can be made up by imports from the California State Water Project, which is already bringing some water into the San Diego basin from as far north as the Feather River; however, increased supplies from the State Water Project are contingent upon completion of the Peripheral Canal around the Sacramento–San Joaquin delta east of San Francisco, and construction of the canal is being held up by a determined coalition of environmentalists and local farmers who feel that it may damage the delta beyond repair. Thus, because of a battle going on more than five hundred miles north of them, San Diegoans may soon be facing some very dry summers. The sea looms right on the city's doorstep, brimful and tempting beyond measure, but as yet no one has figured out how to economically and efficiently desalt the sea.

Greenwich, Connecticut: Just over the Connecticut line to the east of New York City, this green and prosperous suburb of sixty thousand people, situated in a coastal rainbelt which receives better than forty inches of rain a year, might seem a strange place for a water shortage. Yet the shortage is there. The Connecticut-American Water Company, which serves the city, is facing an estimated 100-million-gallon-per-day shortfall by the year 2000, due largely to an aging, too-small reservoir network which has not been updated since the early 1950s. One hundred million gallons per day amounts to one third of the city's projected daily demand. Already the pinch is being felt: during the drought winter of 1980–81, consumers had to be ordered to cut their use by sixty percent under threat of a $100 fine and a potential jail sentence, and a national news magazine reported finding "suburban matrons guard[ing] water like Bedouins . . . [while] town officials lay plans for slit-trench latrines against the not-too-distant day when the reservoirs may run dry."

There are several reasons why a nation of city dwellers is particularly prone to face water shortages.

To begin with—and for whatever reason—city dwellers seem to use more water per capita than their small-town cousins. Across America, the average amount of water used daily by each citizen in 1980 was approximately 90 gallons. But in New York it was 190 gallons; in Tucson, 140; in Denver, 230; and in Sacramento, a whopping 280 gallons, or better than three times the national average. No one is quite sure just why this discrepancy should exist. Do city dwellers water their lawns more often than others? Do they use more air conditioning, take more baths, flush their toilets more often? Do their faucets leak? The cause is obscure, but the effect is quite real, and it vastly complicates attempts to solve city water problems.

Consider, for example, the cost-management headaches involved for the water system of a growing city. Because of the escalated demands of city residents, the water system must expand at a rate significantly faster than the growth of the population area it serves. This means that capital costs go up far faster than growth figures alone would indicate, which in turn means that the system either must charge more per gallon than it did when it served a small town or must raise money in some other fashion—a greater drag on the city taxes, annual bond issues, or the like. But these are usually highly unpopular with the city's residents, who fail to understand why water must cost so much more than it did back when the town was young. Hence, many water companies find themselves starved for operating and development funds, and their systems—and their service—gradually deteriorate.

A second reason for city water shortages is the location in major population centers of large numbers of water-consuming industries. Most industrial plants use water at the rate of several hundred thousand gallons per day; this includes those with such dry-seeming functions as producing pencils, making leather products and turning out eyeglasses. Some, of course, are greater users than others. Tire and rubber manufacturers draw a daily average of about half a million gallons per plant; chemical plants use more than one million, and a good-size lumber mill will take up to two million. Large office buildings, too, use hefty supplies of water, especially in the summer when their air-conditioning systems are gulping tens of thousands of gallons daily. It is sophistic to say, as some do, that if these industrial plants and office buildings were located in small towns they would be using just as much water as they do today in the cities; many supply products or services which are in much greater demand in a city than in a small town, and if the cities weren't there there would be little reason for the plants. A prime example of this is water itself. Because of the greater per-capita demands made by city residents, city systems require proportionately larger pipelines, filtration equipment, and supplies of treatment chemicals—all of which themselves cost water to manufacture. And it is also misleading to suggest that because many industrial plants have their own sources of water, independent of city systems, their effects can be divorced from the shortages faced by the cities' residents. In fact, nothing in the water-supply field is independent. A well punched down by a manufacturing plant will go into the same aquifer as the wells of the city system; a surface-water intake will deplete the streamflow of the same river. Thus, water used by the plant is water taken from the city's supply, and it matters little whether or not it was pumped through city-owned pipes to get there.

Finally, and perhaps most importantly, there is the problem of concentration, the result of crowding overwhelming numbers of people, and their water demands, into the relatively tiny spaces of cities. We touched on this point briefly back in Chapter 2: it deserves a further look now.

Cities are not only bigger than small towns: they are also more densely packed. High-rise apartment buildings cram many more people into a square block than do suburban single-family dwellings; and most cities also have a significant commuter population, the members of which—although counted as residents of nearby communities—work in tight concentrations in the city's office buildings and manufacturing plants and must have city services provided to them during the eight hours or more a day they are present. The impacts of this on cities' water systems are twofold. First, they must somehow find sources for the huge amounts of water per square mile they are called upon to deliver; and, second, they must build massive and exceedingly complex filter plants and pipeline systems to process and distribute that water. So-called "economics of scale" are irrelevant here: most city systems have grown far beyond the point where size helps them, and instead of the economics of scale they are feeling the agonies of scale, a condition one writer on water subjects, historian T. C. Watkins, once compared to "a victim of elephantiasis carrying his privates about in a wheelbarrow."

Forced to put all of their capital-improvement funds into building new parts of the system to keep up with the demand for more and more water, water companies cannot repair the pipelines they have in place, leading to significant system-wide deterioration. In New York, estimates of leakage due to deteriorated pipes run as high as fifteen percent; in Boston, the figure may be as much as three times that. Some towns in New Jersey are still using wooden pipe dating from before the turn of the century; here, the leakage cannot even be estimated. And though they may not leak, the new parts of the systems have troubles of their own. Dense development and high water demands require big pipes, and these, water officials are quick to point out, are far more costly than small ones. "A two-inch difference in the size of the pipe alone can be a huge amount of money," says one utility spokesman, Frank Brooks of Tucson Water. "The difference between, say, a forty-eight-inch pipe and a fifty-four-inch pipe is six inches. Doesn't sound like much, in terms of difference—but it's like a hundred dollars a foot. And if you're going to run it two miles, you're talking about a bundle of money."

Often development plans are so complex and come from

so many different directions that water officials have difficulty sorting them out enough to provide a plan of their own. "There's a lot of confusion," sighs Brooks. "They're not giving us definite numbers and figures to go by, and you need those to plan how to implement your system. You want to be right." The problem is, of course, that with the complex, dense interlocking weave of developments that is a modern city, deciding what is right is virtually impossible.

But even more difficult than the tricky business of distributing all that water is the extremely important task of finding enough to distribute in the first place. As John Cunningham of the New York City water department puts it, "The big problem with city water systems is, if you need additional resources, where do you go? Which direction do you go? You've got problems any way you turn." These problems are not small. To supply the water demanded by a great city, even in an area of heavy rains, drainage basins must be immense—more than a thousand square miles for a place the size of a New York or a Los Angeles. To find enough water, therefore, cities must go far afield. This often involves interference with other cities: it is a sobering thought to realize, for instance, that more than thirteen percent of the nation's population is dependent, in one form or another, on the strictly limited water supplies of the Delaware River. When that much demand is placed on a single resource, it is totally unavoidable that someone is going to get shortchanged.

One way to avoid tapping other peoples' rivers is to tap groundwater instead. But groundwater exploitation by a major city has its own special set of problems. The volume of water that a city demands from its wells often exceeds the flow rate that the aquifer into which the well is drilled can deliver: water simply can't move fast enough through the little gaps in the permeable material the aquifer is made of. This results in a so-called "cone of depression," with depressed groundwater levels centered on the well and extending far out on all sides—often overlapping the cone of depression of the well of a neighboring city and drawing both down even farther. Thus even under the ground cities struggle with one another over the same water supply. "When an industrial pump is turned on in Jesup," commented Georgia state geologist William H. McLemore in a recent issue of *Newsweek*, "the effects are felt in Savannah." Savannah and Jesup are fifty miles apart, but they are located over the same aquifer.

Not everyone would agree that the picture of city water demands should be quite so gloomy as I have painted it here. In Los Angeles, for example, water department official Dwayne Georgeson told me frankly that he thought I was wrong to blame city growth as a factor in water shortages. "Los Angeles," he pointed out, "is thought to be this monster using all the water, and our insatiable, rapidly growing demand is drying up the Western rivers. Well, the water use in Los Angeles today is what it was ten years ago, and ten years from now it will be very similar to what it is today. We have a vigorous economic growth in Los Angeles, but it's kind of a reconversion of land, which tends to develop it with relatively little increase in water use. You take a single-family home, for instance, and put an apartment on the same lot, and you eliminate a big percentage of the lawn. And the apartment dweller uses maybe one-fourth the amount of water as the person who lives in the home. So water use in Los Angeles is growing very slowly."

This is encouraging. It is also largely irrelevant. The principal problem is not Los Angeles: it is all the cities that aspire to *be* Los Angeles. Los Angeles may have most of its water growth behind it, but its imitators do not. They must still expand. But there is nowhere to expand to.

So far, unfortunately, our city-worshiping culture has blinded us to this fact. We go merrily forward, agglutinating our cities, abandoning or paving over the countryside, building our water-dependent industries, our water-dependent homes, our water-dependent lifestyles—and using up the water. The huge size of our metropolitan areas, the increasing percentage of our population that insists on living within them, and the escalating water demands that each citizen makes on the city he or she lives in have joined together to create a situation that is on the brink of being totally out of control. Every city wants its day in the sun; but cities in the sun, we are finding, can get terribly thirsty.

CHAPTER 4

Fields of Feast, Fields of Famine

THE URBANIZATION OF America has created severe water-supply problems. But the cities are not the only place where these problems are being felt. Increasingly, the burden of water shortages is falling on that portion of the nation's economy that can probably least afford it: the much-maligned, absolutely indispensable American farm.

Forget Calvin Coolidge's observation that "the business of America is business." Despite the fact that nearly three fourths of us live in the cities—and ninety-five percent of us make our living there—the backbone of the American economy is still agricultural production. More than twice as much capital is invested in farming as in all other American industries put together. Besides producing the foods we eat, agriculture provides us with significant portions of the raw materials for the manufacture of products ranging from cigarettes and textiles through pharmaceuticals and other household chemicals to paint, paper, and floor tile. It is also a leading item of international trade: the United States ranks first among all nations in the world in agricultural exports, with one dollar in every five made in the worldwide food-products market coming home to American farmers. Our fields are fields of feast, from an economic as well as a culinary standpoint. One significant—if rather ironic—sign of the economic value of the American farm is the size of the American city, which could not exist in anything remotely resembling its current bloated state without the production of huge food surpluses on the part of the farmers. Cities are parasites on their surrounding farmland, and ours have fed well.

If the farm is the backbone of American economic life, water is the backbone of the farm. Crop plants are almost uniformly heavy water users—one thinks of watermelons, for example, as opposed to tumbleweeds—and although most domestic animals found on the farm came originally from moderately dry savanna habitats, only the cat in the barn has desert-dwelling ancestors. In the rain-rich East, where ponds and streams abound and the soil is always damp a few inches below the surface, the farm's heavy dependence on water creates few problems for the farmer. But in the wide-open deserts of the West—where farming has increasingly moved since World War II—the specter of this dependence looms large and crucial. The crops and the animals that the farmers raise need every bit as much water in the West as they do in the East; but in the West that water is much, much harder to come by.

Lifting off from Washington's National Airport for a June flight west across the continent, you look down upon green. The valleys of Virginia are green; so are the ancient, eroded ridges of the Alleghenies, and the broad parallel troughs between them, and the water gaps that slice them. Westward the plane passes over green Ohio and green Indiana and green Illinois, vaults the broad brown ribbon of the Mississippi, arrows onward over the fertile fields of green Missouri. Somewhere over Missouri you begin to notice the change; and by the time you have flashed past the Missouri River into eastern Kansas, you are sure of it. The green is fading. The vibrant, misty blue-greens of the Eastern Seaboard give way to gray-greens, and then to yellow-greens; somewhere over Kansas, the greens fade out altogether. By the time you hit Colorado airspace, the land beneath you is brown.

But not entirely brown. Here and there, sometimes widely scattered, sometimes bunched together like patterns on a bed quilt, there are geometrical shapes and patches of green. Some are circular; some are square; some lie in long thin strips; and a few have no shape at all. In appearance they are vibrantly, almost obscenely alive, and they stand out amid all that deadness like jewels at a poorhouse ball. These are the fields of the West, the source of nearly two thirds of the nation's food, and their existence in this land of little rain would not be possible at all if it were not for a small human miracle called irrigation.

An irrigation system diverts water from a river or pumps it out of an aquifer and uses it to wet down the soil of a field so that the crop planted in that field can use it in place of the rain that does not fall. In a sense, it is a reversal of nature: where the natural course of events is for rain to fall on a piece of land and either soak into the ground or run off in little rivulets, which coalesce into a series of bigger and bigger rivulets and run into a river, an irrigation system either pumps water back out of the ground or withdraws it from the river through a series of smaller and smaller rivulets which eventually spread out on the field and, through the process of evapotranspiration from the leaves of the crop plants, vault back into the air. On its way, this hydrologic cycle in reverse may transform huge areas of land on a scale that rivals the transformations of cataclysmic natural events such as earthquakes and volcanic eruptions. In my book *The Carson Factor* (Hawthorn Books, 1979) I described in detail the almost overwhelming changes that irrigation brought to the lands of Oregon's Klamath Basin. A pair of huge but shallow natural lakes were drained and turned into fields of potatoes and clover and alfalfa; the mouth of a river was moved eleven miles, from the edge of a lake to the shores of another, larger river; and the water level of the largest lake in Oregon was placed under the control of engineers, who could either divert its overflow onto the fields of the basin or run it down its ancient channel, the Link River, as they saw fit. Such massive transformations have become common all over the West, and they have created an industry which is heavily—and, in this dry area, anomalously—dependent on water. Of the 165 billion gallons of water used daily in the states west of the hundredth meridian, 145 billion—more than eighty-eight percent—will go to irrigation.

Irrigation has created a style of farming quite different from that of nonirrigated areas. Because of the control that is possible over the amount and timing of the water that is supplied to the crop plants, irrigated farms are up to three times more productive per acre than rain-dependent farms, and they can be concentrated into smaller areas; on the other hand, because of the capital needed to build and maintain the irrigation works, larger operations tend to be more cost-effective than smaller ones, and those concentrated, highly productive irrigated fields usually turn out to be the property of a few large landowners rather than being spread out among many small farmers. Thus irrigation and the much-derided "corporate farm" or "agribusiness" turn out to be almost synonymous. The fact that water must be supplied to the fields dictates their shape and distribution pattern much more strictly than might be expected. To an Easterner, a Western farm often looks strange, with its carefully planed and leveled fields separated from each other by the berms of elevated ditches, or—in areas where sprinkler irrigation is practiced—plowed and planted in perfect circles, each one trod endlessly by the huge metallic insect-shape of an automatic sprinkler extending several hundred yards outward from its central pivot and creeping slowly along on wheels twice as tall as a man.

The practice of raising animals, particularly beef cattle, has also been greatly modified by irrigation. On traditional farms, cattle are simply turned out to pasture and allowed to take themselves to their food. Where pasturage is lush, this works well; but on the dry range of the West, where, as one Kansas irrigation-equipment salesman once remarked, "you could put an old steer out on four acres and it'd starve," the amount of land required for range feeding is far too large to be practical. Here, once again, irrigation works miracles by reversing the traditional process: instead of taking the animals to the food, the food is brought to the animals. Confined to small feedlots, the cattle of the West are fed from troughs on corn and other grains grown on intensely farmed, irrigated fields. From a tiny start on an insignificant number of farms in the early 1960s, feedlot-raising has expanded until now, in the early 1980s, it accounts for by far the largest share of beef grown in this country. The industry has been revolutionized, divided into so-called "breeders" and "feeders," the one supplying the cattle—usually from breeding stock raised on traditional pasturage farms—and the other maturing them in feedlots and shipping them to the slaughterhouse when, after a few months' time, they become large enough to eat.

So irrigation has been principally responsible for the transformation of farming into a heavy industry using mechanized mass-production methods to yield large amounts of a relatively uniform product. But, like all industries which have become dependent on a single resource, irrigated industrial farming has a limit beyond which it cannot grow— and all over the West there are signs that this limit has not only been reached but in many cases has been surpassed. Irrigated farming on the scale it has grown to in this country has, it is now clear, been using water in far greater amounts than nature can continue to supply. It is an edifice built on borrowed capital, and it is about to go bankrupt.

The signs of this impending bankruptcy are, like cracks in a dried-up field, appearing in many places at once. In the High Plains states, for example—Nebraska, Kansas, Colorado, Oklahoma, and Texas—corn production dropped by 200,000 acres between 1977 and 1980; potato acreage was slashed by ten percent in Idaho, and cotton plantings declined nationally by more than one million acres, during the same period. All of these are heavily water-dependent crops whose cultivation is done primarily or completely on irrigated acreage. In western Kansas, irrigated land once brought double the price of dry range on the real-estate market; it has now lost its premium status and goes for the same per-acre value as any other land, always providing that you can sell it at all. In New Mexico, where water rights—the legal permits required to remove water from a stream for irrigation or other purposes—may be bought and sold like any other commodity, prices for those rights have skyrocketed by one thousand percent and more in the last twenty years; rights that once sold for $200 to $300 an acre-foot may now go for as much as $5,000.

"It's a gradual movement—like a cloud across the sun," comments irrigation specialist Ray Bogle of Kansas State University. "Soon irrigation will be blotted out."

As the shadow line of water shortages creeps forward, its effects are felt far more broadly than most people realize. The price of food, of course, bounds upward. So does the price of cotton and other natural textile products. Since more and more energy is required to bring the increasingly scarce water to the irrigated fields, there is less and less energy available for other uses, and energy prices inflate. As irrigation costs increase, the smaller, marginally productive farms are driven out of business; their lands either are converted to other uses—shrinking the country's agricultural land base dangerously—or are snapped up by the large farming conglomerates which are the only ones that can operate on the tiny profit margins these lands produce. Either way, the centralization of the American farming industry is materially advanced, and the small farmer pays the price.

The taxpayer also pays. Much of the water used to irrigate crops in the West comes from federally built and operated projects like Washington's Grand Coulee Dam or California's Central Valley Project. Water from these projects is typically provided to users at far below cost: Central Valley farmers, for example, pay approximately $3.50 an acre-foot for flows whose delivery costs run in excess of $150, a discrepancy which amounts to an $1,100 per acre subsidy and costs the federal treasury several billion dollars annually in lost revenues.

The biggest loss from irrigated farming, however, may not be a monetary loss at all. It may be the loss of options.

As the farms of the West come closer and closer to using all the available water, the supply that can be set aside for other uses shrinks further and further. Industrial growth is curtailed; city expansion grinds to a halt. Acrimonious conflicts develop, on a scale that makes the wars over water holes in the old West look like canasta tournaments. The current fight over oil-shale development in Colorado and Wyoming is largely a fight between agriculture and industry over water; so is the battle over coal mining in the northern plains states, and the argument over the MX missiles in Utah and Nevada, and the struggle over the Peripheral Canal in California. We will deal with some of these issues in greater detail later; here it should be sufficient to point out that they are real, they are very large, and they are deeply and intricately complex. And they are not likely to go away soon.

The situation in Arizona may be instructive. Arizona is feeling the brunt of the Sun Belt immigration boom; statewide, the population ballooned upward by some fifty-three percent—mostly transplanted Northerners and Easterners—in the decade between 1970 and 1980. All these extra people, of course, require extra water; and in the dry climate of the Southwest, extra water for one use must of necessity be borrowed from another use. Arizona has a brand-new and extremely stringent law, passed in the summer of 1980, to control this borrowing. At this writing (August 1981), it is still too soon to predict how the new law will work, but it is already obvious where the main burden of it will be felt. Says Wesley Steiner, the state's "water czar," "The problem isn't people or immigration. It's agriculture."

It is clear, from this and similar statements, that when it comes to a choice between domestic water supply and agricultural water supply, Americans are likely to choose to be able to have enough water to drink.

It is less clear just what we intend to eat.

CHAPTER 5

The Flowers
of the Forest Floor

FOR MANY AMERICANS, the natural world has become
an abstraction. Living in concrete apartment buildings, eating prepared foods, and coming no closer to nature than an
evening of *Wild Kingdom* or the pages of a Sierra Club cal-
endar, we tend to think of the natural world as something
Out There—aesthetically attractive, chic to protect, but
largely irrelevant to our daily lives. Nature is the Other
Land, the place that is left over after we have built our cities
and planted our farms. The birds and the bugs and the bunnies live there, and although it would be nice to keep as
many birds and bugs and bunnies around us as possible, for
as long as possible, it really won't hurt anything when they
go. It is this attitude that is largely responsible both for much
of our body of environmental law and for many of the attacks
on it. The discomfort index often turns out to be the only
thing separating so-called Environmentalists from the heavily derided Rapers of the Environment, who differ from the
Environmentalists only in the levels at which they believe
that discomfort begins.

Nevertheless, there is a true environmental ethic, held by

a small but growing number of people. These people realize that the natural world is much more than just a home for birds and bugs and bunnies, or a place to go to on vacation and take pretty pictures to hang on the living-room wall. It is a great scientific laboratory, a continuing experiment whose results, properly interpreted by trained scientists, may hold the answer to many of the problems plaguing our well-meaning but still terribly benighted race. It is a genetic bank, the holder of species of plants and animals yet unguessed at, many of which may prove extremely valuable to us: although we tend to forget the fact, every one of our domestic species was once wild. The natural world is a vast automatic air conditioner: it is always several degrees more temperate in the forest than on the farm or in the city, largely because of the respiration of the trees, and it is probable—if not already proved—that the currently ongoing wholesale destruction of the earth's forest will bring with it a permanent rise in summer temperatures and a drop in winter ones. And perhaps most important of all, the natural world is a source of water.

Or maybe "source" is the wrong term. Stretches of unmodified land do not precisely produce water: that is solely the job of the hydrologic cycle, and although forests and other natural areas contribute to that cycle—through evapotranspiration of water from their leaves—they do not drive it. But they do something that is very nearly as important. The hydrologic cycle normally delivers its water in big bursts which we call storms. The natural world—the mantle of life that covers most of the earth where man hasn't yet had a chance to get to it—stretches those bursts out, so that instead of running directly off into the rivers and out to sea again they trickle out slowly over a long period of time. The tangle of plant material, stems above the earth and roots below, holds back the runoff so that it can soak into the ground for storage. It also cools the earth's surface, lowering evaporation rates and keeping water in the ground-based portion of the hydrologic cycle which would otherwise leap back up into the air as soon as the storm stopped. The plant materials on the earth, and the earth itself, filter the water, taking out suspended solids; the trees overhanging a natural stream shade the water and keep it cool, and the boulders in the streambed fling it noisily into the air, filling it with oxygen and destroying the anaerobic bacteria which are the causes of most waterborne disease. The result is a relatively constant flow of cool, clean water—precisely what we want for our agricultural and municipal water supplies. It is for this reason that so many cities—among them Portland (Oregon), Akron (Ohio), New York, and Seattle—strictly protect their municipal watersheds, preserving them from development, from timber harvest, and even in many cases from recreational use.

But if the unmodified, natural world is important for water, water is also important for the unmodified, natural world. The flowers of the forest floor need water every bit as much as the flowers in a city window box do, and the increasing scarcity of good water is affecting the wilderness as seriously as it is affecting the farm and the city. Or perhaps more so: the farm, the city, and the wilderness are under equal attack, but the wilderness cannot fight back.

Human ingenuity has allowed us to use water in nearly identical ways wherever we are. If there is plenty of rain, we collect the rain; if there is not, we either import water or dig it out of the ground. If the water is too dirty, we clean it; if it is too warm we cool it, and if it is too salty we distill it. By doing these things, we have always managed to keep pretty much the same water level in our lifestyle, whether we live deep in a tropical rain forest or out in the middle of the Mojave Desert. But in the natural world, it isn't like that. In the natural world, living things either adapt or die. These days, many of them are dying.

In the Santa Cruz Valley of Arizona, in the San Joaquin Valley of California, and on the Texas High Plains around Lubbock, Plainview, and Amarillo, native vegetation is vanishing—the victim of groundwater overpumping which has lowered the water table to the point where the roots of plants can no longer reach it.

In New York, the Croton River has disappeared down the gullets of thirsty Manhattanites, leaving high and dry the rich aquatic life it once supported.

In the eastern Sierra, stream diversions by the Los Angeles Department of Water and Power have lowered the level of ancient Mono Lake, converting Negit Island into a peninsula and turning mainland predators such as coyotes loose to wreak havoc among the island's thousands of nesting gulls.

In Wisconsin, New Hampshire, Ontario, Maine, and many other places, polluted rain has acidified lakes, ripping apart food chains and decimating fisheries. Among the more notable victims: New York State's Lake Tear of the Clouds—the source of the Hudson—and the wilderness waters of Minnesota's Boundary Waters Canoe Area.

If these problems were isolated, we might accept them as unfortunate but necessary side effects of civilization. But they are not isolated. The last few decades have seen the emergence of broad patterns of water abuse, misuse, and overuse, threatening the entire natural fabric of the continent. Streamflow overappropriations exist in every Western state—and many Eastern ones—as irrigation and municipal demands claim more water than the rivers can produce; the Potomac runs nearly empty in the summer, the Platte and the Delaware have been the subjects of interstate lawsuits over streamflow levels, and the Colorado has not flowed into the sea for years. Estimates of the number of lakes threatened by acidification run into the tens of thousands. Impoundments, channelizations and withdrawals in California have reduced spawning gravels in the state's streams to a fraction of a percent of their original extent, and fish production has plummeted. The Montana legislature has found it necessary to pass legislation limiting withdrawals from the Yellowstone to keep that historic and extremely scenic piece of Americana from drying up altogether.

The destruction of vegetation by groundwater withdrawals is perhaps the most worrisome of all. According to a 1981 report by the President's Council on Environmental Quality, this process is currently taking place on at least ten percent of America's land, and is imminent on another ten percent, making a total of one fifth of the United States in which water-table changes could eliminate or drastically alter the native vegetation. The CEQ report terms the process "desertification," which is catchy but misleading: a true desert supports a surprisingly flourishing community of plants, but even these dryland-adapted plant species cannot for the most part survive in the areas where human use has drastically dropped the water table. Mesquite, for instance, is a hardy bush whose questing roots can reach up to one hundred feet into the ground after the elusive desert water table; but in the heavily used groundwater basins of Arizona, water-table depths have declined in many places to more than 150 feet, and even the mesquite is dying.

Desertification is an accidental byproduct of humanity's increasingly frantic search for water. Along the watercourses of the Southwest, however, plants are also being killed on purpose as a result of that search. The problem here is the presence of phreatophytes, or water-loving plants. Phreatophytes are characterized by high rates of evapotranspiration, and thus send remarkable amounts of water skyward each day from the rivers they grow along. To keep that water in those rivers for human use, water managers are cutting them down.

At Southern Oregon State College in Ashland, I asked limnologist Wayne Linn what he thought of solving water shortages by eliminating phreatophytes. The answer was, clearly, not much. "To begin with," he pointed out, "it's obvious that when you cut out the phreatophytes, you eliminate that as an ecosystem. You're going to influence soil structure, bank stability, and all the organisms which fit in there, which may in turn influence the food chains for other animals. If you take all the vegetation out, it would just be devastating for the animals that use the river. The cover wouldn't be there, so they wouldn't use it as much, or at all." The loss of shade would heat the water; dust and dirt would be blown into it because the plants weren't in the way of the wind, and this would increase siltation and turbidity. "You might as well forget about fishing it," Linn concluded grimly.

In many places, laws have been enacted that are supposed to protect environmental values against too-zealous water appropriation. Arizona, for example, has recently passed a model groundwater law; New York State now has some legal protection for its streamflows, and the previously mentioned Montana law protecting the Yellowstone also affords some guardianship for the rest of the state's rivers. Other states have, or will soon have, followed suit. But these laws are human instruments, and when push comes to shove and what the environment needs must be taken from what humans want, these well-meaning protective ordinances usually prove to have all the backbone of a ten-day-old noodle. Oregon, for instance, has some very thorny-looking legal devices to protect what are known in the trade as "instream minimum flows"—legalese for the amount of water needed to allow fish to get from pool to pool in a river without donning roller skates. But in 1974, when the state was threatened by a record drought, Oregon farmers sought—and got—suspension of the instream minimums in order to keep their irrigation ditches flowing. In theory, the fish were protected; in reality, they were dying.

It remains to be seen whether the laws of Arizona, Montana, New York, and elsewhere will stand up to the pressure or will prove to be made of the same sturdy cellophane as Oregon's.

The natural world tends to arrange itself according to the availability of water. Desert plants and animals live only in the desert; grassland species are limited to the grasslands, tundra species to the tundra, and rain-forest species to the rain forest. We humans do not abide by these distinctions. Taking our same water-dependent lifestyle anywhere we go —and using more than our share everywhere we are—we are upsetting the delicate water balance achieved by our wild areas over millennia of adjustment. In most cases, to upset is to destroy. The costs of this destruction in human terms are not yet clearly seen, but they are bound to be not very pretty—even supposing we have the moral right to demand all that water in the first place.

...II

CHAPTER **6**

The Lawns of Arizona

SKIRTING THE SOUTHERN edge of downtown Phoenix, sundering the South Mountain residential areas from the main part of the city, and for a short distance forming the boundary between Phoenix and neighboring Tempe—home of the Arizona State University Sun Devils—there is a broad, dry expanse of stones and sand known as the Salt River. Except during floods, the river has absolutely no water in it whatsoever. The southbound lanes of U.S. Highway 89, sweeping busily out of town through Tempe and Mesa toward distant Tucson, cross the Salt on a long, many-pillared cement bridge, looking rather silly up there above the bone-dry river; beside them, the more recently built northbound lanes stick primly and sensibly to the gravels of the riverbed, devoid, even in the high-runoff month of March, of so much as a puddle.

A few blocks away, arrowing northward across flat Phoenix toward the distant mountains, First Street knifes through the city's financial district, past the Post Office, past the birthplace of Barry Goldwater, past the glass-and-steel explosion of the Arizona Bank Building, tallest in the state. Palm trees shade the sidewalks, swaying gracefully above wide parking

71

strips. The parking strips are planted to lawn. The lawns are green.

It is there that the Salt River has gone. There, to the lawns and the palm trees; there, to the Arizona Bank Building's air conditioners; there, to the sparkling, exuberant array of fountains in front of the spanking-new Civic Center over on Second Street; there, to the lawns and the gardens and the air coolers and the backyard swimming pools of 800,000 Phoenix-area residents. There to the cotton fields and melon gardens surrounding the city; there to the region's sixty golf courses, with their carefully manicured fairways and emerald, billiard-table-smooth putting greens. There to the lagoon at nearby Fountain Hills, where three powerful pumps force seven thousand gallons of water a minute through a hole in a one-ton metal casting, creating an artificial geyser 560 feet high which is ballyhooed—with reason—as the World's Highest Fountain.

It is, I suppose, the right of the citizens of Phoenix to have green lawns. But it is the lawns of Phoenix that lie at the heart of our national problem with water.

I do not wish to be too hard on Phoenix, which is a beautiful city and which is not alone in using more water than it really needs. New Yorkers overuse it, too, running it—it is said—through their taps all day so that it will always be cold when they want to drink a glassful. Bostonites lose it through the holes in the pipes under their streets. In Los Angeles, which has no more water to spare than Phoenix does, I have watched gardeners use hoses running full bore to blast leaves off sidewalks and into gutters, a process referred to contemptuously by southern-California environmentalists as "irrigating pavement." In my own corner of the state of Oregon, during a summer in which the governor declared a drought emergency and the rivers mimicked the Salt, I have watched my neighbors wash their cars and water their lawns. I have done a bit of car washing and lawn watering myself. We are all, every one of us, prodigious users of water. We use it as if there were no tomorrow—and the way we are going through it, there probably won't be.

Americans are water hogs. As with so many other resources, we use far more of it per capita than the people of
most other cultures do. Our ninety gallons per person per
day of domestic water use is approximately three times that
of the world as a whole, and fifteen to twenty times that of
most third-world countries; at the extreme, residents of parts
of Haiti squeeze by on little more than a gallon a day apiece.
And our use is constantly rising: though the growth curves
have leveled out somewhat recently, water use in the United
States since 1900 has shown an overall expansion rate nearly
four times as great as that of the user population. In 1900,
when our population was 76 million persons, the total
amount of water we used for all purposes—agriculture, industry, and household—was 40 billion gallons per day. By
1950, our population had almost precisely doubled, to 152
million; but water use was up by five times, to slightly over
200 billion gallons per day. Today, as our population approaches 250 million, our daily water use hovers around 500
billion gallons. Population is up 320 percent since 1900;
water use, about 1,250 percent.

Has this increased water use brought with it an increased
standard of living? Some of it has, certainly; there is no deny-
ing that the bulk of us are better off than the bulk of the
American population was eighty years ago. But consider
these figures: Back then in 1900, our gross national product
—expressed in 1972 dollars—was $116 billion, or about
eight tenths of a cent for every gallon of water used that year.
By 1970, the GNP had climbed to more than $1 trillion; but
the amount of money squeezed out of each gallon of water
had fallen to 0.57 cent. Measured in dollar terms, our water
use during the past three quarters of a century has under-
gone a decrease in efficiency of nearly thirty percent.

Why such a profound dropoff? It would be easy—and
tempting—to blame waste; but in the complex world of
water management, things are just not that simple.

To begin with, it is infernally difficult to determine precisely what the word "waste" means when applied to water.
We all have different definitions, depending on our individ-

ual points of view. To an engineer building an irrigation dam, "waste water" might mean the water that flows down the spillway; since it isn't being used to irrigate anything, it is being wasted. To a fisheries biologist looking at the same dam, however, the "waste water" might be the irrigation water itself, especially if it is going to keep a golf course green while fish in the dried-up river are dying. To health and sanitation professionals, "waste water" is water that has already been used once; it flows off the far end of irrigated fields, pours out of sewage-plant outfalls, and runs down storm sewers. Agricultural engineers use a fourth definition; environmentalists, a fifth. "To an ag engineer, waste has a very specific technical meaning," points out San Francisco water activist Dan Sullivan. "It's the ratio of evapotranspiration of applied water to the total amount of applied water. The theory is that evapotranspiration is essential, and it's only when you're applying more than that, that waste occurs.

"The environmentalist's view is more that waste is in terms of the dollar production—if you can get the same value of production with less water, then that's what you should do. If you're not spreading your water out as far as possible, then it's a waste. So there's a lot of difficulty in communication among people, because the same terms have different meanings."

But even after we agree on a definition of waste water— and let's say, for the moment, that we can—then we are still in trouble. Suppose we define "waste water," for the purposes of this book, as water that is withdrawn from a stream or an aquifer but is not put to beneficial use. (There will immediately be arguments over what is or is not "beneficial," of course, but let us sidetrack those for the moment.) Suppose further that everyone agrees that waste, as defined in this manner, is bad and should be eliminated. As an abstract idea, tossed about in a conversation or on the printed page, that is all very well; but as soon as you try to carry it out in concrete terms you will run into three very solid obstructions which will demonstrate to you just how apt the word "concrete" is.

To begin with, there is the problem of economics. Change can be costly, and even if one wishes to eliminate waste he cannot always afford to. It does little good to point out to a factory owner, for instance, that a new piece of equipment will allow him to cut his water use by fifty percent, if the piece of equipment costs a quarter of a million dollars and his credit rating is good for only $100,000. Similarly, it doesn't help a farmer at all to know that corn uses more water than milo wheat if he can make a profit on corn but will lose money growing milo. Water, even scarce water, is a cheap commodity, and as long as this holds true it is always going to be more cost-effective to waste a little—or even a lot— than to spend money to save it.

"The problem," says Pima College's Doug Shakel, "and this is where we got into trouble with oil, is that most things that you pump out of the ground are not priced for what their value is—they're priced for what the cost is of getting them out of the ground and distributing them. Water is basically free." As long as that holds true, water is likely to be the last thing conserved, even by people who recognize and applaud the need for conservation.

Along with economics, there is the problem of laws and regulations. Water-rights law, in the West especially, is a mess. The basic scaffolding is the so-called riparian doctrine, a holdover from the common laws of England—that wet little island—which says that a landowner has the right to withdraw as much water as he needs from any stream on or bordering his own property. On top of that, or sometimes supplanting it, is the doctrine of prior appropriation. Prior appropriation is basically a complicated legalistic version of finders, keepers: it says that people can continue to take water from a river as long as there is water to be taken, but when the river begins to dry up the last person to connect a ditch to it will be the first person to lose his water.

Well and good: you may grouse a bit if your drinking water is cut off while your neighbor with slightly earlier rights fills his swimming pool, but without getting into the tricky world of moralistic judgments about what water, once paid for, is

to be used for—an un-American issue if there ever was one
—it is probably about as fair as any system for appropriating
a scarce resource could be. Nevertheless, it has one extremely serious problem. What happens when a water right
dating to, say, 1859 is not being used, while later rights are?
Under strict prior-appropriation doctrine, the active later
rights would have to be cut off while the unused water in
the earlier right flowed merrily past the intakes and out to
sea.

Faced with this problem, the legislatures and the courts in
the seventeen Western states have come up with what is
essentially seventeen variations on the same solution. Earlier rights should take precedence over later rights, it has
been decided, only as long as the earlier rights are being
used. Unused, a right can be declared vacated and given to
the next user up the line.

Again, well and good—except for one small problem. For
the most part, parts of rights have been treated under the
abandonment statutes as if they were whole rights. This
means, for example, that if you have a right to fifteen cubic
feet per second of water from the Colorado River, and you
use only twelve of it, you lose the right to the other three.
Not just for this year—forever. And this effectively stifles any
significant efforts to cut waste. If you are a good citizen and
cut back from fifteen cubic feet per second to twelve to help
the community weather a drought, you will never see fifteen
feet again.

Under these circumstances, of course, water users in the
West—especially big water users, like municipalities or corporate farms—are extremely reluctant to cut back on what
others might view as waste. "They argue that under existing
law they cannot afford to indulge in conservation first," says
George Pring, a water-law expert at the University of Denver
School of Law. "They have to go straight to the hardware
projects, develop the reservoirs, develop the pipelines—and
then, fifty years down the road instead of now, they will have
developed enough to hang on to their water rights, and they
can go to conservation."

So economics and water-rights laws are barriers to conservation in this country. They are major barriers. But there is an even bigger barrier: it is called habit.

We are all well habituated to using more water than we really need to. And of all things in the world, engrained habit is absolutely the most difficult to turn around.

A few years ago, the city of Ashland, Oregon, where I live and work, was hit by a major flood. The flood wiped out the city's water-treatment plant, and for a full week, in the middle of one of the worst rainstorms on record, we were without water to drink, to cook with, or to bathe in. On the evening of the first day of this disaster, I stood in the kitchen, discussing with my wife the hardships we were about to face. As we talked about the fact that we had no water, I opened a can of cat food, fed our two cats—and then, before my horrified wife could stop me, proceeded to use a pint or so of the precious stuff to wash out the cat-food can before placing it in the garbage.

Habits are like that. We do them without thinking; they are lower-cortex activities, pathways of neurons built up so thoroughly over long years of use that they are almost like instincts. The lawns of Arizona are like the cat-food can in my drought-stricken kitchen: a product of something we might call we-have-always-done-it-this-way. Our houses have always had green lawns, so when we build a house in the desert we put in a green lawn and the devil take the incongruity. We have always had golf courses, and our golf courses have had green lawns, too. In hot weather we have always liked to go swimming, and you have to have water to swim in, don't you? If New York has steel-and-glass skyscrapers, isn't that the mark of a great city, and shouldn't Phoenix have them, even though the heat-producing ability of this fishbowl type of construction makes it hopelessly impractical as a desert structure? If we escape from it all to the Sun Belt, is there any reason why we shouldn't bring it all with us?

The truth is harsh, but we must face it. We are water

junkies. We are hooked on the stuff—and, like any addict, we will go to incredible lengths to satisfy our craving for a fix. The expense doesn't matter. "People scream bloody murder about twenty billion to go to the moon," snorts Doug Shakel, "but they don't even *twitch* over three billion to bring water to towns that don't need it."

As we'll see in the next few chapters, the rearrangements that have taken place in the name of water supply in this country border on absurdist fiction: three-million-year-old water pumped out of the ground to be flushed down toilets in Kansas, a river run backward to keep from fouling the expensive beachfronts of Chicago with industrial and human excrement, snowmelt from the Rockies imported over a distance of nearly a thousand miles to sprinkle on strawberries in southern California . . . Wonderful feats, to be sure. But there is a limit even to wonderful feats. We cannot go on replumbing the continent forever. Somewhere, sometime, we must stop assuming that the answer to water shortages is to go out and find more water, and begin wondering instead if we shouldn't just use less.

Maybe all those green lawns in Arizona are all right; maybe the golf courses and the swimming pools, the cotton fields and the melon patches, and the glass-and-steel, air-conditioned buildings are all right, too. Maybe we should turn the desert into a sunny version of Memphis. Maybe. But somehow I can't help wondering if, someplace along the line, a point hasn't been missed. We have always asked for all the uses of water we could afford. Isn't it about time to start asking if we can afford all the uses?

Just outside Phoenix, within spitting distance of the banks of the Salt River, there is a phenomenon called Big Surf. At Big Surf, there is an artificial ocean containing upward of 4.5 million gallons of pure, fresh water. Every ninety seconds, all day long—as long as the doors remain open and the customers stay—fifteen floodgates spring suddenly downward, sending a five-foot-high wave across the artificial ocean toward four acres of beach surmounted by palm trees and bearing a curious resemblance to the set for a budget version of

South Pacific. As the wave rolls forward, swimmers and sur-
fers splash and yell. The sands of the beach are wet. Outside
the walls, over there in the riverbed, the sands of the Salt
River are dry as dust.

CHAPTER 7

Across Mountain and Prairie

I HAVE A friend who lives in a small walk-up apartment in New York City's Greenwich Village. It is a comfortable apartment, loaded with books and paintings and good music, but it is not a particularly fancy one: a single room plus kitchen and bath, simply furnished, the plaster falling in places, the steam heat loud and largely uncontrollable. All the little things which demonstrate that the resident, whatever his other good qualities might be, is not a wealthy man.

Despite its lack of ostentation, however, there is one thing that my friend's apartment has in common with the most elegant penthouses up on Fifth Avenue. It has, in the kitchen and the bath, a total of four sets of controls to the largest and most intricate machine in Eastern North America. The controls are called faucets. The machine is the New York City water system.

When my friend turns his tap to draw a glass of water, he sets in motion a chain of events that will be felt as far away as the upper Delaware River, 120 miles and more to the northwest. In the walls of his building, water moves in

pipes; beneath the street, water gurgles in mains. Deep in
the stony roots of Manhattan, masses of water in two large
tunnels move ever so slightly. The reservoirs that feed the
tunnels ripple and draw down a fraction of a centimeter; the
aqueducts that feed the reservoirs fill them back up. The
machine sighs into a new equilibrium—until one of the
seven million New Yorkers who hold the controls disturbs it
once again.

The New York City water system is huge. It draws water
from the Croton, a tributary of the Hudson which enters the
main river a few miles above Manhattan (or used to enter:
the lower Croton, these days, is virtually dry). It draws water
from the Schoharie, another Hudson tributary, which enters,
via the Mohawk, on the north side of the distant Catskills. It
draws from the Delaware, which isn't a Hudson tributary at
all and never comes closer to the city than Matamoras, Pennsylvania, fifty-five miles to the northwest. All in all, it draws
water from more than one thousand streams, large and small,
with a total drainage area nearly twice the size of the state of
Rhode Island. The amount of rain that falls on this area is
immense; in a good year, it would fill a lake one hundred
feet deep, a mile across, and more than one hundred miles
long.

To transport these massive quantities of water into the
city, New York's water engineers have constructed an entire
artificial river system. More than 350 miles of aqueducts
thread the New York State countryside or pierce like caverns
through the dark heart of the Catskills. Twenty-seven man-
made lakes glisten in the sun. The flow in the concrete-lined,
unnatural riverbeds pulses in and out of the twenty-seven
lakes at an average rate of around 1.5 billion gallons per day
—about the same as the flow of the upper Hudson, or of the
Red River as it forms the boundary between Minnesota and
North Dakota, or of the Colorado at the Arizona-Colorado
line. One and a half billion gallons per day.

If New Yorkers stopped using water for a week, they could
raise the level of Long Island Sound by eight feet.

City of New York Water Supply Systems

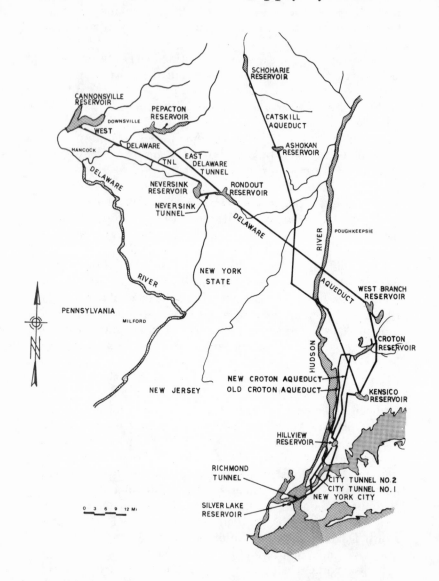

When first encountered in all its complex and glorious immensity, New York City's water-gathering system seems extraordinary indeed. The most extraordinary thing about it, however, is that it is not extraordinary at all. The aqueducts of New York are huge, but they are in no way unusual. Across the mountains and prairies of the United States are flung hundreds of these artificial river systems, large and small, conveying trillions of gallons of water to and fro over the landscape on a scale rivaling in size the natural systems they mimic—and rob. Oklahoma City transports water from reservoirs in Oklahoma's hilly southeastern corner, 125 miles and more away. Fort Worth, Texas, pipes its city supplies in from Richland Creek, seventy-five miles distant; San Francisco sucks its water out of Hetch Hetchy Valley in Yosemite National Park, 150 miles to the east. Denver has bored a tunnel under the Rocky Mountains to tap the headwaters of the distant Colorado, making part of that river, as environmental writer Marc Reisner points out, "flow toward the Gulf of Mexico instead of toward its normal destination, the Pacific Ocean." Water for Portland, Oregon, travels nearly fifty miles, from the Bull Run watershed in the shadow of Mount Hood to the half-million or so Portlandites clustered in the lower end of the wet Willamette Valley: the wet Willamette, it turns out, is not wet enough.

Even cities which get their water from wells—a source that we usually think of as highly localized—may pipe it some distance before using it. Wichita's wells, as we have already seen, are twenty-five miles from the city; Tucson gets some of its water from wells in the Avra Valley, on the far side of the Tucson Mountains; and Los Angeles—among the many gyrations it goes through to keep water flowing through its system—pipes some groundwater in from the Owens Valley, east of the Sierra and close to three hundred miles away.

Like the water for cities, the water for irrigated farms often travels great distances. Hundreds of miles of canals lace the Nebraska plains near the Platte River and feather out over the Columbia Basin south of Grand Coulee Dam in the state of Washington. Agriculture in Utah and Nevada relies almost exclusively on irrigation. In Southern California's Imperial Valley, farmers at the turn of the century built more than two hundred miles of canal to bring the waters of the Colorado to their fertile but dessicated fields; a breach in the canal's embankment in 1905 sent the Colorado sprawling out over the valley, creating the three-hundred-square-mile Salton Sea, but the breach was repaired and the water still flows to the remaining farmland.

In Arizona, the Superstition Mountains cup the reservoirs of the Salt River Project, the nation's oldest federal irrigation works. It is this project which is largely responsible for the current dry state of the Salt River: in addition to supplying domestic water to the residents of Phoenix and its suburbs, it waters the surrounding fields over canals that in some cases follow paths laid out for them by America's first irrigators, the Hohokam Indians, nearly two thousand years ago.

In many ways, of course, all of this makes sense. If there is not enough water where you are, the logical thing to do is go to a spot where there is more than enough and bring some back. This is the policy that humans have been following for millennia, but it is past its prime. Mile after thirsty mile, the pipelines have gone snuffling out across the landscape in search of water, draining the rivers, tapping the aquifers, sucking the earth dry in bigger and bigger circles around our cities and our fields, until the circles have interlocked and there is almost no place left to go to. Between them, the farm aqueducts and the city aqueducts have the country tied up in water-transport devices like Christmas ribbons. The rearrangement of drainage patterns is nearly total: sometimes it seems as though no drop of rain can fall anywhere in the country without being waylaid, bound, gagged, shipped off, and spewed out of a faucet several counties away from its original destination.

Nowhere is the paucity of possibilities more apparent than in our national symbol of growth-gone-wild: southern California, particularly the so-called South Coast Basin area, stretching from Los Angeles to the Mexican border along the beaches of the blue Pacific. Here amid the sunshine and palm trees and everpresent smog live—well, the figure is uncertain, depending upon where you draw the boundary, and whom you are talking to, and the time of day, but it is roughly half the state's population. They have come to revel in the balmy climate, but it is precisely that balmy climate that is their biggest problem. Half the state's population is approximately twelve million people. The basin's rainfall is enough to support a little over 100,000.

Faced with deficiencies of that nature (for those who haven't done the arithmetic themselves, it works out to about a 12,000 percent overdraft), southern Californians—it should surprise no one—have become massive importers of water. They bring it in from the Colorado River, 170 airline miles to the east. They bring it in from the Owens Valley, three hundred miles to the northeast, and from the Mono Basin, one hundred miles beyond that. They bring it in, through an amazing, intricate, and extremely expensive combination of canals, conduits, pumping stations, and in-river transport, from the northern Sierra. The Feather River, which heads out in the Caribou Peak Wilderness beside Lassen Volcanic National Park, and which is nominally a tributary of the Sacramento, now empties large portions of its water into San Diego Bay.

Draining the state into Los Angeles and environs has not been without its difficulties. The engineering problems have been immense. The 770-foot-high Oroville Dam, which impounds the waters of the Feather to send them south, is the tallest earthfill structure in the United States. California Aqueduct water, aided by pumps, must flow uphill for more than two thousand feet over its five-hundred-mile course; and a large part of the Trinity River, whose natural outflow is into the Pacific via the Klamath River near the north-coast community of Eureka, has been made to flow backward through the Trinity Alps into the Central Valley, where it is piped south to irrigate fields around Fresno and Visalia and Bakersfield.

Energy use is also extreme: one publication of the California Department of Water Resources states calmly that the State Water Project consumes "more than half of all electricity used in the State of California," mostly to pump water over the Tehachapi Mountains on the northern rim of the South Coast Basin. And the sheer dollar costs are, to put it mildly, incredible. The Owens Valley aqueduct cost the city of Los Angeles $25 million back in 1913, and estimates of the completed cost of the State Water Project start at $2.5 billion and go upward from there (one link alone in the State Water Project, the Peripheral Canal, has had cost estimates of as high as $23 billion).

Needless to say, the controversy has also been huge.

"Every time we have to manipulate the waters," says limnologist Wayne Linn, "it's a monument to man's inability to manage it right in the first place." A limnologist is a biologist who specializes in freshwater life forms. Linn, who is well known for his work on the fisheries resources of the developing countries of Africa, is currently a member of the biology faculty at Southern Oregon State College in Ashland, and an adamant foe of California's water-transport philosophy. He speaks scornfully of "the technology we're locked into": rather than solving problems, he feels, it is now contributing to them, by encouraging us to think of water as a limitless resource. The draining of northern California has been "a disaster." The drainers themselves? Linn snorts. "They're just so self-righteous. Once water policy gets set, it takes an act of God to change it."

Biologically, the costs of this fossilized policy are not easily measurable, but there is no question that they are serious. Not long before our conversation, Dr. Linn had been called on to verify the discovery of a species of fish in the waters of southwestern Oregon that had never been seen there before; he theorizes that it probably came in from the Klamath Basin, over the mountains to the east, via irrigation canals. "So that's one impact," he told me, "extending the range of species you might not want extended. There are times you might transport organisms you wouldn't want. To coin a

phrase, we might call it biological transfer." The chemistry
of water coming in from another area is often different from
the chemistry of the native waters, and this too can have an
effect. If the native plants have trouble using the alien water,
the plant community might change. This is particularly a
problem when the imports are significantly higher in dissolved solids. "There is enough variability in organisms to
sustain themselves against different chemistries in the water
in most cases," Linn is quick to point out. "Still, it's something that cannot be ignored.

"Where I see the real danger, though, is not where the
water is taken to but on the other side of the coin—where
it's taken from. This is particularly true of the Owens Valley.
That area is being deprived of its natural volumes of water,
and that's where the serious problems can develop. What
you're doing is, you're robbing the other side, and if you take
a lot, you won't have the seepage, you won't have nearly the
buildup in the aquifers, so you won't get recharge in your
wells. If it's done on a long sustained basis, the whole area
can be influenced by a reduction in available water. And I
think it could also have an influence on climate, because
you've removed the water for evaporation and transpiration,
and your normal amount of water for hydrological uses isn't
there anymore. That's a serious concern that's been voiced,
but probably not heard very well. I think it's already happened in places like Owens Valley, but it happens so slowly
we don't see it."

Water managers, of course, disagree with these conten-
tions.

In downtown Los Angeles, on top of a hill overlooking the
old city center on the edge of the dry Los Angeles River, a
sparkling, modern, multistory building surrounded by a full
moat of water serves as headquarters for the Los Angeles
Department of Water and Power—the "DWP" of many an
environmentalist's nightmares. Here, in his fourteenth-floor
office, Dwayne Georgeson, the lanky, affable, and articulate
chief engineer for the Los Angeles Aqueduct, props his el-
bows on the arm of his chair, steeples his fingers together,

and skillfully parries Linn's concerns. Drainage of the Owens Valley, he points out, has been going on since the First World War, but farming is still carried on there. The ecology has been changed, but not necessarily degraded. The recent addition of groundwater pumping to the long-standing diversion of the river waters hasn't really altered this. "The plants that live off the water table," he explains with just a touch of irony, "used to be known as water-wasting plants. Well, in our environmentally sensitive era, to pull the water table down away from the roots of those plants is known as environmental degradation. And if you were to set a standard whereby you didn't affect any of those plants, you couldn't pump a *drop* out of the Owens Valley.

"It stands to reason, of course, that if the groundwater table is going to be lowered over a portion of the valley for the next fifty years, there probably will be some impact on vegetation. And since it's never been a concern to anybody prior to this, nobody's made any particular study on what the effects of groundwater pumping are on a basin that's full. And so it's impossible, frankly, to predict with any kind of accuracy what the effects are going to be. You know, to my mind, a reasonable person would say the effects are insignificant. But to somebody who's concerned with the plants, and there are a few of those in the valley, I mean, concerned very intimately with each and every plant—they think it's outrageous to say that the effects are insignificant."

But if the effects of the transport are, as Georgeson maintains, "insignificant," the same cannot be said about the controversy: it has, in fact, flared heavily almost everywhere the pipes have tried to reach. Southern Californians have been called "water imperialists" by their north-state brethren for seeking to divert the waters of the north-coast rivers—the Eel, the Klamath, the Trinity, and the Smith, all five hundred miles and more upstate—into the California State Water Project. They have fought bitterly with neighboring Arizona over the rights to Colorado River water—a fight that finally ended in 1964, but not before giving the United States Supreme Court the biggest case, in terms of sheer paperwork, of its entire two-hundred-year history (the record of proceedings in this case, *State of Arizona, Complainant, v. State of California et al.*, fills more than one hundred volumes). For nearly three decades now, they have carried on a running battle with agricultural interests, environmentalists, and San Francisco–area residents over completion of the Peripheral Canal, a project which southern-California water managers claim is essential for the South Coast Basin area's continued growth and prosperity, and which San Francisco claims will destroy its famous bay.

Both are probably correct. The canal—or, as the water managers prefer to call it, the "isolated transport facility"—would siphon off up to eighty percent of the flow of the Sacramento River at the town of Hood, a few miles below Sacramento, and carry it around the eastern edge of the Sacramento–San Joaquin delta to the head of the California Aqueduct, where it would be dumped in for transport south. Canal backers point out that most of this water is going south anyway, transported through the winding natural channels of the delta and pumped out on the south edge, at the Clifton Court Forebay: the canal, they say, is necessary to manage the flow more efficiently and thus firm up the yield of the State Water Project. The canal will be wider at its intake than at its mouth, so that it sucks up more water than it can deliver; spillways at several points along its route will deliver the excess water into the eastern edge of the delta, thus providing for the delta's preservation. Critics grant all these points, but make a few of their own. Moving the water through the delta has kept the delta channels full of fresh water; moving the water around the delta will remove most of that. The releases will provide the delta with up to 1,800 cubic feet per second of fresh water, but scientists of the United States Geologic Survey have calculated that at least twice, and probably three times, that amount is necessary to prevent the infiltration of salt water from San Francisco Bay up the delta channels. And no one denies that the canal will move more water south than is currently being moved. There is a strong chance—some say a certainty—that depriving the bay of this extra inflow of water will prevent it from flushing pollutants out to sea through the Golden Gate, converting one of the world's most beautiful anchorages into nothing much better than a stagnant cesspool.

They have fought over all these things, and the fights have been hot, and heavy, and long. Most of all, though—hottest, heaviest, and longest—they have fought over the fate of an extraordinary valley on the east side of the Sierra Nevada range, that magnificent rain-catcher and water-producer that John Muir referred to as the "range of light." This valley is called the Mono Basin.

Just off Wilshire Boulevard in the western portion of Los Angeles, not far from the UCLA campus, a small white stucco building with a Spanish-style central courtyard holds the Los Angeles headquarters of the Mono Lake Committee. Ten miles away, on top of its hill and surrounded by its modern version of the medieval moat, stands the headquarters of the DWP. And between these two headquarters yawns a gulf far greater than physical distance, or size, or style of architecture would suggest. The gulf concerns Mono Lake. The DWP says that it is shrinking the lake. The Mono Lake Committee says that the DWP is killing it.

Mono Lake is spectacular. Four hundred miles north of Los Angeles and a little to the east, it gleams in the trans-Sierran desert like a blue ghost. Around it rise volcanic cinder cones and strange, unnatural-looking formations of salt-encrusted tufa. The cinder cones are young. The lake is old. Geologists say that it has been there for at least half a million years, perhaps twice that; it is, they say, the oldest continuously existing body of water in North America.

Just to the west, looming over the lake and its desert like a great blue wall, towers the Yosemite section of the Sierra crest. Down this wall, tumbling and pell-melling toward the lake, rush the streams of the eastern Yosemite highlands—Rush Creek, Mill Creek, Walker Creek, and Lee Vining Creek, counterparts of the more famous west-slope streams like the Tolumne and the Merced. In ancient times, when Mono Lake was young, these streams and their now-van-

ished companions supplied enough flow to create an inland
sea that may have reached all the way into the Owens Valley,
a hundred miles to the south; but by the time white men
came along in the middle of the nineteenth century they had
shrunk to a fraction of that flow. The lake had shrunk, too,
but it was still impressive: ninety square miles of achingly
blue water, almost perfectly round, cloudy with flocks of
gulls, and saltier than the sea.

That was the way things stood until 1940. In that year the
Los Angeles Aqueduct came snuffling up over the low divide
to the south, looking for new sources of water to feed into
the apparently limitless maw of the rapidly growing city by
the sea four hundred miles away. The Owens River had
been sucked dry, and the massive quantities of Colorado
River water that had just started to come into the South Coast
Basin via the Colorado Aqueduct had to be shared with the
other cities of the basin and were thus strictly limited. (This
is probably as good a time as any to point out that the city of
Los Angeles, whatever its other sins might be, does not now
and has never in the past imported any water from the Colorado. That honor belongs to the Metropolitan Water District, or MWD, which serves the sprawl of communities
surrounding Los Angeles. Los Angeles does buy some water
from the MWD, but in most years it is a scarcely significant
amount.) The waters of the Mono Basin were an attractive
possibility. The lake itself couldn't be used—it was far too
salty—but the streams feeding it could and were. A large
dam across Rush Creek blocked its flow, creating a storage
reservoir called Grant Lake. Small dams on Walker and Lee
Vining Creeks diverted their waters into Grant Lake, where
they could be picked up by an eleven-mile-long tunnel
under the Mono Craters and spat out into the upper end of
the Owens River. This left only Mill Creek still flowing un-
fettered to Mono Lake, and although overflows from Grant
Lake would often pour down the bed of Rush Creek into
their old destination, half of the basin's water supply was
now going south. The ancient lake began to shrink percep-
tibly.

For the next thirty years this shrinkage slowly continued,

the lake level dropping six to twelve inches a year, the shore-
line creeping down away from the town of Lee Vining, exposing acres of bare, salt-encrusted sediments. Winds picked
up the drying sediments and sent them whirling in stinging
blasts through the town. The citizens began to mutter. They
were still muttering in 1970, as Los Angeles, still short of
water, completed construction on the so-called "second barrel": a second Los Angeles Aqueduct, parallel to the first
one, that could double the flow from the Owens Valley to
the city. Since the Mono Lake Extension fed into the Owens
Valley system, that meant that its exports could be doubled,
too. They were. The overflows from Grant Lake virtually
stopped; the lake's shrinkage rate jumped enormously.

So did the criticism.

"The Los Angeles Department of Water and Power,"
states Tom Cassidy with barely controlled anger, "is a classic
example of a very narrowly oriented utility whose sole job is
to provide power and water to the city of Los Angeles at the
lowest possible rate and with no consideration for the environmental consequences of their actions." Cassidy, a stocky,
intense young man with a quick smile, is the director and
entire staff of the Los Angeles office of the Mono Lake Committee. He considers the DWP's actions at Mono Lake "a
catastrophe of the first magnitude." The lake level, he points
out, has been dropping for forty years—a foot a year from
1940 to 1970, eighteen inches to two feet a year since. This
has dramatically increased the water's salinity. The lake is
inhabited by brine shrimp, which live in the salty water, and
by gulls, which live on islands and feed on the brine shrimp.
Like all simple ecosystems, this one is inherently unstable,
and there is some question how much longer it can last in
the face of the DWP diversions. Already, signs of stress are
appearing. "The scientists who are studying the brine
shrimp are very concerned about the long-term effects. In
forty years, the salt content has doubled. That is an extraor-
dinarily huge change. And we don't know when we are
going to achieve a threshold point with the salinity. There is
a lake in Africa, Lake Nkuru, that was drying up, and becom-

ing ever more saline. And studies of the invertebrates
showed they were doing just fine. As it got more salty their
population increased. And studies show that that's the case
in Mono Lake: as it becomes saltier, to a certain extent, the
reproduction rate of the brine shrimp goes up. At a certain
point, though, it begins to fall. And in Lake Nkuru, it collapsed like *that*. Everything died. There wasn't a gradual
die-off, there was an immediate collapse in the whole ecosystem. And we're very concerned about that happening in
Mono Lake." There is also a question about the gulls. Gulls
like to nest on islands, cut off from land-based predators; and
when, in 1979, the waters of the lake fell to the point where
Negit Island became an exposed peninsula, "the rookery
was entirely abandoned. Instead of a historical nesting of
more than thirty thousand gulls, no gulls nested on Negit
Island. Fish and Game constructed a fence. That fence was
successful in that it kept coyotes off the island. It was not
successful in convincing gulls that peninsulas are a safe
place to nest. Ten gulls—there were ten nesting gulls on
Negit Island. But the gulls are really not the bottom-line
biological concern. The bottom-line biological concern is the
effects of increased salinity. The gulls are merely an indication that something is very wrong."

Down at DWP headquarters, Dwayne Georgeson gazes
out his fourteenth-floor window at the distant San Bernardino Mountains and counters Cassidy's charges. "At the risk
of sounding overly defensive on Mono Lake," he begins,
"we start with the fact that, because we divert a lot of the
streams that used to flow into the lake, the lake is unques-
tionably going down because of our diversions. That fact we
agree to. And there's general agreement that the lake's going
to continue to get smaller until it's about half its present size.
The facts that don't come out very well are that the lake has
been going down for forty years, and the bird population has
been *increasing* over that period of time. The brine shrimp
populations show every indication of increasing also, for a
while, as the lake gets saltier. So there is no immediate threat
to the ecosystem of the lake.

"I think we approach the whole question from the stand-point that Mono Lake is not the only water problem that's threatening California, or southern California, or Los Angeles. And thus we're disinclined to be stampeded into simplistic solutions. I think there's reason to believe that at some point the salinity will start to have a negative effect on the production of the brine shrimp. The thing that people lose sight of is that that's many years off. There are many options, I think, which might be found in the next few decades, in terms of protecting discrete parts of the ecosystem —the birds, and the brine shrimp—but the focus has been on what my attorney friend calls 'cosmic solutions,' which ignore the fact that you would aggravate environmental problems elsewhere, where the replacement water would come from."

And so we return to the crux of the problem. Where is the replacement water coming from? If Los Angeles stops diverting water from the Mono Basin, to provide for the brine shrimp, where are they going to go to provide for the people? Not to the Owens Valley: the Owens River is already all going south anyway, and though there is some groundwater in the basin, Los Angeles is already pumping it out at a rate that has Owens Valley residents suing them. Not to the Colorado: southern California is already drawing more than its share of Colorado River water, and the courts have ruled that these imports must be dramatically cut within the next decade. Not to the south: there isn't any water to the south. And not to the north either, though there is some water there. Going north means expanding the California State Water Project, and building the Peripheral Canal, and that is tied up in at least as much controversy as is the Mono Basin itself. Where to? And where to next? Where do we go when all the where-tos have been used up?

This is the problem we face all over the country. All our where-tos have been used up. Aside from the costs, and the engineering problems, and the biological implications, there are real questions of limits involved in any further extension of water-transfer activities. It may be physically possible to build the aqueducts, and float the bonds, and satisfy the environmentalists, but what good is it all if there isn't any water at the other end of the pipe? If all you can do with your straw is to dip it into somebody else's drinking glass, what good are more straws?

And yet it is more straws that water-supply experts persist in dreaming about. They talk of pipelines everywhere. They talk of a pipeline across Kansas, transporting Missouri River water uphill from Kansas City to the high-plains region of the Kansas-Colorado border. They talk of a pipeline from Oregon to Arizona, transporting Columbia River water southward to Phoenix. They talk of a pipeline along the Gulf Coast of Texas, running from Louisiana to Mexico and sweeping up rivers as it goes, to deposit all the water in the fertile but dry valley of the lower Rio Grande. They talk of pipelines from the Adirondacks to New York, and of converting Long Island Sound into a freshwater lake. And when they really get wound up, and well into their subject—or into their cups—they talk about NAWAPA.

NAWAPA, to put it mildly, is a whopper. It is the heaven that all good water engineers would like to go to when they die. The brainchild of Donald McCord Baker, an engineer and water official from—where else?—Los Angeles County, NAWAPA, or, to use its official full-length name, the North American Water and Power Alliance, is basically a scheme for picking up the North American continent by the North Pole and making all its northern rivers run backward. Great dams would be placed on the Mackenzie, the Yukon, the Coppermine, and virtually every other north-flowing river above the 55th parallel. One hundred ten million acre-feet of water per year, once tributary to the Arctic Ocean and the Bering Strait, would be piped southward instead, to water cornfields and flush toilets and wash cars as far south as Mexico. The scheme calls for a man-made reservoir five hundred miles long, made by damming both ends of the Rocky Mountain Trench in northeastern British Columbia. It calls for a tunnel eighty feet in diameter and fifty miles long to transport water under one of the little barriers that is in its way: the state of Idaho. It calls for a canal into the Great Lakes, and another into the Missouri, to use them as water storage and transport devices.

It calls, in short, for a total rearrangement of the drainage system of North America.

In its twenty years of serious existence as a proposal, NAWAPA has had some enthusiastic and dedicated supporters. One of them is Congressman Jim Wright of Texas. "NAWAPA has an almost limitless potential if we possess the courage and the foresight to grasp it," Wright wrote in his 1964 book *The Coming Water Famine.* ". . . There is to the north of us a stupendous supply of water, enough to satisfy most of our predictable wants for years to come, which is simply going to waste. We need the water. We need to develop the means of getting that water."

Maybe. Maybe we do need all that water; maybe it is simply going to waste by filling up the Arctic Ocean. Maybe we can live with the climatic changes that are sure to occur when we shift the continent's point of water balance that far south. Maybe all the people who live in the Rocky Mountain Trench, in McBride and Dunster and Raush Valley and Dome Creek and all the other picturesque little towns along the Yellowhead Highway, can be convinced that they should abandon their homes so that we can drop the Mackenzie River on top of them to create a capitalist Lake Baikal. Maybe the price tag—an estimated $100 billion in 1964, sure to be much more today—is not outrageous in the face of the possible consequences of not acting. Maybe. But if so—and this is important—*what do we do next?*

What do we do when we have moved the Arctic Ocean to Kansas? What do we do after the Mackenzie and the Peace and the Yukon have become tributary to Los Angeles Bay? This question is not lightly asked. Where do we go for water when we run out next time? Which continent do we re-plumb, which ocean do we steal, which five-hundred-mile-long valley do we turn into a reservoir? Consider: 110 million acre-feet of water is four months' supply. Eighty years from now, if our growth rate continues at the same pace as it has for the last eighty years, it will be one *week's* supply. Coupled with the water we're currently using, that's three weeks' supply. What do we do for the other forty-nine weeks?

Sooner or later, we are going to have to come to grips with that problem. Sooner, actually, because the earlier we do it, the more room we will have for sensible solutions.

In the late summer of 1981, several months after my conversations with Tom Cassidy and Dwayne Georgeson, word spread from the Mono Basin that the ecosystem collapse feared so strongly by the environmentalists had finally taken place. Biologists David Winkler and Petra Lenz of the University of California reported that the brine-shrimp hatch in the lake had suddenly declined by eighty-five to ninety-five percent, and virtually all the baby gulls born that spring had died, principally from starvation. "If the spring shrimp populations do not recover to their former levels," Winkler wrote, "it is highly improbable that the lake will be able to support large numbers of nesting gulls again." The Mono Lake birds represent ninety-five percent of California's breeding population of gulls. Gulls are a primary predator of field mice, one of the state's principal crop pests. The thought of a future without them is frightening: their loss will have literally incalculable ramifications for California agriculture.

Was the extra water for Los Angeles worth it? Can we really afford to keep on with business-as-usual?

As reports and articles on the deaths of the gulls collected in my study in the fall of 1981, I remembered wrenchingly the last words Tom Cassidy had said to me the spring before in Los Angeles. "I think we have to recognize that there are limits to our resources," he had said, leaning back in his chair in his little office off Wilshire Boulevard and putting his hands behind his head, "and we are certainly facing the limits of our resources in water. The utilities should not further the delusion that we live in New Zealand, here in a semiarid area. We can go on with our wasteful ways—we can continue to take water from the Mono Basin, and we can continue irrigating pavement in Los Angeles. We can continue irrigating pavement in San Diego or Sacramento. And yet all that this leads to is saying, well, we'll go on, and get water from some other place, we'll get water from the Eel, or we'll get water from the Columbia, or we'll get water from the Yukon. . . ." He had paused here, gesturing emphatically, chopping the air with his hands to emphasize each word. "Sometime, someday, we're going to have to realize that there just *isn't—any—more.*"

CHAPTER **8**

The Water Miners

WEST OF WICHITA, U.S. Highway 54 spears toward the
setting sun, dipping now and then to cross the muddy, meandering Ninnescah River, but for the most part staying high
and level, the sky cupped over it like a blue dome, the plains
sweeping out to infinity beyond the gravel shoulders. At dec-
orous intervals, small, tidy towns—Kingman, Pratt, Greensburg—come and go, their brick streets and green parks and
cupola-crowned buildings solid and dignified and warm. In
the spring, the air is sweet with new growth; in the fall, ripe
and bountiful with the scent of harvest.

At Mullinville the road splits. The main fork veers south,
through Meade and Liberal and on into Oklahoma; the alter-
nate route, labeled 154, continues due west. A few miles
north of Bucklin it turns northwestward, toward Ford. Here
it picks up the broad, shallow Arkansas River, oozing slug-
gishly eastward across the plain from its birthplace in the
distant, dreamlike Rockies. The highway turns upstream,
following the line of cottonwoods that marks the river. In
fifteen minutes or so, the eye picks out the skyscraperlike
shapes of grain elevators silhouetted against the distance.
Dodge City is close at hand.

To many Americans, Dodge City has an almost mythical

significance. This is the Great Cowtown, the Wild West Wal-
halla of the nineteenth century, where men were hard and
money and women were easy, where gamblers died with
their boots on and where hired guns lit out for the Territory
ahead of flinty-eyed lawmen like Matt Dillon and Wyatt
Earp and Bat Masterson. The legend is not entirely fraudu-
lent. Hollywood has embellished the stories, but Hollywood
did not create them: Matt Dillon never existed, but Earp and
Masterson were real enough, and both were once sheriffs
here.

Dodge City today enjoys its Wild-West image—Dodge
City, you might say, revels in it—but the image remains just
that: an image. Behind the tourist traps that line Front Street,
behind the hype of Boot Hill and the cutesy street names—
Wyatt Earp Avenue, Gunsmoke Avenue, Matt Dillon Drive
—lies a typical middle-American farming community, another Pratt or Kingman or Greensburg. Above the warm,
shallow Arkansas the residential districts march neatly up
the bluff, well-kept frame houses lining tree-shaded brick
streets, to the edge of the open and all-encompassing plain.
This is the country of spacious skies and amber waves of
grain, mile upon mile of it, rolling off to the distant, flat
horizon like an earthen ocean. There is water in that ocean,
too, but it is underground, laced through a vast deposit of
ancient sands and gravels known as the Ogallala Aquifer.
And for Dodge City—and hundreds of other cities, west
to the Rockies, north to the Dakotas and south to the
Rio Grande—the waters of the Ogallala are the waters of
life.

The American High Plains have a long history of seeming
to be inhospitable to human settlement. Early explorers
passed this region by; the maps they brought back with them
called it the "Great American Desert." "We do not hesitate
in giving the opinion that it is almost wholly unfit for cultivation and, of course, uninhabitable by a people depending
upon agriculture for their subsistence," wrote Stephen H.
Long, surveying the area for the United States Army in 1819.

Oregon-bound Conestoga wagons lumbered through and did not stay. What, in this godforsaken land of empty horizons and tough, sparse grasses, could there possibly be to stay for?

And yet, in time—inevitably—there were those who settled here. Cattlemen were the first, coming into the area on the heels of the Civil War and finding in its broad, unfenced grasslands a place for great roaming herds of a size undreamed of in the small-horizoned East—herds big enough to supply whole states with meat, herds that could make a man rich for the rest of his life. The cattle industry needed a support network; cowtowns sprung up, went through brief youthful flings of thumb-your-nose, flaunt-the-law machismo, and settled down to a staid middle age. The towns attracted farmers, and the farmers survived—barely. Given enough water, they found, the land would produce bountifully; but all too often there was not enough water. Some years the rains would come and some years they would not. This is, in fact, the boundary of the arid lands, the midcontinental line, transected by the hundredth meridian and haunted by drought. If only there could be water . . .

It was the water-lean years of the 1930s, the Dustbowl years, that led to the great discovery. The water *was* there: you had to dig to find it, but it was there. Deep under those dry plains, bursting the seams of the Ogallala Aquifer, there was more water than you could dream of. By happy coincidence—or by Providential design—the eastern border of this rich lode of water coincided almost precisely with the hundredth meridian, supplying from beneath the ground what the rains refused to supply from above. Well drilling was suddenly big business. Down went the questing pipes, each topped by a whirling windmill; up came the water, pouring into the stock trough, onto the vegetable garden, and eventually onto the cash crop of corn or milo or wheat or cotton that they had said couldn't be grown out here. It was a boom time, a time for building, a paradise come true. The water would make it so.

Where did all that water come from? No one was quite

sure. Prevailing opinion held that it was part of a vast underground stream carrying runoff from the melted snows of the Rockies to the distant Gulf of Mexico. Others, less secure in their geomorphology, thought it might be sinking into the ground from the Platte and the Arkansas and the other rivers that sprawled across this empty land. Or perhaps it was being made down there. At any rate, it seemed limitless. There were Cassandras who warned otherwise, but they could be safely ignored; in a bull market, no one has time for Cassandras. One by one the windmills came down, replaced by gasoline-powered submersibles of much greater pumping capacity. Big center-pivot irrigation systems bristled out of the ground from San Antonio to the South Dakota border. In 1935, west-Texas farmers pumped 8.4 billion gallons of water out of the Ogallala onto their fields; fifteen years later, pumpage had increased to more than 350 billion gallons. Nebraska had no significant acreage irrigated by wells in 1920; by the early 1960s, pumps were supplying Ogallala water to more than two million acres in the western and central parts of the state. The story was the same in western Kansas, in eastern Colorado, and in the Oklahoma panhandle—all underlain by the Ogallala. On the market, irrigated lands went for double the price per acre of dry range, and speculators reaped small fortunes.

In Dodge City, and in surrounding Ford County, the pattern was the same as elsewhere in the six-state High Plains region. "In 1938," says Mike Dealy of the Southwest Kansas Groundwater Management District No. 3 in nearby Garden City, "Ford County had 197 irrigation wells irrigating about 2,800 acres. In 1980 there were 850 wells irrigating some 85,000 acres of land. The Ogallala is the primary aquifer." The amount of water pumped jumped thirtyfold in this period, from 4,800 acre-feet—about 1.6 billion gallons—to 144,000 acre-feet.

At the same time, however, attitudes toward the Ogallala in Dodge City, and elsewhere on the High Plains, have changed dramatically. Few new wells are being drilled these days: the booming optimism of the 1940s and 1950s has been replaced by a wariness, a watchfulness, even a little fear.

The Cassandras, you see, were right.

John Gries, a transplanted Texan who has taught geology at Wichita State University since 1972, is among the Cassandras. Sitting in his cluttered office in the Wichita campus's old brick McKinley Hall on a cool March Wednesday, the rain misting down outside, I listened while he described the geology of the Ogallala aquifer. It was a fascinating and in many ways an amazing tale. The Ogallala, it seems, is a geological holdover, the buried remnant of a vast alluvial plain stretching eastward from what once were Himalaya-sized Rocky Mountains. The climate was cooler and wetter then; there were great glaciers among the high peaks, and the Arkansas and its sisters to the north and south ran brimful across the porous deposits of gravel and rock and sand washed down from the eroding mountains. Rains fell on the eastern slopes of the peaks, trickled into the upper end of the sloping alluvium, and flowed slowly out under the plain. Gradually, like a giant sponge, the earth of the plain filled with water.

Then the climate changed. The rains lessened; the glaciers retreated. In the mountains, erosion slowed, and the north- and south-flowing streams along the base of the Front Range—tributaries of the ancestral Arkansas and Platte and Canadian and Pecos—began to cut down through the alluvium faster than it could be deposited. The Ogallala was beheaded, cut off from its recharge areas and deprived of the runoff water from the Rockies. At the same time, out on the plains themselves, the drastically reduced rainfall led to a process called "calichefication"—a cementing of the soil particles together by minerals left behind by evaporating groundwater. This process, somewhat akin to baking potters' clay in a kiln, created a thick, watertight roof over the alluvium; what little rain fell could no longer flow into it. The Ogallala was trapped, preserved unchanged through the ages; with next to nothing flowing out or in, the water in the aquifer had become, to all intents and purposes, a fossil.

"The problem over much of the Ogallala," says Gries, "is that the original recharge area in the Rockies is gone, and the conduit between here and there has eroded out. Those beds extended clear up into the high parts of the Front Range, and the main part of the water that's in there is from that time. There are some areas where you still get some recharge, but unfortunately they are not in the areas that are being heavily used."

How long ago did the connections to the recharge areas exist? Gries ponders. "Let's see, now," he says, "our problem is probably when it *ceased* to exist. In other words, when the last things were cut." He pauses, lost in thought. "I'd probably have to go with the late Pleiocene or early Pleistocene," he says at last. "You're probably talking three million years."

The farmers on the High Plains are irrigating their crops with three-million-year-old water, the fruit of rains that fell in the ancient Rockies at about the same time that the first brute ancestor of early man walked the warm green earth of Africa.

The meaning of this statement, for the six states whose agricultures depend partially or wholly on this ancient lode of stored water, is clear. If you are pumping something out of a reservoir, and not putting anything back in, eventually that reservoir is going to run dry. The fossil water of the Ogallala is exactly like fossil fuels elsewhere: a limited resource. You can build an economy around it as long as you can keep taking it out of the ground, but when it is gone the economy will go with it, leaving behind the ghost towns that accompany any played-out mineral deposit. Agriculture here, in other words, is an extractive industry: as Mike Dealy puts it, "the water is being mined."

The Ogallala is not the only place in America where water mining is being practiced: in most places around the nation, in fact, water tables are falling. In North Carolina, Arkansas, Indiana and Hawaii wells and springs are drying up, their flow rates significantly diminished or gone altogether. The water in the wells supplying the town of Nogadoches, in east Texas—an area of relatively heavy rainfall—fell sixty-five feet in one recent ten-year period. Des Moines's wells are down; so are those serving Long Island, and New Jersey, and Savannah, Georgia. In California's San Joaquin Valley, pumping has lowered the water table so far that the ground surface above it has collapsed, falling by as much as twenty-five feet since the 1920s.

The scope of the groundwater-supply crisis is demonstrated with remarkable clarity by the current state of flowing artesian wells in this country. A "flowing artesian well" is a well punched into an aquifer which is sitting with one end tipped up higher than the other: when the overlying caprock is punctured, the weight of stored water in the upper end causes water from the lower end to flow, or even spout, out onto the surface of the ground. A good healthy majority of the wells drilled in this country used to be flowing artesian, and it is a measure of what we are doing to our continental water supply that today such wells have become next to non-existent. Not only are few new ones being drilled; the old ones have stopped flowing, most of them so long ago that were it not for written records, there would be only a dim sort of racial memory to indicate that they ever flowed at all. Montgomery, Alabama, lost its artesian pressure at the turn of the century, and by 1950 the formerly overflowing wells were being pumped from static levels one hundred feet and more below the surface. City wells in Miami, Oklahoma, were flowing in 1907; fifty years later the static level in the wells had dropped more than five hundred feet. Green Bay, Wisconsin, had flowing artesian wells late in the nineteenth century, but by the middle of the twentieth century the water level was more than three hundred feet down, and in 1964 the town had to abandon the wells altogether when the pumps began bringing up air instead of water. Green Bay now gets its water from Lake Michigan. Previously flowing wells are down more than five hundred feet in the Dallas–Fort Worth area of Texas. When the first deep well was drilled in Chicago, in 1864, water shot eighty feet into the air; today, in the same area, some wells must pump from as much as eight hundred feet below the surface. We are wringing the continent dry like an old shirt, using up in a few short decades stores of water that have been accumulating under the earth for generations. Fifty percent of our drinking water —and twenty-five percent of the water we use for all purposes—comes from beneath the ground. But the ground is increasingly unwilling to give it up.

Aside from the Ogallala, the place where groundwater mining is being practiced most assiduously is undoubtedly Arizona—particularly southern Arizona, in the Santa Cruz Valley around Tucson. Here, in the heart of the Gadsden Purchase, the last piece of land to be added to the contiguous United States, half a million people live and work amid ancient, eroded mountains under skies that can best be described as Mexican blue. It does rain in Tucson, but, at barely eleven inches a year, rain is rare enough to be an Event; mostly the sun shines, and the dry, beautiful city sparkles in the dry, beautiful air.

Because it *is* dry—so dry that the surrounding mountains bear forests of saguaro cactus instead of trees—water supply has always been a problem for the residents of Tucson and the surrounding communities of Pima County. The Santa Cruz River is no help; once it was a real river, with cottonwoods and fish and beaver, but that was so long ago that it no longer matters. Mining and irrigation activities in the late nineteenth century were the culprits. The water was all gone by 1890; today, except during one of its rare floods, the Santa Cruz River is dry as a bone. There are no other rivers. A few springs and seeps around the edge of the valley, at the base of the mountains, provide a tiny amount of flowing water that can loosely be called a surface water supply; other than that, the name of the game is groundwater.

Fortunately, there is a lot of groundwater. The mountains around Tucson are very, very old, and they have been eroding for a long time. Gravity has pulled the detritus from the

MAJOR AQUIFERS

OGALLALA

COLUMBIA BASALTS

OTHER MAJOR AQUIFERS

GROUNDWATER OVERDRAFT

REGIONAL OVERDRAFT

LOCAL OVERDRAFT

erosion down to the mountains' feet, and, with no significant flows of water to carry it farther, it has accumulated there, growing to extraordinary depths. Tucson sits on a plain of this debris that is probably half a mile deep. The debris is very loosely packed, and it is full of water.

Or *was* full of water. The homes and farms and mines of Pima County have been sucking it out, drop by stream by gusher. Since 1940, when population growth in this area began in earnest, the average water level in the wells has fallen by around 150 feet. And the people of Tucson are getting worried.

"We have," says Frank Brooks of Tucson Water, "a diminishing resource." Brooks is a silver-haired, grandfatherly figure who has been working for the city for a long time. Currently he is in charge of public relations, a job which translates, these days, into convincing Tucson residents that clean cars and green lawns are at least Semi-Pelagial, if not Original, sins. Conservation, he feels, must be a long-term thing, because "we can't afford for it not to be. You can't go on sticking your head into the wringer year after year. The nature of the thing is, we don't have unlimited water. We have limited water."

He ticks off the figures. Wells throughout the city dropping anywhere from two to eight feet per year. An annual evaporation rate eight times the region's annual rainfall. A water demand, without conservation, of 200 million gallons per day; a total in the aquifer of about 30 million acre-feet, or 130 years' supply at the nonconservation-use level. That use level, by the way, includes agriculture and industry, which is part of the problem. "All urban use," says Brooks, "represents only about ten per cent of the water use in the basin. So if people didn't use *anything* there wouldn't be a significant effect on the problem. Agriculture is the largest user. People and industry use about the same—but it's consumptive use you're worried about. Of domestic water, fifty percent is returned to the underground. Most of the agricultural and industrial water is used up." Mined. Gone.

And after it's gone . . . well, it was a nice place for a city.

And maybe the tourists will enjoy coming to look at the ghost town, if they bring their own water.

Still, Tucson is lucky, in a way. They know how much water is down there, and 130 years is a long time. Time to breathe; time, perhaps, to come up with some solutions. These solutions may not be possible; they may not be practical; but at least they know what kind of problem they're dealing with.

Up in the Columbia Basin, around my old home town of Pullman, Washington, they're not so sure.

Asked how much groundwater there is in storage in the aquifers beneath Pullman, Jim Crosby leans back in his chair, looks at his visitor calmly, and says in a quiet voice, "I haven't got the vaguest idea."

Coming from anyone else, that response would be precisely what was expected; but coming from Crosby, it registers as a bit of a shocker. He is a basalt hydrologist—a specialist in precisely the type of aquifer that underlies the city—and he has lived and worked and studied there, as a member of the Washington State University geology faculty, for nearly thirty years. The amount of water in the aquifer, it would seem, would be one of the first things a basalt hydrologist would want to discover. Hasn't the matter been studied?

Crosby, a short, balding man who looks like the Hollywood stereotype of a middle-aged small businessman, exhales a bit tiredly. "Oh, we've tried to study it," he says, "but the thing is, there are just these untouchable parameters. You know, we've got areas now where the amount of work that has been done on the system just totally *buries* the amount of work that's been done on the Pullman area, and still in *those* areas we don't really have a good understanding of what's going on. You get a dozen basalt hydrologists together to talk about the system, and basically about all they'll do is disagree." The problem is not one of lack of interest, or lack of expertise, or lack of man-hours spent. The problem is the aquifers themselves. They are deeply buried, and structurally complex, and they do not give up their secrets easily. Often they do not give them up at all.

The term "basalt hydrology" is in some ways self-contradictory. Basalt is among the least-permeable materials on earth; it does not make aquifers, it closes them off. Water cannot run through it, period. To talk about a functioning basalt aquifer seems on the face of it to make no sense at all. What's the use of talking about water where no water can be?

And yet the water is there. Not in the basalt itself—no miracle could produce that—but in what Crosby calls "interflow zones," layers of soil or gravel or volcanic ash or ancient vegetable material, locked between separate flows of the Columbia Basin basalts and of the neighboring Snake River Plain. Together, these basalt formations cover several thousand square miles in eastern Washington and eastern Oregon and central and southern Idaho. The soil above them is very fertile. The rainfall is scant. To develop this three-state region into what it is today, one of the leading agricultural areas in the nation, its people have had to rely heavily on the water in those paradoxical basalts. And, unfortunately, there are signs, here as on the Ogallala, that this reliance cannot be counted on much longer.

There is, to begin with, the age of the water. Carbon-14 tests place it at about twenty thousand years—nowhere near the age of the Ogallala water, but still, by human terms, very old. It is, Crosby believes, water that was laid down at the end of the last ice age, the runoff from glaciers that are no longer there. In that case, it is not likely to be renewed for several thousand years. It is fossil water, and it is being mined.

Tending to bear this out is the behavior of the water level in the wells. Pullman's wells have dropped sixty feet in the last thirty years, and they are not the only ones that have been losing pressure. "A lot of domestic wells here have dried up since I arrived," says Crosby. "Over in the Ritzville-Odessa area, sixty-five miles or so to the northwest of us, they've got one well where the static level dropped 120 feet last year. There are some wells out there where the static level is now in the neighborhood of 750 feet. And, you know, when you start getting down there to 750 feet for a static level, well, you can still afford to pump it for drinking water and municipal supply, but that must be getting awfully close to the cutoff point for irrigation, unless you see a big upswing in the value of the crops that you have. And my feeling is that basalt hydrology is sufficiently homogeneous in its bulk effects that what you see happening in one place, in basalt terrain, you'd better think in terms of how that might also pertain to your particular area. Because the storage properties of these basalts are very, very peculiar.

"We'd like to have a parameter on how long the supply will last. We don't, frankly, have it."

In some ways, of course, as with water transfer and storage activities, all of this makes a certain amount of sense. Groundwater mining is not all bad; in fact, a pretty good case can be made for doing a substantial amount of it. For one thing, fossil water is generally of very high quality. Tucson's, according to Pima College's Doug Shakel, serves as the national minimum standard for low levels of organic contaminants; others are of similar purity. These waters can be used domestically with substantially no treatment, and that can save a city a great deal of money. Pullman's water system is typical of groundwater systems, but it is substantially different from a surface system; there is no filter plant, no settling basin, no precipitator, none of the paraphernalia that cities which use surface waters must regularly invest in. "We add a little chlorine," says Gordon Fish of the Pullman Water Department. "That's all."

Groundwater mining offers a local, and locally controllable, water source that is independent of both rainfall and river flow. It is relatively inexpensive; water can be pumped from five hundred feet below the surface for many, many years before the pumping costs begin to equal the construction costs of a California Aqueduct or a Central Arizona Project. And though we worry about using it up, there is no real point in not doing so; the result of stopping the pumps will mean that the water will stop flowing whether or not any remains in the well. As New Mexico state engineer Steve Reynolds told *National Geographic* reporter Thomas Canby a few years ago, "With an aquifer like the Ogallala, whose recharge rate is so slow as to be negligible, if you use it at all you are going to mine it. The alternative is to leave it underground and simply enjoy knowing it's there."

But if there is, as Reynolds insists, nothing "intrinsically evil" about mining groundwater, there *is* something disturbing—seriously disturbing—about our dependence on it. To depend on fossil water is to plan, ultimately, to run out. And to knowingly build an economy around a precious resource that will, in the predictable future, not be there any longer is to build an economy that cannot survive—at least, not in its present form. Growing corn on the High Plains is a splendid idea as long as the Ogallala remains there to be used. But to structure your farm economy around that corn—to assume that, because it grows there now, it will always grow there—is to invite disaster. Forty percent of our beef cattle are now feedlot-raised on High Plains corn. What, in twenty years, will that do to the price of hamburger?

This point has not been entirely lost on the water miners themselves, of course. They are in a better position than anyone else to see what is happening, and they are not blind. The falling water levels in their wells, the diminishing flow from their pumps, and the increasing energy costs to do the pumping all concern them, and they are seriously searching for answers. Unfortunately, the answers they have managed to find so far in this serious search cannot themselves be taken very seriously. There are plans, but the plans border on fantasy. The trouble is that the planners have been stubbornly unwilling to face the fact that solutions might involve changing lifestyles. Once a cornfield, they imply, always a cornfield. If the corn cannot be watered from below, some way must be found to water it from above.

And so the calls go out for aqueducts, for reservoirs, for canals, for pipelines, for the same transfer and storage devices that, as we have seen, have already tied the country up into such a web of interlocking knots that they are squeezing it dry. If the Columbia basalts run out, use the Columbia River. If the Santa Cruz isn't big enough, go get the Colorado. If corn on the High Plains needs watering, and the Ogallala is gone, why let the Mississippi run into the sea?

In his Wichita office, John Gries strokes his beard and muses on this last point. "Some years back," he says, "Texas devised this grandiose Texas Water Plan, which was going to take water from the Mississippi and bring it on west to the High Plains. But as soon as they started really running studies on it, they came up with some problems besides just getting that water in the first place. Pull it out of a major river system like that, which carries a large silt load—what do you do with the silt? It's going to settle out immediately. What do you do with it? And then you start looking at pumping costs, and energy for pumping the stuff uphill—and in that case, you were looking at thirty-five hundred or four thousand feet—you're talking a tremendous cost for the water. And that thing sort of died on the vine.

"The thing is, you have to change. Certainly on the current system, the people who are doing the current operations, they're going down like Rome. You've got to change the base of what you do. Go back to dry-land farming, or grazing, or whatever your particular property is good for otherwise. And that will certainly change the amount of revenue that you take out of a particular unit area of land, by vast amounts. But it's really the only way."

The only way. Will we see that in time? Or will our feeling that the water *has* to be available—because it always has been, because the land grows things so nicely, because God wouldn't have made it so fertile if He hadn't wanted it to be used—keep us always searching beyond the golden horizon for the elusive faucet to eternity that is not there? At this point, it is too early to tell. In Arizona, the Central Arizona Project grinds toward completion, already too small for Tucson's needs. In Pullman, Jim Crosby says—with fingers crossed—that the cone of depression around the city well may have expanded outward to Union Flat Creek, giving the aquifer a chance to recharge and staving off the day of depletion for a little while yet, but that "there are so damn many unknowns" that no one can be sure. On the High Plains, they notch their wells into the bedrock beneath the Ogallala in an effort to squeeze every last drop out of it. Beneath that there is another, very thin aquifer called the Dakota Sandstone; beneath that, nothing. Some wells are already tapping the Dakota Sandstone. "I don't know what people out here are going to do," says one western-Kansas groundwater management official, a little wistfully. "It's going to get awfully thirsty."

CHAPTER **9**

Out of the Endless Seas

SOUTH OF MIAMI, Florida, U.S. Highway 1 puts out to sea, vaulting from landfall to landfall along the long, sickle-shaped chain of islands known as the Florida Keys. At the far end of this Overseas Highway, more than 120 miles out into the blue Caribbean, closer to Cuba than to the American mainland, sits an ancient pirate stronghold and modern-day tourist mecca called Key West. Old, cosmopolitan, and aggressively tropical, Key West clings proudly to its title of "southernmost city in the United States," even though this is no longer true and has not been for the more than twenty years since Hawaii achieved statehood in 1959. They process seafood there (the city is the site of one of the world's largest turtle canneries), and they go about the business of governing sprawling Monroe County, which includes part of the mainland and for which Key West is the county seat; but the biggest industry, far and away, is tourism, and most of the city's thirty thousand residents make their living in some way from the tourist trade.

And therein lies a problem.

For tourists, the principal drawing cards in Key West have

always been the city's saltwater attractions. Saltwater it has in abundance. Freshwater it does not. A small, flat hunk of land, way out in the middle of the ocean, the island of Key West has no streams or lakes and nothing much in the way of springs. Wells more than a few feet deep bring up brine. The rain helps, but the rain is not overabundant: Key West has two inches less annual rainfall than New York City. Finding enough water for the city's residents has always been difficult; finding enough for the tourists who practically double the population during the winter months is nearly impossible.

Or was until 1967. In that year, Key West achieved a kind of historic immortality. With great expectations, and with even greater hype, the city opened a desalinization plant, becoming the first American community to draw its principal supplies of freshwater from the salt sea. The dawn had broken, and the day stretched forward, bright with promise. In the water-supply field, a new frontier seemed to open; the oceans, the ultimate water source, had been tapped at last.

It was only later that the tarnish on that bright promise began to be apparent.

Desalinization—or, as some would have it, "desalination" (both terms are correct)—is one of humanity's ancient dreams, on a par with flying, or the exploration of the moon, or the transmutation of dross into gold. The argument is simple. More than ninety percent of the water on earth is cupped in the ocean basins, splendid for catching fish and for floating upon in ships, but useless for anything else, due to its overwhelming proportion of dissolved solids—principally sodium chloride, otherwise known as table salt. If some efficient, cost-effective means could be found of removing this salt, the oceans could be converted to freshwater. Then we would never run out. Out of the endless seas would come endless supplies for drinking, and washing, and irrigation, and all the other myriads of uses to which we put this wonderful and irreplaceable liquid; the deserts would bloom, and the Millennium would arrive.

It is a tantalizing problem, and one which has come tantalizingly close to being solved, not just once but several times. There is, for example, the process of distillation—the oldest approach to desalinization, and still one of the best. Distillation is simply an artificial means of accelerating the hydrologic cycle. Saltwater is heated, driving off clouds of water vapor. As the water evaporates, it leaves its load of dissolved solids behind; if you catch the vapor and condense it back into liquid, the result is a pool of absolutely pure water. Devices for distilling water, called "stills," have been built for centuries, and have been quite successful on a limited scale. The problem lies in that word "limited." Because of water's extremely high specific heat, it takes huge amounts of energy to change it from a liquid to a vapor. If you are after only a small amount of water, those huge amounts of energy are still manageable. If you want a large amount, though, forget it: you will be burning coal, or pushing electricity, or whatever it is you are doing to put energy into the system, from now till Doomsday. Thus, to make desalinization commercially effective you have to do one of two things. You have to find a way to make an end run around the energy requirements of distillation; or, alternatively, you have to find a different way to accomplish the desalting process.

Each approach has its merits and its disciples, and each has been quite extensively tried.

To get around the high energy requirements of the distillation process, a technique called "flash distillation" is used. Flash distillation takes advantage of the fact that if you lower the air pressure, you also lower the amount of energy required to vaporize a given amount of water. This is why water boils at a lower temperature when you are camping in the mountains than when you are home cooking on your kitchen stove. In a flash-distillation plant, water is heated under pressure and then injected into a low-pressure chamber. It immediately "flashes" into steam, which is caught and condensed. Since it is possible to flash a single pressurized hot-water source into several chambers simultaneously, relatively large amounts of water can be produced this way, improving the method's efficiency; and since the technology involved is quite simple, a flash distillery tends to be extremely dependable. For these two reasons, most commercial desalinization plants currently in operation, including the pioneer plant at Key West, are of the flash-distillation type.

Despite its improvement over straightforward distillation, however, flash distillation remains an energy hog; and so attempts have been made for a long time to find some means other than the vaporization/condensation cycle to remove the salt from saltwater. To date, three alternative methods have been found which show some promise of being cost-effective. Technically, these three methods are known as freeze distillation, electrodialysis, and reverse osmosis; non-technically, we might call them simply freezing, shocking, and squeezing.

Freeze distillation, or "freezing," depends on the fact that saltwater freezes at a lower temperature than fresh—meaning that most ice, even on saltwater bodies, is freshwater. In freeze distillation, one freezes saltwater, skims the ice off the top of the concentrated brine that remains, washes it to remove clinging salt particles, and remelts it. Unfortunately, unless one lives in a very cold climate, it takes almost as much energy to freeze water as it does to vaporize it, and this, coupled with the fact that the ice has only a reduced salt content—not a totally eliminated one—has kept freeze distillation from becoming anything much more than a laboratory toy.

Electrodialysis is better. Shocking saltwater into submission may sound like cruel and unusual punishment, but it works. The process depends on a rather esoteric fact about saltwater: the salt is not present in the water as sodium-chloride molecules, but as separate, incomplete atoms of sodium and chlorine known as "ions." Each ion carries a minute electrical charge. If an electrode of the proper polarity is lowered into the water, the ions will flock toward it like cats toward an old lady who just bought a fish factory; therefore, if you build a series of electrodes in the shape of screens and pass saltwater through them, the salt ions will collect on the screens, and the water that comes out the far end will be fresh.

Electrodialysis is good enough to have seen a fair amount of commercial use. In fact, there has been an electrodialysis plant in operation at Buckeye, Arizona, since 1962—a full five years before Key West's groundbreaking flash-distillation plant. (Buckeye, far from tidewater, uses its plant not to desalt the sea but to render palatable the brackish waters of the Gila River.) But the energy requirements are still high, and the process is far from millennial. Lately, attention in the desalinization field has tended to shift elsewhere; "elsewhere," in this context, meaning, predominantly, reverse osmosis.

Like electrodialysis, reverse osmosis may strike delicate sensibilities as somewhat kinky; it consists, essentially, of squeezing a batch of saltwater until it cries real tears. The tears are freshwater. A reverse-osmosis desalinization facility has two principal parts. One is a filter with holes large enough to pass water molecules but small enough that sodium and chlorine ions are blocked; the other is a device to apply enough pressure to force the water through the tiny holes in the filter at rates that add up to more than a drop or two an hour. The water is poured in; the pressure is applied, and freshwater comes squeezing out the other end like orange juice out of a juicer. Every few minutes, the operation is halted long enough to wash the accumulated salt off the filters; then the pressure is reapplied and the juice comes squeezing through once more. To apply that pressure, of course, requires tremendous levels of energy—levels of energy that are not too far removed from that needed for flash distillation or electrodialysis.

By this time—if you're still with me—you will have begun to see a certain refrain echoing throughout this admittedly nontechnical description of the technical side of desalinization. That refrain is the ever-present need for energy. All means of desalinization take great amounts of it: some more than others, but all more than can possibly be practical under any but the most marginal of circumstances. Energy is expensive, so desalted water, because of its energy requirements, is also expensive—around a dollar per hundred gallons, as opposed to a nationwide average cost, for home-delivered water, of around fifteen cents. If we are ever to fulfill our age-old dream of unlimited freshwater from the oceans, some way is going to have to be found to dramatically cut those energy requirements.

All of which brings us, curiously enough, to one of the most unlikely spots that can be conceived of for a breakthrough in desalinization technology: a suburban kitchen in Flagstaff, Arizona.

Flagstaff, three hundred miles inland from the Pacific, nestled in a pine forest nearly eight thousand feet up on the side of the San Francisco Peaks, seems a strange place indeed to come to find out about using the ocean as a source of freshwater. Nevertheless, here I am. We have spent the day, Dave Gore and I, hiking around on the rim of the Grand Canyon through four inches of fresh March snow; now, while a very un-Arizona blizzard howls by outside, we are snuggled down in front of a blazing pine log in Dave's kitchen fireplace, discussing ways and means, practical and impractical, of taking the salt out of the salt sea.

Dave, a slight blond man who bears a faint resemblance to singer John Denver, comes from a family of inventors. His brother, chemist Robert Gore, was the principal developer of Gore-Tex, the breathable waterproof fabric now widely used for backpacking and skiing clothing and gear; his father, W. L. Gore, was an early worker in Teflon. Dave, after a period of youthful wandering, has settled down with a wife and family and gone to work for his father's firm in Flagstaff, where he has combined a long-term interest in water-supply problems with one of his father's inventions and come up with the impossible: a low-energy, solar-powered still.

"The trouble with earlier solar stills," he is saying now, "is that you had to boil the water, and that took expensive, high-temperature energy. This process uses diffusion, and that lowers the energy costs dramatically." At the sink, he fills a cup with hot water, stirs in a copious amount of salt, and places a thin membrane of what looks like white plastic over the cup's mouth, securing it with rubber bands. "That membrane," he states, "is twenty percent Teflon and eighty percent air. Now watch." He inverts the cup and holds it up to the light. The salty water stays put; but, silhouetted against the light, clouds of vapor emanate from the membrane and curl upward around the cup and the hand that holds it.

"The vapor, as you see," he points out, "passes through the membrane easily. The water, due to the peculiar behavior of water on a Teflon surface, does not. Now we need something cold." The cup is turned right side up once more, and a piece of ordinary Saran Wrap–type plastic goes over the Teflon membrane; the membrane and the plastic are pushed down until the membrane comes into contact with the surface of the hot water, forming a hollow in the top of the cup above the Saran Wrap. Dave pours cold water into the hollow, adding salt "just to prove that what you're drinking doesn't come from here." A layer of water immediately begins forming between the two membranes. After a few moments, Dave lifts off the Saran Wrap and invites me to taste the puddle of water sitting on the sheet of expanded Teflon. The water is fresh. The inventor grins like a proud papa.

How practical is this? Dave is serious again. "We've run experiments," he says, "that show that just by using the thermal difference between warm ocean water on the surface and cold ocean water from the depths, you can produce five gallons of water per square foot per day." That's hardly Niagara Falls, but it's enough to be useful. The driving force is not heat per se, but differential vapor pressure: the greater the differential, the faster the operation. Heat differences create the vapor–pressure differences. Adding a solar collector can increase the output of the still enormously.

All of this sounds as though that long-awaited Millennium has arrived; and yet, as the bus carries me away from Flagstaff the next morning, my mood is oddly sober. Suppose that it's true; suppose the key has at last been found to cheaply and efficiently convert saltwater to fresh. Where does that leave us? How does it fit into the total water-supply picture in the United States? It may be a boon to Los Angeles, and San Diego, and New York, but what does it do for Kansas? Depending on the oceans for our freshwater needs is, when you stop to think about it, remarkably like depending on NAWAPA; the source may be adequate, but the transportation problems will be immense. It will just be another huge water-transfer scheme, not materially different from the California Water Plan, and it will suffer all the problems that this implies. Can we really recharge the Ogallala from the oceans, or refill the declining levels in the Great Lakes by pumping the St. Lawrence backward? Can water from Puget Sound grow crops in the Columbia Basin? Can the citizens of Tucson drink the Gulf of California?

I wonder.

Of course, not all salty water is in the ocean. There is Great Salt Lake, and the Salton Sea, and Mono Lake; there are saline rivers (Arizona's Salt River is not named that lightly), and there are salt marshes. Deep underground, underlying most freshwater aquifers, are vast quantities of saltwater; these could be mined. And there are polluted waters which need to be cleaned up. Will Dave Gore's magic still help us do all those things?

Perhaps; but Dave doesn't think so. "The technology I'm working on," he wrote to me some time after my visit, "has its greatest value where the feed water is high in salinity, where the product water must be very pure, and/or where low-temperature thermal energy is readily available. For most cases of heavy pollution of drinking water, reverse osmosis in combination with filtration and activated carbon works just as well. For low-salinity feeds, reverse osmosis is a highly energy-efficient desalinization technique."

Oceanic thermal energy, Dave points out, is restricted to certain areas, mostly in the tropics. Solar collectors are useful as long as the sun is shining, but that is less than half the time; for times when the sun is not shining, the expensive collectors sit there depreciating but doing little else. Waste heat from power plants represents a possible energy source for use with the still, but studies have indicated that this too is limited; it may be able to supply the domestic water for coastal cities, but industrial and agricultural needs will remain unmet. "I believe the invention has great potential for water production in desert areas near the sea, especially where solar and oceanic thermal-energy sources are available," he sums up. "But really cheap, pure water will always be in short supply."

And even if Dave is wrong—even if his still does turn out to be useful for pollution cleanup, and brackish-water treatment, and other applications he has not yet foreseen—there will remain that nagging problem of transportation. It is not enough to produce the water; as anyone in the Los Angeles Department of Water and Power can tell you, you must also get it where it is going to be used. And this is always going to be a stumbling block to anything we try in the way of getting more water.

And not only over long distances. Key West and its neighbors in the Florida Keys have just found that out—the hard way. In January of 1981, the Florida Keys Aqueduct Authority opened a big new desalinization plant in Key West, designed to spread the blessings of desalinated water up and down the chain of keys through an aqueduct system not unlike that which carries Owens Valley water to Los Angeles, although somewhat smaller. The new plant worked very well. Too well, in fact. All up and down the keys, rotted pipes and plumbing fixtures gave way under the pressures of having adequate water in them for the first time in memory. The plant cost $10 million; the needed repairs on the water system, it is estimated, will cost at least five times that. Meanwhile, a million gallons a day of that nice, expensively desalinated seawater is pouring out of the leaky pipelines— and back into the sea.

Our problems with water are not always problems of supply. Sometimes, perhaps most of the time, they are problems with distribution. And when the problems are problems with distribution, even the endless seas will not save us.

CHAPTER **10**

The Human Factors

NATURE CONTROLS HUMANITY'S water supply, producing it via the hydrologic cycle and distributing it by means of weather patterns, the topography of river basins, and the formation and filling of aquifers. But nature is not alone in its work: we humans also control our own water supply. We do it through laws, regulations, customs, and technology—through the means we have chosen to gather water and to distribute it, and the decisions we have made as to whom it should belong to. At their best, these human factors can be sophisticated, efficient, and excitingly creative. More often, though—much more often—they are none of these things. More often they are hidebound, unimaginative, and smothered so thoroughly in political horsefeathers that it becomes a thing of wonderment that they can move at all. Our water-supply networks and the regulations that govern them have a disturbing tendency to become their own worst enemies, and the solution to this problem is not readily in sight.

There is, at first glance, a bewildering variety to human approaches to water management. Each state has its own set of water laws, and they are different from those of every other state. Within the framework of the state laws there are county and municipal ordinances; coordinating the laws and ordinances, directing them, and at times overriding them, there are several more or less discrete layers of federal regulations. This hodgepodge regulatory activity is administered by an equally hodgepodge group of agencies: pollution-control bodies, and dam-building bodies, and water-power bodies, and fisheries bodies, and water-resources boards, and soil-conservation boards, and county governing councils, and upward of several dozen others. The 1981 edition of *Congressional Quarterly*'s *Federal Regulatory Handbook* devotes an entire page of its brief index to the subject of water, with listings for thirteen separate federal bureaucracies ranging from the Environmental Protection Agency through the Army Corps of Engineers and the Bureau of Reclamation to the Geologic Survey and the National Atmospheric and Oceanic Administration. And even this listing is far from complete: missing are such water-related bodies as the Federal Energy Regulatory Commission (water power and associated supply and quality problems), the Bureau of Sports Fisheries (pollution standards affecting riverine life), and the Office of the Surgeon General (waterborne epidemics and related health problems).

Add a like list for each of the fifty states and the upward of several thousand local governing bodies spangled across the American landscape like freckles on a ten-year-old, and you begin to sense the scope of the problem.

These agencies often have confusingly overlapping jurisdictions, not only among themselves but within themselves. Under the Environmental Protection Agency's generalized umbrella, for example, there are at least five quasi-independent offices, reporting to three separate deputy administrators and acting under the terms of at least eight federal laws, all dealing in some form or another with the single problem of water pollution; these offices must coordinate with one another as well as with the various other agencies, federal, state, and local, which have some say in pollution-control activities. Often the goals of these agencies and the laws they administer conflict with one another, a situation which creates massive confusion and which, needless to say, leads to no end of headaches for local water administrators. Examples of these headaches and this confusion are distressingly common. In one small Western city, for example, the combination of a small-capacity reservoir and a heavily eroding watershed requires the water department to flush silt from the storage system on a yearly basis. For many years this was done by sluicing the reservoir during the spring high-water time, sending the silt load over the dam and downstream. In the early 1970s, however, the city was ordered to suspend its sluicing operation due to violation of water-quality standards downstream. City officials protested that the reservoir would silt up if something weren't done; they found the regulatory agencies sympathetic but impotent, agreeing in principle to the need to do something but bound up in a welter of disagreement about what that something should be.

The state Department of Environmental Quality held out for resuming the sluicing but only during a strictly limited period of highest spring streamflow, so that its turbidity standards would not be violated.

State and federal fisheries agencies insisted that if the sluicing was done at all, it should be done in November so that their standards concerning siltation of spring spawning beds could be upheld.

The federal Environmental Protection Agency suggested that the city buy a dredge, anchor it permanently in the reservoir, dredge out the silt instead of sluicing it, and dispose of it on land. They did not suggest where the money to purchase the dredge was to come from, however, and when contacted about it, the various federal funding agencies—including EPA's own grant program for upgrading city water systems—threw up their hands in horror.

The shelf of thick, thorny-looking documents concerning the case grew and grew: federal environmental-impact statements, independently commissioned studies, Fish and Wildlife Commission studies, state water-quality-control strategies, county water plans, hearings records, and on and on into the dark, legalistic night. The silt load increased; the reservoir shrank. An emergency, stopgap dredging operation was done, in August because that was the only time the Army Corps of Engineers could loan the city a dredge; the resulting turbidity silted up downstream spawning beds, wiping out a whole year's production of summer steelhead. Finally, nearly ten years after the city had been ordered to cease sluicing the reservoir in the spring, city officials emerged out of the other end of the thicket with a federal permit in hand specifying that the best way for them to solve the siltation problem was—to sluice the reservoir in the spring.

"So now," growls the city watermaster, shuffling the papers on his well-laden desk, "we're under permit from the government to go back to the same goddamn thing we've been doing for fifty years. Except we have to submit monthly reports to the EPA, and about twice a year they lose the reports, and we get docked." He sighs. "I don't really mind the EPA, I guess," he continues after a moment. "The thing I don't like is, we're working with strangers we never see, and they don't know a damn thing about what we're facing."

Networking among water-supply agencies is at least as bad as it is among water-quality regulators.

Agencies dealing with water supply are highly stratified. The low man on the totem pole is the body directly responsible for getting water into the pipes leading into your home: the municipal water company, the one that fixes the leaking mains and sends the man around to read your meter. Municipal water companies are usually banded together into regional associations, often corporations in their own right which wield considerable power over their member companies. The regional associations are under the thumb of state oversight agencies; the state agencies, in their turn, are subject to federal regulations of diverse forms administered by agencies as far apart from each other in apparent function as the Department of Commerce and the United States Army. A glass of water, it turns out, is not just a glass of water: it is a technological and regulatory end product which depends on an intricate intermeshing of bureaucratic machinery of almost overwhelming size. In Los Angeles—to pick a random example—a partial list of agencies which have had a hand in the production and distribution of that glass of water would include the Los Angeles Department of Water and Power; a regional supply agency called the Metropolitan Water District; the California Department of Water Resources and its parent body, the Natural Resource Agency of the State of California; the Colorado River Basin Commission; the Interstate Commerce Commission; and the United States Bureau of Reclamation. And that's just the supply side of the water picture: if we got into the quality side, we would have to bring in an even longer list of diverse agencies, a list ranging from the Los Angeles Department of Public Health to the Federal Maritime Commerce Commission, a list that would be—except at the very bottom—entirely different from the supply-side list.

Given this mountain of proliferating bureaucracy, there is little wonder that the regulatory process often seems to move with worse-than-glacial slowness. The diversity of regulating agencies, the lack of coordination between them, and the massive piles of regulations each is weighed down beneath guarantee that things in the water field will get done slowly if at all. Still, it is not this maddening and stultifying variety that is the real problem with our human approach to water; it is the even more maddening and stultifying sameness that underlies it.

The diversity of water agencies is a sham. Underneath, they are all alike, far too alike for anyone's good, including, most distinctly, their own.

The surface wrangling among water agencies comes as a result of their differing emphases: pollution control, or fisheries, or city supply, or farm supply, or what have you. The sameness that underlies the writhing upper layers comes from the basic, unquestioned assumption that is common coin among all agencies, the assumption that underlies all the differences and determines each agency's approach to its own peculiar aspect of the overall water problem. It is comfortable, this assumption: simple, and straightforward, and totally and mercilessly unchanged since Appius Claudius

Caecus stretched the first tentative length of Roman aqueduct toward the sweet water of the distant Apennines. In its most elemental, three-word form, it is this: demand is king. Supply is only a handmaid, running hither and yon to bring the king what he wants, curtsying when the royal finger is lifted, and, in the time-honored way of kings and handmaids, getting discreetly raped whenever the opportunity presents itself.

North to south, mountain to prairie, dry Denver to wet Wilmington, the situation repeats and repeats. Always an alphabet-soup agency—a DWP, or a DWB, or a DEP, or whatever the local initial scoop has brought up out of the common bowl. Always the same plans, and the same projections, and the same construction projects and bond issues and legislative patchworks. Always the same terribly earnest bureaucrats pushing the same terribly outmoded solutions. The infighting among water agencies, God knows, is bad enough; the fact that they are fighting over what is essentially a wrongheaded course of action makes it ten times worse.

It is also, unfortunately, inevitable. Because until supply is freed of its subsidiary relationship to demand—until it is broadly recognized that different parts of the country have different amounts of water availability, and that this is a given which must be planned *with* instead of planned *around*—the wrangling and the infighting are going to go on. Because all those diverse and seemingly contradictory laws and regulations and ordinances really have only one purpose: to take a generalized policy born in the distant water-rich past and to Procrusteanize it into submission. Water-regulatory reform? Certainly. But unless we understand what we are doing—unless we question the underlying assumptions as well as the overlying detail—any real reform we manage to accomplish will be strictly accidental.

The most important of the human factors standing in the way of water is not the means we use to obtain the ends. It is the way we define the ends.

...III

CHAPTER **11**

Nor Any Drop
to Drink

ONE EARLY MARCH Tuesday in 1969, while preparations
for the first manned moon flight went feverishly forward at
Cape Canaveral, the inventor and philosopher R. Buckminster Fuller, possessor of what is surely one of the most original and unconventional minds of this or any age, sat at a
table in a Senate hearing room in Washington, D.C., and
lectured the assembled senators on the word "synergy."

"I have been a visitor at 320 universities and colleges
around the world," stated Fuller, "and have always asked
those university audiences 'How many of you are familiar
with the word "synergy"?' I can say authoritatively that less
than ten percent of university audiences and less than one
percent of nonuniversity audiences are familiar with the
word and meaning of 'synergy.' . . . The word 'synergy'
means behavior of whole systems unpredicted by behavior
of any of the systems' parts. Nature is comprehensively synergetic. Since 'synergy' is the only word having that meaning and we have proven experimentally that it is not used by
the public, we may conclude that society does not understand nature."

Nature persists in operating as a unit; humans persist in treating it as a collection of spare parts. Nature unifies; humans divide. Unless this is changed, the usually buoyant Fuller concluded with uncharacteristic pessimism, "I think man may readily not make it on this particular planet."

Nowhere is this gloomy view better justified than in discussions of water resources. For decades—for generations, even—humans have persisted in putting on blinders before they tackled problems of water supply. Straight-line, engineering, $A + B = C$ approaches have always been adopted. We have put our water problems into little compartments and placed labels on them: drought, flood, aridity, distribution, waste, pollution. But nature does not compartmentalize this way. Nature is synergetic; and nonsynergetic, compartmentalized approaches to it simply won't work.

We think of our "water supply" as the amount we have collected, but it is more than that. Water merely collected is no good. It must also be distributed—passed out to those who are going to use it, where they are going to use it, when they need it. It must not be wasted; water thrown away is no longer part of the water supply. And, perhaps most important of all, it must be usable.

A water supply too dirty to use for anything can no longer be considered a water supply. Pollution destroys. As Sam Sage, a Syracuse, New York, resident and longtime chairman of the Sierra Club's National Water Committee, puts it, "Water quality and water quantity are not separable issues." Like the images in funhouse mirrors, they appear different, but they are really just varying reflections of the same fundamental concern.

Up to this point, we have been discussing water in this book strictly from the standpoint of raw water supply; of going out and building the pipelines, mining the aquifers, desalting the sea, doing whatever is necessary to corral those gallons and get them back to the people who need them. It is now time to get synergistic. It is time to realize that one major, overwhelming reason why we are running out of water is that we are killing the water we have.

When Samuel Taylor Coleridge wanted to torture the old sailor in *The Rime of the Ancient Mariner,* he put him on a raft out in the middle of the ocean and surrounded him with water, none of which he could consume. As a nation, we are swiftly putting ourselves on that same raft; like Coleridge's Mariner, we may soon have

> Water, water everywhere,
> Nor any drop to drink.

Water pollution, these days, is not the popular topic it was a few years ago. Most people today, in fact, probably believe that the subject is a bit passé: that it was once a serious problem, but is now under control. That is a comfortable illusion, but it is an illusion just the same. Water pollution today is as bad as or worse than it has ever been. We are losing ground, not gaining it. In our streams, fish are still dying; algal blooms continue to cloud once-pristine lakes; and clean drinking water, one of modern America's greatest technological accomplishments, is swiftly on its way to becoming an historical curiosity.

To be sure, there have been some notable successes in pollution control. Lake Erie, once declared dead, is now slowly reviving; fish are returning to the Detroit River, where not so long ago ducks would die from the effects of merely landing on the surface; and the lower Potomac, where coliform-bacteria counts once ranged up to ten thousand times the safe level for swimming, is seeing summer sports activities again. Pollution in Oregon's Willamette has been cut ninety percent since 1968. The Háckensack in New Jersey, the St. Johns in Florida, and the Cuyahoga in Ohio are pleasant adjuncts to their cities once more instead of open sores; the city of Seattle no longer has to forbid children to play in Lake Washington. Pushed by the stiff-toed boot of some tough-minded federal legislation—the Clean Water Act, the Safe Drinking Water Act—cities and industries nationwide have been cleaning up their waste outfalls remarkably. Water-treatment technology has advanced to the point where waters containing once-dangerous levels of pollutants can be routinely cleaned up and used in city water systems. We have done much, and we have much to be proud of.

But this pride must not lead to complacency. The battle is not over; the battle has just begun. Behind every showcase success loom a hundred hidden failures, and the general quality level of our waters has been going down, not up. "Since about 1970," reported the federal Water Resources Council in its *Second National Water Assessment* (1978),

> the incidence of waterborne illnesses seems to have been increasing. . . . At least 4,000 cases of waterborne illness, primarily of bacterial or viral origin, are reported each year. The actual number of cases, including the more-difficult-to-identify chemical poisonings, could be as much as ten times higher.

All across the nation, the cool detachment of this statement translates into local anguish as city and state governments attempt to deal with the problem. In Michigan, an EPA spokesman calls pollution levels in the Great Lakes "scary"; tests of their waters show the presence of between three and four hundred different varieties of toxins, most of which have unknown long-term effects. In Oregon's Jackson County, water officials report the pollutant level in Bear Creek—a major tributary of the Rogue River, and the county's principal urban waterway—"about the same" as they were ten years ago, despite strenuous efforts at control. In New Jersey, a consultant's report for the Department of Environmental Protection notes that the state "faces an immense problem in assessing and attempting the after-the-fact control and abatement of water contamination." Arnold Schiffman, the state's outspoken director of water resources, agrees with that gloomy prognosis. "The problems are so great," he told me in the spring of 1981, "that they're beginning to cripple the state. I've had to issue boil-water orders. Can you imagine that in this day and age?"

Improvements in the technology of the plants that treat our drinking water have helped. But water-treatment technology has one major drawback that severely limits its effectiveness as a tool to combat pollution. As the chief research engineer for one major Midwestern city water system explained it, "The trouble is, you've got to define the problem before you can look for solutions." Because different pollutants often require widely varying treatments, water-treatment plants can generally remove only the pollutants that are known to be present in a water source. This means that pollution removal depends on pollution detection—and that, unfortunately, is still not very good. Technologically, we have the ability to detect ever more minute presences of ever more esoteric chemicals; practically, we cannot use it. Most of the tests are far too costly and complicated for routine application. How many small-town water systems own their own gas chromatographs? How many water systems of any size have organic chemists on their staffs?

We are losing our waters to pollution at an accelerating rate. There is every reason to believe that we will continue to do so until and unless drastic steps are taken to reverse current trends. And that, unfortunately, does not appear to be a step that will soon be taken.

In his speech to that Senate subcommittee back in 1969, Buckminster Fuller concluded with a touching and beautiful image of humanity as a baby bird, just coming out of its nurturing egg of clean waters, vast spaces, and fossil fuels, and having to learn to function in the world beyond. "The new little bird," he said, "exhausting the nutriment inside the shell, impulsively pecks at the eggshell, it breaks open, and there is the little bird, suddenly moving about on its own legs, beautifully prepared to operate on an entirely new basis. I see that all humanity thus far has been guarded by such an innocence-tolerating nutriment. . . . I think we are at that critical historical moment in which we have just broken our shell of permitted ignorance and henceforth we can survive only by learning to operate in our universe in a very different way."

As we take the next few chapters to examine the specter of pollution eating into our national water supply, it will be important to remember that.

Humans, like birds, will die when they can no longer drink.

CHAPTER **12**

The Sewers
of Louisville

AT 5:16 in the morning of Friday, February 13, 1981, two
women in a small late-model car with a malfunctioning,
overheating catalytic converter approached an underpass in
the south-central portion of Louisville, Kentucky, on their
way to early-bird jobs in the city's central district. The
weather was bitterly cold, and the driver, aware of the ice
which often forms in the low places beneath underpasses,
slowed carefully as her car nosed under this one. Suddenly,
there was a tremendous explosion; the car was picked up
and flung violently sideways against the underpass supports.
Shaken but not seriously injured, the two women listened in
amazement as a series of answering explosions ripped away
from them through the predawn darkness, echoing down the
long streets toward the black Ohio River.

A few blocks away, reporter Jim Detjen was still sleeping
—the heavy, dreamless sleep of the very weary—when the
telephone jolted him awake at 6:30 A.M. He had been out
late the night before, working on a story for his employer,
the *Louisville Courier-Journal*, and hadn't made it to bed till
about 3:30 in the morning: now, barely three hours later,

there was the damn telephone buzzing at him. Groggily, he picked up the receiver and found himself talking to his editor. "He said," remembers Detjen, " 'There's been an explosion, and it seems to be in your area. Why don't you check it out?' So I sort of stumbled out the door—I hadn't heard anything, I'd been so beat I slept right through it—and about a block and a half away there was this amazing crater in the street. I was just overwhelmed by the size of it."

The law of averages, as one observer put it succinctly a few days later, had finally caught up with the sewers of Louisville.

Perhaps that is being unfair. The Louisville sewer system, after all, is not materially different from that of most other urban areas, large and small, around the United States. Run by an alphabet-soup agency called the MSD (for Metropolitan Sewer District), it is basically a water system in reverse. Drain pipes finger out from homes and businesses and industrial plants; these are gathered in mains beneath the streets. The mains, in turn, are gathered into large pipes known as "trunk lines," which carry great volumes of sewage to riverbank treatment plants where it is processed to remove as many of its poisons and disease-causing organisms as possible before being dumped into the river. This is all old, well-tested technology. Like most American cities, Louisville has had indoor plumbing since well before the turn of the century; virtually the entire city is on sewers, and the Southern Outfall, the trunk line that transfers the south-central district's collected wastes to the MSD's big Morris-Forman Treatment Plant on the banks of the Ohio, was constructed around 1910.

Louisville is a heavily industrialized city, and the greatest volume of sewage running through the Southern Outfall comes from industrial plants. Among these, the largest single contributer is a soybean-processing installation run by the Ralston-Purina Company on South Floyd Street; and it was here, apparently, that the series of events which led to the Great Louisville Sewer Explosion began. As investigators from the MSD later reconstructed it, the culprit was a volatile, highly explosive solvent called hexane, used by Ralston to extract the soybeans' valuable oil. The Floyd Street plant uses a great deal of hexane. Normally, the substance is caught before it enters the sewers, separated from the plant's waste water by a device called a "containment basin," and piped back for reuse; but because of the cold weather, the plant's machinery was malfunctioning, and quantities of hexane vastly greater than normal were finding their way to the containment basin. The basin was overwhelmed. An undetermined amount of hexane (the company says approximately a hundred gallons; MSD investigators estimate upward of several thousand) got loose into the sewers. Soon its volatile gases were leaking out of holes in manhole covers and pooling in low places in the streets, such as in underpasses. The faulty catalytic converter did the rest.

The explosions were spectacularly destructive. Witnesses reported manhole covers popping like champagne corks, lofting Frisbee-like as high as two stories above the pavement. Great holes opened in a number of major thoroughfares. Two miles of the Southern Outfall were ripped to pieces; they would have to be torn up and almost completely replaced. A number of south-central-area residents had to be evacuated from their homes, and several schools, including the University of Louisville, were temporarily closed.

Water supplies were hit hard. In some areas pipes were cracked, allowing effluent from the shattered sewer to leak in; residents in those areas were forced to boil their water until the pipes could be repaired. The Morris-Forman Treatment Plant was miraculously undamaged, but fear of further explosions forced the MSD to temporarily bypass it, and for twelve hours raw sewage poured into the Ohio at the rate of several million gallons per hour. Downstream communities such as Evansville, Indiana, drawing their water from the river, had to either shut down their intakes or keep going with their fingers crossed, hoping that their water-treatment facilities were up to the job. Louisville officials began receiving irate phone calls from downriver.

All in all, the score was quite impressive. Ten million dollars or more in damages; four injuries (none, fortunately, serious); scores of forced evacuations; months of disruptions as sewers and streets were repaired. At least sixty million gallons of extra pollutants in the Ohio River. But as MSD representatives, Ralston officials, and weary local citizens sorted through the facts surrounding the incident over the next few days and weeks, the question that seemed most agonizingly clear was not Why did it happen? but Why didn't it happen sooner?

Ralston was really not at fault. Louisville's sewers were a mess.

"None of us really knows what's going into the sewers," says Bruce Lane, stabbing a finger into the air for emphasis, "and I don't think *MSD* knows what's going into their sewers." Lane is the chief of the Environmental Health branch of the Jefferson County Health Department. Jefferson County contains Louisville. Lane has been worrying about the Louisville sewers for years.

There has been much to worry about. Most of us probably think of sewers as carrying primarily human wastes, but in Louisville, as in most industrial cities, that is simply not true. The city's industrial plants are connected to the sewage system along with the houses, and they send their waste products into the sewers, often in overwhelming volumes. The result is a stream of sewage that is a bewildering witches' brew of ingredients, many of them toxic, mixing together and sloshing around and fermenting into still more potent compounds on their journey to the treatment plant. Wastes from the manufacture of synthetic rubber fall into the sewers on top of paint ingredients and pharmaceutical leftovers. Acids and ammonias gurgle together. An MSD study in 1979 found 118 industries regularly discharging toxics of various strengths and consistencies into the sewers—not counting "accidental discharges," or spills, of which there are an average of about six per month.

Some of these discharges are relatively harmless: soap,

motor oil, animal fats, what have you. Some are not. In May of 1980, nine months before the Great Sewer Explosion, residents of western Louisville's Vermont Avenue district had to be briefly evacuated due to a leak from a solvent-reclaiming firm which had filled their sewers with explosive gases; and two months before that, the MSD had been required to go to court to force a local chemical firm to reduce the amount of acid it was washing down its drains. The sewer company charged that the acid was eroding its concrete trunk lines, a charge Bruce Lane agrees with. "Those sewers," he says, "are *gone*. There's a large pipe in the center of the city that's been pretty well eaten away, and the sewage is leaking out and contaminating the surrounding aquifer." The fact that this aquifer is not currently being used as a water supply does not make this leakage any less serious. In the wet Ohio Valley, most aquifers flow fairly rapidly, and what goes in at one end will eventually come out the other. Then the groundwater supply will become a surface water supply—still carrying its nice little load of pollutants.

Along with the planned and the accidental spills are the blatantly illegal ones—the so-called "midnight dumpers." Around Louisville, the king of the midnight dumpers is probably a man named Donald L. Distler, proprietor of a firm called Kentucky Liquid Recycling. In the early 1970s, Distler's firm was being paid by a number of industrial plants, some as far away as Memphis, Tennessee, to haul their hazardous wastes away and dispose of them. On several occasions, the method of disposal chosen by the firm was simply to lift a manhole cover in the western end of Louisville and dump the stuff into the sewers. "There were tons of it," says Jim Detjen, who covered Distler's 1978 trial on illegal dumping charges for the *Courier-Journal*. "It killed the bacteria in the secondary-sewage-treatment plant at Morris-Forman, and tens of millions of gallons of raw sewage ended up in the Ohio. It's been three years now, and the plant still isn't fully back to normal. A number of downstream communities are suing us." Distler was convicted, fined $50,000, and sentenced to two years in prison. (In one of life's nice little ironies, that conviction was upheld by a federal appeals court in Cincinnati less than twenty-four hours before the Great Sewer Explosion brought Louisville's sewers into the news once again.)

Aside from its overtones of illegality, not to mention stupidity (how long did he think he could reasonably expect to get away with a dumping scheme on that order of magnitude without detection, anyway?), the Distler story demonstrates with remarkable clarity one of the central problems sewage systems face today. When you dump hazardous chemicals down them, what happens to those chemicals? In Distler's case the dumping was, shall we say, extracurricular; but in a larger sense this is probably irrelevant. There are plenty of perfectly legal ways of getting exotic chemicals into a sewer. Householders wash them down sinks and flush them down toilets; manufacturers spill overloads, dump defective batches, and wash working surfaces into floor drains. Called to spills on city streets, firemen routinely wash them into manholes and storm sewers. What happens to them after that?

The answer to that question, of course, is almost insultingly simple. Things washed into sewers end up in sewage-treatment plants. Everyone knows that. Unfortunately, however, ending up in a sewage-treatment plant is not always a solution. All too often, as the results of Distler's dump demonstrate, ending up in a sewage-treatment plant is a large part of the problem.

Sewage plants are designed primarily to handle human wastes. By and large, they do a fine job of it. But what comes through city sewers today, as we have seen, often has very little to do with human wastes. The human-waste-oriented plants can't handle it. A great deal of it comes out the other side of the plant almost completely unchanged.

And in Louisville—as with hundreds of other communities in the Midwest—"out the other side" means into the Ohio River.

"The Ohio," insists Steve Hubbs, "is not as dirty as it is imputed to be." Hubbs is an engineer with the Louisville

Water Department. Louisville gets its water directly out of the Ohio, and pollution in the river is a serious concern for the city. Hubbs, however, is not too worried. "We test the water a lot," he says, "and most of the time I can't put a number on the pollutant levels because our instruments aren't calibrated that low. The river's volume is its greatest ally. Most of the pollutants that enter it just get lost."

Louisville's water intake, of course, is upstream from its sewage outfall ("Nobody spits upwind," Hubbs explains laconically). Still, the test findings are encouraging. Louisville, after all, is not the only city to disgorge pollutants into the Ohio. The river serves as the cloaca for much of industrial America. Above Louisville there is Cincinnati; above Cincinnati is Huntington; and above Huntington is Wheeling. Between Huntington and Wheeling is the mouth of the Kanawha, and astride the Kanawha a few dozen miles up is Charleston. At the very head of the Ohio, where the river is born out of the waters of the Allegheny and the Monongahela, looms Pittsburgh. All these, and dozens more, drop wastes into the river. According to Environmental Protection Agency (EPA) records, at least 1,800 industrial firms hold permits to pollute the Ohio. At least two thirds of these are above Louisville. Given these facts, Hubbs's statements about the quality of the city's drinking water are extremely encouraging.

They are also, unfortunately, suspect. As Hubbs himself admits, "We aren't looking for everything in the river, but only for that narrow band our instruments can detect. For ninety percent of the chemicals in the water, we don't even know how to test for them."

When sensitive tests are carried out, the results tend to be alarming. The EPA estimates that "between 300 and 600" different exotic chemicals are present in the Ohio at all times. More than three hundred of these have been identified in Cincinnati's public water system—and, as Jim Detjen has pointed out, Louisville's system is similar enough to Cincinnati's that if Cincinnati has them, Louisville probably has them, too. Tending to bear out Detjen's fears are studies such as the one done on Ohio River PCB levels by the EPA in 1977. PCBs, or polychlorinated biphenyls, are a chemical once widely used in the insulation of electric transformers. They are now known to be powerful carcinogens, and their use has been banned since the mid-1970s. In its 1977 study, the EPA took samples from ten spots along the banks of the Ohio. In all ten spots they found small amounts of PCBs. And the highest concentrations were found in the samples taken adjacent to the intake for the Louisville Water Works.

Barge traffic on the river provides an additional worry. An estimated six thousand loads of toxic chemicals forge up and down the Ohio each year, bearing their deadly cargoes a hull's width away from the drinking-water supplies for more than one million people in the Ohio Valley. Sometimes those cargoes spill. In March 1978, for example, between 10,000 and 25,000 gallons of phenol leaked from a barge at Cincinnati, forcing water-treatment plants to shut down in two downstream Indiana counties. A few months prior to that, a massive carbon-tetrachloride spill at Charleston had caused Cincinnati itself to close down its water intakes. "There are frightening amounts of relatively scary compounds going up and down that river," comments Hubbs, admitting to having nightmares about the situation. "A leaking barge moored in the river would be the worst horror story. If it was in the wrong place, we could get practically all of it in the intake."

I have picked on Louisville heavily in the last few pages largely because it has been convenient to do so; events in that city demonstrate with remarkable clarity the interconnectedness between problems of waste disposal and problems of water supply. Louisville residents should take heart, however; they are not alone. Similar problems crop up wherever you look around the nation. A fistful of recent examples follows.

Forbestown, California: A typical "wide spot in the road," so small it doesn't even appear on many highway maps, Forbestown languishes beside the South Fork of the Feather

River a few miles upstream from the reservoir behind Oroville Dam. Nearby on the river is a small dam and an electrical-power-generating station, the Forbestown Power Plant, run by the Oroville-Wyandotte Irrigation District. In 1967, the power plant was hit by lightning, damaging one of its transformers and forcing the removal of some 250 gallons of oily-textured PCBs. At that time, the tight link between PCBs and cancer had not yet been demonstrated. Unaware of any danger, and uncertain what else to do with the stuff, the power-plant crew scattered it along two miles of gravel road beside the river in an effort to hold down the dust. Over the ensuing years, rains washed the material off the road and down the bank toward the water.

In the summer of 1980, California's Central Valley Regional Water Quality Control Board began testing the Feather near Forbestown for PCBs; and in December of that year, board spokesman Don Rothenbaum announced the results. In the soil of the riverbank, a few feet above the waterline, the board had found PCB concentrations in excess of ten parts per million (ppm)—five times the national standard "safe" level of 2 ppm. In fish taken from the river, concentrations had been measured at nearly 8 ppm. Perhaps most frightening of all was the finding of PCBs in excess of the 2 ppm "safety" level in fish from Oroville Reservoir itself. Oroville Reservoir is a key component of the California Water Plan. The Forbestown Power Plant's improper waste-disposal practices thus had at least the potential of affecting irrigation and drinking-water supplies as far away as Los Angeles.

Escanaba, Michigan: In the center of Longfellow's (and Pabst Beer's) "land of sky-blue waters"—the woodlands nearby are part of Hiawatha National Forest—Escanaba sits on the shores of an inlet called Little Bay de Noc on the northwest shore of Lake Michigan. With a population of fifteen thousand, it is a center of commerce for Michigan's so-called Upper Peninsula (actually, an isthmus between Lakes Michigan and Superior). The Upper Peninsula State Fair is held there each year; the city is a lumber- and iron-ore-shipping port, and the county seat of Delta County.

Residents of an area famous for its waters, Escanaba residents have always been proud of theirs. In May 1981, however, that pride was eroded somewhat. Toward the end of that month, heavy concentrations of industrial-strength ammonia suddenly began showing up in the city's tap water. A patron at one of the city's restaurants was hospitalized with chemical burns in his mouth; the Public Safety Department warned residents to sniff their water before using it. Where did the ammonia come from? If the department knew, it wasn't telling. UPI dispatches accused local officials of "refusing to say." Nevertheless, one thing was quite clear: in this portion of Hiawatha's country, the waters were no longer quite so sky blue.

Cincinnati, Ohio: One hundred fifty miles up the Ohio from Louisville, Cincinnati—as we have already mentioned —shows a remarkably similar set of water and sewer problems to those of its sister city. On February 19, 1981, that similarity was strikingly driven home, as, less than a week after the Great Louisville Sewer Explosion, a section of sewer in downtown Cincinnati collapsed, leaving a crater twenty-four feet wide and thirty feet deep in the middle of the street. Sewer workers sent to the scene to make repairs noticed their shovels and other metal tools turning green. They also turned a bit green themselves; headaches, mucous-membrane irritation, and dizziness were common, and four men suffered severe nausea and vomiting and had to climb out of the sewer. Investigators from the city health department and the National Institute for Occupational Safety and Health discovered high levels of acids, chlorides, and volatile organic solvents coming out of the effluent pipes at a nearby pigment-manufacturing plant. Readings for these contaminants in the sewer lines below the plant showed concentrations as much as one million times higher than readings taken above the plant. The plant had wastewater-treatment facilities, but they were either malfunctioning or being bypassed; the firm's equipment for monitoring acid levels in its outfall was inoperable. Cincinnati's sewers, of course, lead eventually into the Ohio River, and from there into a number of water systems—including Louisville's.

Olympia, Washington: Washington's state capital is a picturesque little city of sixty thousand nestled among low evergreen-covered hills above Budd Inlet, the southernmost arm of Puget Sound. On June 2, 1981, the state's Department of Fisheries released some two million baby salmon "fingerlings" (so called because at this stage of their lives they are about the size of a human finger) into Budd Inlet from downtown Olympia's Capitol Lake. A few hours later, at least fifty thousand of the little fish were dead. Noting that the kill was centered near a City of Olympia sewage-plant outfall, fisheries officials did some investigating and discovered that over the course of the previous week that outfall had discharged some 500,000 gallons of beer—the result of a decision by the managers of a nearby brewery that beer in that batch didn't meet the company's quality standards. Brewery officials insisted that there was "nothing toxic" in the beer that could have harmed the fish; nevertheless, it seemed pretty clear that, whatever the old stein songs might say about the joys of swimming in beer, to actually do so could be acutely hazardous to your health.

Medford, Oregon: The manufacturing and distribution center for a large area which includes most of southern Oregon and part of northern California, this city of forty thousand sits on the floor of the broad, flat Bear Creek Valley between the towering Cascade and Siskiyou mountain ranges, ten miles or so south of the Rogue River. The surrounding mountains are full of forests and lakes; the Rogue is famous for its whitewater. Statewide firms usually find appointments to their Medford branches eagerly sought after.

Though Bear Creek, which flows through the center of the city, is heavily polluted (see Chapter 11), fish are usually able to survive in it; and thus it caused a certain sense of alarm when, on April 29, 1981, employees of the Jackson County Irrigation District found several hundred dead fish washed against the screen across one of their intakes a few miles below Medford. Called to the scene, county health officials traced the fish kill to a thick blue-white fluid with a smell described as "ammonia-like," entering the creek from a storm drain at Tenth Street, near the city center, at a rate of ten gallons per minute. Reckoning backward to the estimated time of the fish kill, the health officials determined that nearly six thousand gallons of the unidentified substance had entered the creek. Downstream, the cities of Grants Pass and Gold Hill, which take their municipal water supplies from the Rogue, had to close down their intakes for three hours until state public-health officials determined that the danger had passed. "We've had a lot of these recently," an angry health official charged. "We just have more and more things being dumped down the storm drain system as if Bear Creek was a conveyance for toxic chemicals. People use that for drinking water and irrigation. We'd hate to have anybody hurt."

These events, which all took place over a single six-month period, should not be considered unusual. Similar reports could be made for all sections of the country. In New Jersey, where one state official describes the Passaic River as "all sewage," twenty-five percent of all municipal water intakes are downstream from someone else's sewage plant ("We're the number-one state in the nation for recycling water," says the same official. "We didn't plan it that way, but we are.") In Illinois, Chicago had its own version of the Great Louisville Sewer Explosion in the early 1970s. In Indiana, ten thousand gallons of the chemical monochlorobenzol, a paint thinner and perfume base, leaked from a derailed tank car into Storm Creek near the city of Seymour, killing several thousand fish in the nearby Muscatuck Wildlife Refuge. Monochlorobenzol does not break down in the environment, and officials were unsure how to clean it up. In Utah, a sixty-one percent population rise in the Salt Lake Valley during the last ten years has seriously overburdened sewage-treatment plants; the plants are discharging untreated sewage into the Jordan River, which one local source has referred to as a "cesspool." These examples could probably be extended indefinitely.

In late July 1981, the Environmental Protection Agency released a list of thirty-four metropolitan areas in twenty-three states whose water supplies contain "potential toxic pollutants." The list reads like a travel gazetteer of some of the nation's most desirable cities: it includes, among many others, Baton Rouge, Louisiana; Coeur d'Alene, Idaho; Hartford, Connecticut; Lincoln, Nebraska; Syracuse, New York; and Portland, Oregon.

Why is there so much filth in our lakes and streams? Why, years after the passage of the Clean Water Act and the Safe Drinking Water Act, are we still having so much trouble finding clean, safe water? Why are the few successes in pollution control so overwhelmed by the failures? Why is New York City, with one of the largest rivers in the nation flowing past its front door, still afraid to drink it?

Part of the problem, certainly, is that our production technology is far ahead of our disposal technology. We can figure out ways to make things we want far better than we can figure out how to get rid of the things we don't want. It is tempting to blame the good old capitalist profit motive for this (everybody knows that the Henry Fords among us make more money than the trashmen): however, such scapegoating ignores the Russian experience, which is remarkably similar to our own. The supposedly nonprofit-oriented Soviet industry has managed, in a few short decades, to turn Siberia's mile-deep, three-hundred-mile-long Lake Baikal into a virtual dead sea. Lake Baikal contains fully twenty percent of all lake water in the world. By comparison, our heavy-handed treatment of the Great Lakes seems almost gentle. Rather than blame the profit motive, therefore, we should probably blame our very understandable human desire to get rid of unpleasant things as fast as possible. If haste makes waste, we can also say with certainty that waste makes haste—and things disposed of hastily are not going to be disposed of very carefully.

A far more important reason for the increasing pollution of our surface waters, though, is the greater and greater amounts of pollutants we are producing each year. Though we seldom stop to think about it, as per-capita water use increases inside the home, sewage volume must also increase; every drop that comes out of the faucet in the kitchen or the bathroom eventually ends up, in one form or another, going down the drain. And production of industrial wastes is increasing even faster than production of home wastes. According to author Michael Brown *(Laying Waste)*, hazardous-wastes loads pouring from our factories increased by nearly six hundred percent in the decade between 1970 and 1980; at that rate, our production of ten million metric tons of these wastes in 1970 could become a production of 360 million metric tons by 1990. Obviously, as the amount of waste we produce increases so drastically, finding places to put it becomes more and more difficult.

The problem is—literally—overwhelming us.

In Louisville, the MSD points proudly to its system's numerous safety measures, designed to reduce the risk of cataclysmic events like the Great Sewer Explosion and to make certain that the city's outfall into the Ohio is as clean as possible. Sensors have been placed in the lines above the Morris-Forman plant to detect particularly hazardous or explosive components in the sewage stream. An extensive sampling program is carried out; local firms know that MSD inspectors are likely to descend at any time, unannounced, to take samples of their outfalls and run them through laboratory tests to discover whether or not hazardous or illegal substances are being discharged. The agency has authority to fine polluters up to $10,000 per day. In the works is a network of remote sensors like the ones above the treatment plant, designed to monitor the various parts of the system at all times and make tracing illegal dumps or accidental spills simpler. The Louisville system is far from shoddy; in many ways, it is a model for the nation.

None of these safety devices, however—planned or in place—tackles what may be the most serious problem of all: the sheer volume of the effluent. Louisville produces sixty million gallons of sewage per day. That is nearly one hundred cubic feet per second—greater than the total flow of many Western rivers. It is still far below the Ohio's 100,000 cubic feet, but it is gaining on it. And Louisville is not the only, or even the biggest, city that pours sewage into the Ohio. There are also Cincinnati, and Pittsburgh, and Huntington, and Evansville, and so on and so forth, down the long list of Ohio riverfront communities. At what point does the volume of this sewage—clean or not—become significant? When do all of America's rivers stop being rivers of water and start, like the Passaic, being rivers of sewage? If their character is changed in this manner, can we safely use them for drinking?

In the water-supply field, this is one of the most important questions we can ask. Unfortunately, however, the answer to it may pose severe problems of its own. If the volume of our wastes is too great to be absorbed by our rivers, we must stop dumping them into our rivers. But if we don't dump them into the rivers, what do we do with them?

One answer is to bury them in the ground. But burying wastes in the ground—as we shall see in the next chapter—may also be acutely hazardous to our drinking-water supplies.

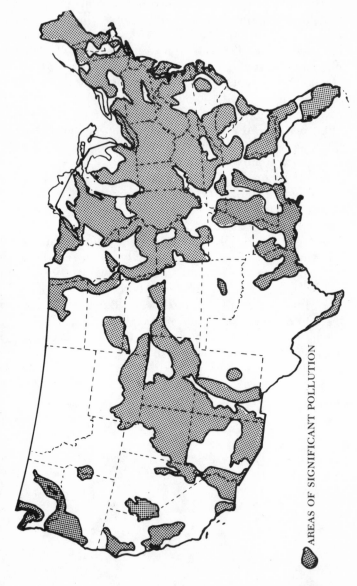

SURFACE WATER POLLUTION

AREAS OF SIGNIFICANT POLLUTION

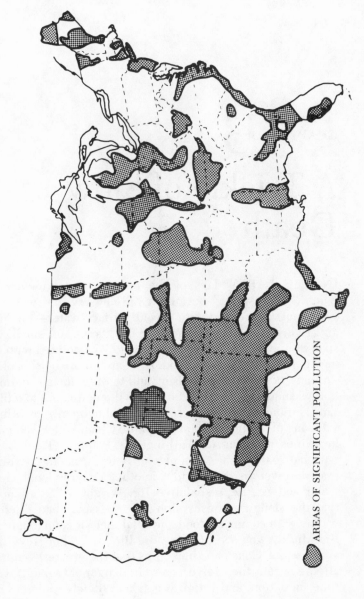

GROUNDWATER POLLUTION

AREAS OF SIGNIFICANT POLLUTION

CHAPTER **13**

A Trickle of Slow Death

IN THE EARLY days of the environmental movement, when "clean water" became a rallying cry, the water we were most concerned with was all surface water—the lakes and rivers and streams and marshes, large and small, that spangle the face of the American land. We pointed with dismay to the suffocation of Lake Erie, and to the horrors of the "Albany Pool" on the Hudson, and to the human excrement that washed over the Falls of the Willamette, and to a thousand similar cases. Representative John Blatnik of Minnesota, one of the prime sponsors of the Clean Water Act, made headlines referring to Washington's Potomac Tidal Basin, with its wealth of blossoming cherry trees, as "the best-decorated sewer in the world"; another congressional clean-water activist, Representative Jim Wright of Texas, noted that the slaughterhouses along the Missouri had filled its waters with so much blood and offal that "it is no longer the Big Muddy, you see. It is the Big Bloody." Thor Heyerdahl and Jacques Cousteau showed us that the greatest waters of all, the oceans themselves, were in danger of dying. It was a time for action, and action was taken. Slowly, progress of a

156

kind was achieved, and if today that progress seems to us to have been a bit precarious—teetering on the brink of another plunge—we must not deny that without those early efforts things would surely be considerably worse.

In their overriding concern for surface waters, the pioneer clean-water activists left groundwater almost entirely alone. They considered it largely unassailable by pollution. The slow filtration it received traveling through its miles of underground aquifers, the time it took to make that dark journey through the earth, and the chemical properties of the soils and rocks it remained in constant contact with were thought to constitute a natural water-treatment plant of the highest possible order. Groundwater was "harder" than surface water—that is, it contained more dissolved minerals—but it was also cleaner. Cities which took their municipal water supplies from wells watched, a bit smugly, as their sister cities on surface-water supplies went glumly and heavily into debt in order to install the expensive and uncooperative treatment machinery needed to provide their citizens with potable water. Their own systems, they were sure, weren't going to require any of those things. A little precautionary chlorine, perhaps; that was all.

Today we are beginning to realize that this smug assurance was woefully in error. Groundwater *is* subject to pollution, and of a particularly insidious variety. Polluted groundwater often neither looks nor tastes polluted. It sparkles in the drinking glass; it strides across the palate with the honest hardness of natural mineralization. But the pollution is there. Like a trickle of slow death, the toxic waste products of our chemically sophisticated society have worked their way down into the aquifers and lodged there, unmoving, tainting all the waters that come by. And once an aquifer has been rendered unusable in this manner, most hydrologists agree, there is very little chance that it can ever be made usable again. "With contamination by toxic organic chemicals," notes one government report on the problem, "ground water can remain polluted for hundreds or thousands of years, if not geologic time." Aquifers subject to such contamination must be removed from our catalogue of known water supplies. Permanently.

In hundreds, perhaps thousands, of places across the country, this has already been done.

Fifteen miles northwest of Portland, Maine, near scenic Sebago Lake—Maine's second largest—the little town of Gray nestles amid pine-covered hills next to the Royal River. With a population of less than a thousand, on the road to nowhere, Gray seems the very picture of bucolic New England. But the rural image is a mask: beneath it lies tragedy.

In 1972, Portland's spectacularly beautiful Casco Bay was fouled by an oil spill; and after the shouting had stopped and the cleanup was over, the city was left with thousands of gallons of contaminated oil on its hands. It seemed a shame to throw it out. A contract was arranged with a local firm, the McKin Company, to clean up the oil, reprocess it, and put it back into circulation. The McKin Company's major business up to this point had been cleaning oil drums; they would need a new facility to handle the oil from the Casco Bay spill. After due consideration, they located this new facility on the outskirts of Gray.

The dirty oil came in, was cleaned, departed—and then, because after a while there was no more oil and there was no point in letting a perfectly good facility stand idle, the oil was followed by other materials in need of reprocessing: crankcase oils, machine oils, and a wide variety of industrial solvents. Over the next several years, between 100,000 and 200,000 gallons of these materials came and went at the Gray plant annually.

Gray has a municipal water system; but, like water systems in many other small towns, it is not universally used, and a number of people, especially those living around the perimeter of the community, rely on private wells. Among these were a cluster of sixteen families with homes near the McKin Company facility. In the fall of 1977, five years after the plant had opened, these sixteen families found the water from their wells becoming increasingly noxious. It tasted strange;

at times it would turn orange. When toilets were flushed, dizzying fumes would rise from them. The people themselves began suffering unexplained headaches, nausea, rashes, and loss of equilibrium. Finally, after a young girl from one of the families became seriously ill with a liver disorder, the local health officer, Dr. Robert McNalley, ordered all sixteen wells capped. Tests of the water revealed significant levels of numerous toxic and/or carcinogenic compounds, including trichloroethane, trichloroethylene, freon, acetone, xylene, dimethyl sulfide, and various alcohols. Municipal water lines were constructed to the affected neighborhood; but a month later the municipal system itself had to shut down when trichloroethylene was discovered in it, too. Fortunately, the compound disappeared again, and after an anxious week the water works were able to reopen.

Officers of the McKin Company denied—and continue today to deny—that their firm had anything to do with the well contamination. It is just barely possible that they may be right. The flow of underground contaminants is extremely difficult to predict, and even more difficult to trace once it has happened. But on the McKin property, investigators have found corroded storage tanks and, beneath them, pools of liquid wastes which have leaked out of the tanks and are busily seeping into the ground. The tanks are located in an abandoned sand-and-gravel pit, a remarkably effective instrument for infiltration. And test borings have located traces of contaminants as much as six hundred feet below the surface. Nearby, the closed wells with their high concentrations of toxic man-made compounds bear mute testimony to one irrefutable fact: whether or not McKin can be blamed, something is seriously wrong with the methods used for toxic-wastes disposal in Gray, Maine.

And as the old saying reminds us, as Maine goes, so goes the nation.

"Man, there's a lot of stuff out there," says Dave Burmaster, waving his hand in the general direction of the United States of America. Burmaster, a tall, intense man with a disarming smile and a direct and rapid-fire manner of speaking, is a chemist from Massachusetts who served as a coordinator of drinking-water projects for Jimmy Carter's Council on Environmental Quality. When I met him in March 1981, he was still in Washington, at the CEQ's office suite in the New Executive Office Building a block north of the White House, helping prepare for the transition to the Reagan Administration CEQ team. "In the last two years," he told me, "we at the Council just started picking up newspaper clippings saying that here and there, up and down the East Coast, there were well closures due to contamination by toxic organic chemicals. At first it was a well here, and a well there, a story about Massachusetts, maybe—I read the local paper up there—or a story about New Jersey, and then, all of a sudden, it seemed like opening up a floodgate. There was just a *deluge* of stories in the newspapers about drinking-water wells being shut down because of contamination by toxic organic chemicals. So we started working on that, and we started making phone calls, and all of a sudden people started sending us things. I keep a repository in my office that's filled with newspaper clippings, state reports, laboratory reports, university professor reports—a lot of stuff where people were working kind of one at a time in their local areas, and not realizing that their neighbors twenty miles down the road or across the state line had the same problem."

With others at CEQ, including the agency's chairman, Gus Speth, Burmaster put together a report, *Contamination of Groundwater by Toxic Organic Chemicals*, which was released in January 1981 by the outgoing Carter Administration. The report is a lulu. Case after case of groundwater contamination and well closures is reported, documented, and detailed. The links between groundwater contamination and illness are carefully probed. The picture that emerges is that of a nation slowly poisoning itself, but still unable—or unwilling—to admit it.

The problem is nationwide. In the state of Michigan, 286 wells have been closed because of groundwater contamination, and another 381 are suspect. In California's San Gabriel

Valley, east of Los Angeles, thirty-nine wells supplying water to thirteen cities with a combined population of nearly half a million have been closed due to high concentrations of trichloroethylene, a known carcinogen widely used as a septic-tank cleaner. In Jackson Township in southern New Jersey, one hundred families were without water for more than a year after their wells were found to be full of a chemical soup containing, among other things, toluene, methylene chloride, acetone, ethyl benzene, trichloroethylene, benzene, and chloroform. All in all, the report finds "serious contamination of drinking water wells in 34 states, and there are indications that the true number is at least 40."

Hardest hit of all has probably been Long Island. An ancient glacial moraine, the 118-mile-long island consists entirely of one vast pile of unconsolidated soils and rock fragments, looming in the waters off Connecticut like a huge geological sponge. The sponge is full. Water striking the surface vanishes almost immediately underground; there are few running streams, and the island's four million residents depend entirely on wells to supply their drinking-water needs.

In 1976, chemical contamination was found in several wells in Nassau County, in the central part of the island. Curious, county and state environmental officials initiated a testing program for all public wells in Nassau County and neighboring Suffolk County, which takes in the island's entire eastern half. The results were frightening. Of five hundred wells examined in the two counties, none was entirely free of contaminants; fifteen percent showed levels high enough to call for serious concern. Thirty-six wells, supplying water for more than two million persons, had to be closed. "Shortfalls from closure were made up from other wells," notes the CEQ report, "but in an area which relies almost exclusively on ground water for all purposes, the closures caused a number of substantial dislocations."

The principal cause of groundwater pollution, on Long Island and elsewhere, is contamination by industrial wastes. To point this out is not so much to accuse the contaminating industries of irresponsible practices, however, as it is to lament that as a people we have done so much with so little knowledge of what we were doing. The current deadly state of our underground waters is a legacy of our past failures to understand the dangers we were exposing those waters to. Buoyed by our belief in the unalterable purity of groundwater, we have been incredibly casual in our siting of industrial-waste disposal areas. It was, for instance, a perfectly legal, licensed hazardous-waste dump that caused those one hundred families in Jackson Township, New Jersey, to lose their wells; it turned out to have been located over the Cohansie Aquifer, the largest in New Jersey and the source of all drinking water in that area. (Not all of the Cohansie, it should be pointed out, has been rendered unusable. Groundwater pollution tends to move away from its source as a discrete plume in the direction the aquifer is flowing; wells sunk into this plume are heavily contaminated, while wells a few hundred feet away but outside the plume may remain pure.) The trichloroethylene contamination in California's San Gabriel Valley appears to have been primarily the result of the use of septic-tank cleaners that were for sale, until recently, in nearly every hardware store and supermarket in the nation. On Long Island, the hazardous conditions of the groundwater may be largely traced, ironically enough, to reforms in waste-disposal practices which came about as a result of the Clean Water Act. Prohibited from merely dumping their residues into Long Island Sound, the island's industries began discharging them into the sewers at the rate of nearly ten million gallons per day; this contaminated sewage, its chemical toxins and carcinogens unmodified by conventional waste-treatment practices, was then disposed of by spreading it in landfill areas over the Magothy Aquifer.

Prior to 1970, the Lee's Lane Landfill in Jefferson County, Kentucky, was a major repository for wastes from throughout the Midwest. "They'd just bring the barrels in," remembers one local official, "and if anybody questioned it, they'd just say, 'What's wrong with this stuff? It's ninety percent water.'" Says Jefferson County environmental-health officer

Bruce Lane, "What has gone into the ground down there is anybody's guess. The EPA came down and did some studies with a gas chromatograph, and they found the gas coming out showed forty-five different peaks." Each "peak"—a high point on the gas chromatograph's graphed spectrum—indicates the presence of a separate but not necessarily identifiable compound. "What impact it's had on groundwater," continues Lane, "has never really been assessed. We don't know what toxics are in there. Knowing what we know today, we would never allow landfills over an aquifer again. But they were taking care of a part of the economy that needed to be done at low cost, and in all honesty thought they were doing it well. I don't think we can condemn them."

Today we have a much greater awareness of the problems that can derive from improperly located waste-disposal sites. Many of the old dumps have been closed, and the ones that remain are subject, in most states, to rigid controls. Dumps are now carefully sited to avoid aquifers which are used for drinking water; they are designed with impervious clay floors, and the leachate from the wastes, instead of sinking into the ground, goes to treatment plants especially designed to remove its toxic and carcinogenic compounds before allowing it to flow into an aquifer or a river.

The great care with which we now locate and build these facilities, however, has caused certain problems of its own. Though our waste output continues to grow by leaps and bounds, the places where we can legally dispose of these wastes are actually shrinking. And this has placed the firms that generate the wastes in a serious quandary. What do they do with the stuff? If they can't store it and they can't dump it, where does it go?

"There is currently no licensed hazardous-waste facility at all in the six New England states," points out Dave Burmaster in Washington. "Nevertheless, that is an industrial area, and it generates a significant amount of hazardous wastes. Now, people like Polaroid can afford to spend $125 a barrel and truck their wastes to North Carolina, but there are other companies that are less civic-minded." For those "less civic-minded" companies, there is no practical alternative save one: to entrust their wastes to one of the nation's rapidly growing network of illegal waste-disposal firms, the ones known—as we pointed out in the last chapter—as "midnight dumpers."

Fifteen miles south of Louisville, just over the line into Bullitt County, Kentucky, a tiny Ohio River tributary called Wilson Creek heads out in a small round valley amid low limestone hills. Nearby, a cluster of houses, too small to really be called a town, goes by the name of Brooks. A private golf club, the L&N, spreads beside the tracks of the Louisville & Nashville Railroad, swinging into the valley's head from the south on its way from everywhere else into the city. Hardwoods smooth the hills and soften the ragged edges of the huddled farms. By most measures it is a place of great beauty; and yet it is not beauty, but horror, that has given birth to the name this valley is known by to toxics workers and water activists throughout the nation.

It is called the Valley of the Drums.

One cold, overcast day in the spring of 1981 reporter Jim Detjen of the *Louisville Courier-Journal* took me to see the Valley of the Drums. With my brother Jack—a music professor at the University of Louisville—at the wheel, we drove south out of Louisville down the North–South Expressway to Shepherdsville, turned northwest on a secondary road, and headed toward Wilson Creek through an aptly named place called Gap In Knob. A short distance past the sign marking the L&N Golf Club, Detjen suddenly said, "We turn here." Jack turned. We bumped along a rocky side road for a few moments and then, at Detjen's direction, pulled off into a blocked-off driveway beside an abandoned shed. Before us, grim and gray under the heavy skies, sprawled the valley.

I had seen pictures of the Valley of the Drums, and thought I was prepared; but no picture can convey the sense of reeking malice that reaches its grasping fingers out of that valley to clutch at visitors standing at the brink. Fields of wasted earth gouge the shrinking hills, the raw red soil stained with unearthly chemical blues and greens. Corpses of lifeless trees lift beseeching, skeletal arms skyward. Steel drums, the drums of the valley's name, lie everywhere. Pile upon pile, windrow upon windrow, acre upon acre of mangled, shattered, discolored drums. Beside the path winding down from the shed, the rotting carcass of a dead dog stands silent sentinel.

Jim led the way down the path; Jack and I gingerly followed. For an hour the three of us prowled among drums. Red drums, green drums, yellow drums, blue drums. Drums relatively intact, stacked in long neat rows. Drums thick with corrosion standing in the center of spreading stains. Drums cascading down hillsides like lethal Niagaras; drums humping into rusted and grotesque caricatures of the surrounding hills. Drums everywhere. The sick-sweet smell of solvents hung in the air so heavily that its odor could almost be seen. I worried about the soles of my boots.

In an odd, distant manner, like a tour guide to hell, Jim Detjen told us the story behind the horrors of the valley— the story he and fellow reporter Jim Adams had dug out and exposed in the pages of the *Courier-Journal*. The land we were standing on had once belonged to a man named Mitchell, who had sold it to a man named Taylor, Arthur L. Taylor, to use as a storage site for what Taylor told him were to be bricks and other building materials taken from buildings he had contracts to raze. That was in 1967. The bricks, etc., never appeared: Taylor, who has been characterized by acquaintances as "a harsh man, but honest," had apparently changed his mind. Instead of tearing down buildings, he opened a firm called the A. L. Taylor Drum Cleaning Service. He would buy barrels full of waste from local industries, dispose of the contents, clean the barrels, and sell them for reuse. The barrels would be collected and processed on the land he had bought from Mitchell.

There is some evidence that Taylor had originally meant to keep the operation small. He did not seek permits for waste disposal; he was not a waste-disposer, he was a barrel-cleaner. For a time, he trucked the contents to the Lee's Lane Landfill or other at-that-time-legal waste dumps in the vicinity. But soon the barrels began coming in too rapidly for that. By the early 1970s, he was just emptying them onto the ground; shortly after that, apparently totally overwhelmed by the job of merely collecting and trucking the things, he began simply tossing them into haphazard piles on the property to be dealt with later. Later never came. In 1978, Taylor died of a heart attack, leaving as his legacy to an unaware public a valley full of anywhere from 20,000 to 100,000 decaying, leaking, unmarked barrels. EPA officials, who stumbled on the site a few months later while looking for something else, were awed: it was, they said, the biggest illegal dump site they had ever seen, anywhere in the nation.

They had no idea how to clean it up.

"It's been over a year," Detjen told us, "and not a single barrel has been removed. All they've done is rearrange them into lines and flatten the empties. They still don't know what's in most of them. Look." He pointed to letters painted hastily on the barrels: "S" on some, "L" on others. "The EPA did that," he explained. "The letters stand for 'solid' and 'liquid.' It's really the only thing they know about the contents of most of these things."

At the bottom of the valley's slope, just above Wilson Creek, Detjen showed us an earthen dam with a pool of noxious-looking water behind it. "The EPA put this in last winter," he said. Oily rainbows swirled on the surface; a stone tossed into the center would bring up large, slow bubbles. The fumes were intense. The dam's purpose is to gather the surface water running down the hillside past the barrels. A pump, operated by a switch that turns on when the water in the pool reaches a certain level—like a domestic sump pump, but on a much larger scale—sucks the contents out through a pair of large green boxes, one an ion exchanger, the other an activated-charcoal filter. The cleansed water is then dumped on the ground a few feet from the edge of the creek. "They decided it was necessary after they found thirteen different chemicals in Wilson Creek, and twenty-nine more in the surface runoff above the creek," explained Detjen. "Some of them were in concentrations as high as 100,000 parts per billion. The allowed levels for them tend to be down around five."

"I have a headache," Jack said quietly. Jim nodded. "I always get one when I come out here," he observed. "One of the EPA guys said it best: 'Yea, if I walk through the Valley of the Drums, I shall dissolve.' "

The Valley of the Drums is frightening in many ways. It is frightening for its size; it is frightening for the bewildering variety of chemicals stored there, most of which are unidentifiable without sophisticated tests. It is frightening for the concentrations of exotic chemicals that have found their way into its runoff waters and into Wilson Creek. It is frightening as an example of governmental sloth: records show that surrounding landowners began complaining about the place as early as 1975, and that the county and state authorities, through what they now call an "oversight," failed to follow up on the complaints. The most frightening thing about it, though, is none of these things: the most frightening thing is that the Valley of the Drums is not alone.

A few miles southwest of the Valley of the Drums, where the Salt River runs into the Ohio near the town of West Point, there is a place known as The Brickyard; here more than three thousand barrels of industrial wastes stored without authorization by Donald Distler—the man convicted of pouring toxic wastes down a manhole into Louisville's sewers—were discovered in 1977.

Across the Salt River from The Brickyard, on land owned by Distler's father, one thousand more barrels were found floating in Ohio River floodwaters in December 1978. The younger Distler claims to know nothing about these, and it is still undetermined just how they got there.

Southeast of Distler's farm, near Shepherdsville, a thirty-seven-acre piece of land called Smith's Land Fill and Private Rifle Range holds uncounted thousands of barrels, most of them buried beneath huge piles of earth by bulldozers. More barrels arrive daily. Smith's is licensed to accept solid wastes, but not all the barrels on the property have solid wastes in them; the owners have been cited repeatedly for permit violations involving liquids. The citations have yet to lead to convictions. The dumping goes on.

Outside the Louisville orbit, out in the rest of the Midwest and the rest of the world, the story continues. In Monroe County, Kentucky, on the Tennessee line, 1,500 barrels hauled from a Cincinnati firm were stored illegally in a shed in the late 1970s; some of the barrels burst, and the liquid wastes within crept downward and dissolved a water main buried more than two feet beneath the surface, depriving residents of a nearby town of water. At Seymour, in central Indiana, thirty thousand illegally stored barrels at a place called "Seymour Recycling" polluted a major aquifer. Eastward through Ohio and Pennsylvania and Delaware; southward through Tennessee and Georgia and Florida; northward through Illinois and Michigan; and westward through Iowa, Kansas, Nebraska, Colorado, Oregon, and Washington, at thousands of sites, behind factories, beneath bridges, in ditches, along roadways, the barrels have turned up. "Every day," says Dave Burmaster in Washington, "there are stories in the newspapers about how some state trooper up in the middle of Nowhere, New Hampshire, has found a truck with New Jersey license plates dumping some foul-smelling liquid beside the road." And in Nowhere, Vermont, and Louisiana, and Nevada, and California, and virtually every other state in the Union. Everywhere our industrial wastes are a problem that has gotten away from us; everywhere they are getting into our waters. And everywhere we are drinking them. The ultimate results can only be guessed at.

One measure of the problem may be found in the state of Hawaii. Stuck out in the middle of the ocean, Hawaii is essentially a closed system; wastes produced there must stay there. There is no place else for them to go. And yet, of 100,000 barrels of industrial wastes produced in the islands each year, legitimate dumps can account for only 20,000. Where does the rest of it go? Nobody knows. It is known, however, that much of Hawaii's groundwater is polluted—by toxic organic chemicals.

The illegal dumps—the midnight dumpers, the Valleys of the Drums—that spatter across the nation are a serious problem, and promise to remain one for some time. Still, it is not the illegal dumps, but the legal ones, that tend to concern groundwater professionals the most. Illegal dumps are a problem of law enforcement, and that is a problem, by and large, that we know how to deal with. Legal dumps, on the other hand, are a problem of technology—and there, despite our best efforts, we remain on much shakier ground.

How can we deal with the hazardous waste products of our chemical society? What is the best way to segregate them from the environment and prevent them from harming either it or us? How can we keep them out of our water supplies?

This is perhaps our greatest shame: no one really knows. Despite decades of trying, we have yet to design something that really does the job. We can put a man on the moon, but we still can't find anything to do with the trash the man leaves behind.

In Salem, Oregon, in a small building not far from the State Capitol, I discussed this problem with Ted Groszkiewicz, a hazardous-waste specialist with the state's Department of Environmental Quality (DEQ). A stocky, dark-haired, earnest young man and sometime Sierra Club activist, Groszkiewicz had just finished helping to oversee cleanup activities at the Caron Chemical dump near Sufer, Oregon, in the mid–Willamette Valley a few miles south of the college town of Monmouth. Here, amid green, flat fields that hold the scent of spring most of a good year through, a man named Ron Richmond had begun a solvent-recycling and hazardous-waste-storage operation in early 1978. He had a permit from the state to do this. ("We thought it was a good idea to have a site there," Groszkiewicz says. "Having a site discourages people from just throwing the stuff in the ditch or the river.") But shortly after storage began at Caron, a management decision at the distant Chem-Nuclear Corporation—operators of Oregon's principal hazardous-waste dump, trenched into the Columbia River Basalts near the town of Arlington—doubled their disposal price; and Richmond, who never meant to keep wastes permanently but only to hold them for eventual transport to Arlington, found himself in trouble. He couldn't afford Arlington's new rates; he couldn't keep the stuff where it was, either. The neighbors were complaining. In early 1980, Caron Chemical went out of business, leaving two thousand decaying drums at the site.

The county government had called the EPA, and the EPA had told them it would cost $2 million to clean it up. Groszkiewicz and his colleagues at the DEQ thought that was extravagant. With the cooperation of Caron's former customers, several of whom donated equipment and labor, DEQ crews had gone in and cleaned up the Caron site for $65,000. They had done a good job: tests of surrounding wells in mid-1981 showed no significant contamination. This is one, apparently, that they had caught in time.

Nevertheless, Groszkiewicz remains worried, not just about Caron but about the whole field of hazardous-waste disposal. "Even the spots we've licensed and certified as secure," he muses, "they're as safe and as secure a spot as we can find, but in the long run, who's to say? It's kind of a cut-your-losses situation. It's better to have it there than in the middle of your local shopping center."

State-of-the-art technology in waste disposal involves what are known as "secure landfills." These, Groszkiewicz explains, are specially prepared sites with impervious clay bottoms of plastic liners, or sometimes both, designed to keep chemicals from leaching into the groundwater. The sites have a slight slope. Wastes are placed on the upper end of the slope and covered with earth; as barrels decay and rain leaches the contents out, the leachate runs down the slope and collects in a waste pond known as a lagoon, to be stored until treatment can be arranged for it.

This is, of course, far better than the alternative of just dumping the stuff and forgetting it; yet, at the same time, it is far from perfect. The principal weak spot is the liner. It is called impervious. It is not. Against much of today's waste, nothing can be.

"There is no such thing as a pond that doesn't leak, even if you line it," states Groszkiewicz categorically. "You always have to come to a decision in an industrial area: can you protect the aquifers, or can't you? The answer is generally no. So you have to make a decision to site the plant in an isolated aquifer situation, where the aquifers it contaminates won't be those used for drinking water. And that's sometimes impossible to do."

And even if it were not impossible—even if properly sited secure landfills could do the job for our future trash—what about the legacy of the past? How do we deal with the hazards caused by the improper dumps now in existence? This is not a small problem. According to EPA figures, there are at least fifty thousand active and inactive waste-disposal sites around the nation which contain potentially dangerous amounts of hazardous waste. A map of the United States carrying dots showing these sites looks like a child with a bad case of the measles; there is not a single state without at least one, and most have hundreds. In at least seventy percent the lagoons are unlined; in many cases, these unlined lagoons are located over aquifers that are used for domestic water supplies. It is not known how badly these water supplies are affected, because ninety-five percent of the sites have no means of monitoring groundwater contamination. But the EPA estimates that more than one billion gallons of leachate are lost each year from unlined and leaking industrial-waste lagoons, and that leachate has to go somewhere. Living a long distance from a hazardous-waste facility may not turn out to be a great deal of protection, either: at least thirty square miles of aquifer surrounding the Rocky Mountain Arsenal near Denver, Colorado, have been found to be contaminated, and in Iowa, contamination of wells in Waterloo by arsenic compounds has been traced to a dump located in an abandoned sand-and-gravel pit near the Cedar River, fifty miles away.

What are we doing to our water? What are we doing to ourselves?

Near St. Louis, Missouri, but on the Illinois side of the Missouri River, the 130-acre Earthline hazardous-waste dump has been closed by court order due to threats to the water supply of the nearby town of Wilsonville.

North of Spokane, Washington, wells near the Colbert Landfill have been closed because investigators from the Washington State Department of Ecology found levels of trichloroethane in them approaching ten thousand parts per billion.

In Dover Township, New Jersey, at least 148 wells have been capped due to contamination by man-made organic chemicals since 1974.

In Bedford, Massachusetts, four wells supplying between seventy-five and eighty percent of the municipal water supply had to be closed when tests found contamination levels of up to 2,100 parts per billion of dioxane and 500 parts per billion of trichloroethylene. The discovery was accidental: physicist Dan Oblas, a Bedford resident, was helping to test some new analysis procedures developed by the GTE labs in nearby Waltham. One of the samples they ran through the equipment in the course of the tests came from Oblas' home taps. (After the closure, Bedford began purchasing drinking water from other towns in the vicinity. Unfortunately, this was not necessarily an improvement: wells have been closing in the other towns, too.)

In Helena, Montana, state health officials are wondering what to do about potential contamination of hundreds of wells throughout the state by the pesticide Endrin. A relative of DDT, but considerably more potent, Endrin was sprayed on some 120,000 acres of Montana farmland in the spring of 1981 to control cutworms. Later that year, low levels of the pesticide began showing up in the flesh of game birds: the birding season was almost called off, and director John Drynan of the state health department suggested that the pattern of Endrin's presence in the birds suggested a high potential for a slow creeping of the pesticide into the state's aquifers, with what he termed "mind-boggling ramifications" for the long-term health of Montana residents.

In Westmoreland, California, in one of the most bizarre twists of all, county officials are testing wells to find out whether or not an earthquake has rendered them undrinkable. The quake, in late April 1981, is feared to have opened fissures between a waste dump run by the I-T Corporation, six miles west of town, and the aquifer that provides the town's water supply.

More than fifty percent of the people of the United States get their drinking water from beneath the ground. Where will they get it when the groundwater can no longer be used? How many wells can we close before the shortages caused by the closures begin to damage the American economy? Is it—to paraphrase Bruce Lane—worth writing off our aquifers so that we can dump trash on a short-term basis?

So far there are no answers. There are only the questions —the nagging, unanswerable questions.

CHAPTER 14

On the Wings
of the Wind

IN THE EARLY 1970s, sport fishermen in the western part of New York State's Adirondack Mountains began to notice a strange and unsettling phenomenon: they weren't catching anything.

It was, the evidence suggested, more than just a bad run of fisherman's luck. Always before, the Adirondacks had been superb fishing country. On the east side of the mountains, Lake George had routinely produced record-threatening trout; on the south side, the northern pike in Great Scanadaga Lake had held the world's weight record since Peter Dubuc had pulled in a forty-six-pounder on September 15, 1940. The 2.4-million-acre Adirondack Forest Preserve, in the center of the range, had been set aside as "forever wild" by an amendment to the New York State constitution in 1892: a spectacularly scenic region of sharp granite peaks, shaded forests, rushing brooks, and more than two thousand lakes, it had always been literally teeming with trout. Empty creels just shouldn't happen—not consistently, not here. Still, there they were.

What was causing the declining catches? Pollution, it

seemed, could be safely ruled out; there was nothing there in that wilderness that could pollute. Disease also seemed unlikely. If there was disease there would be deaths, and if there were deaths there would be carcasses. There were none. The fish didn't seem to be dying—they were just disappearing. Where are they going?

Not down into the murky depths, that was certain; there were no murky depths. The water was crystalline, clear as diamond—clear enough to distinguish undecayed twigs and leaves on the bottom twenty feet and more down. Come to think of it, what were *they* doing there? Twigs and leaves submerged in mountain lakes do not, by the nature of things, remain long undecayed. Bacteria consume them; plankton consume the bacteria, insects consume the plankton, and fish consume the insects. An entire food web should have been living in those lakes. What had happened to it? Where had it gone?

The fishermen didn't know, but they were worried. Clearly, there in those sinisterly transparent waters, something funny was going on.

By 1972, the mystery had caught the attention of an ecology professor at Cornell University, Dr. Eugene Likens. To Dr. Likens, the situation in the Adirondack lakes seemed uncannily similar to fifteen-year-old accounts from Scandinavia of lakes losing their primary food webs. There the culprit had proved to be acid. Would it prove so here as well? A piece of blue litmus paper dipped into one of the mysteriously sterile lakes provided the answer; it promptly turned a blushing pink. The pure, sparkling lake water had the litmus characteristics of a glass of tomato juice.

Where had the acid come from? That, at least, was no mystery: there was only one real place it could have come from. Despite the seeming impossibility of pollution in this pristine wilderness environment, it was pollution that was the culprit. The lakes were upstream from virtually everything else in New York, but there was a polluted source above them anyway. That source was the rain.

And that, in turn, meant that we were *really* in trouble.

If there is any single worst place for water pollution to show up in, it would have to be in the rain. Rain is not just water; rain is the mother of waters, the original source of all freshwater on earth. Rivers and aquifers do not give birth to water, they only collect and store what the rain gives them. All the water that we use, all that we drink, or wash with, or cook with, or sprinkle on our crops, or cycle through any of the myriads of industrial processes that depend upon this most important of economic resources—all of this comes, ultimately, from the rain. To pollute the rain, therefore, is to commit the ultimate act of pollution. If the rain is dirty, then all waters are dirty. As an act of vandalism against a nation's water supply, dumping filth into the rain could not possibly have any peer.

But if the rain was polluting the lakes, what was polluting the rain? Guided once more by the work of their predecessors in Scandinavia, Likens and others who had now taken up the work soon came to an answer. The source of the acidification couldn't be the seas: even if, by some quirk, a patch of the Pacific had turned to lemon juice, the acid in it wouldn't be carried aloft in the water vapor. According to the laws of physics, that vapor could only be pure H_2O. The source couldn't be the ground around the lakes, either; tests of the acid proved that. Runoff of the rainfall over and through the ground was indeed contributing some acid to the lakes—as it had been for centuries—but it was tannic acid, the acid of tea, leached from the ground's cover of fallen leaves and pine needles. The predominant ions in the damaged lakes were not those of tannic, but of sulfuric and nitric, acids. This was the stuff, not of forest floors, but of chemistry labs.

Not in the vapor, not on the ground. That meant that the rain had to be picking up its acid load someplace between—sometime after it condensed from vapor and before it landed on the ground or in the lake water. In other words, while it was falling through the air. The polluted rain which was causing the polluted lakes had itself to be the result of polluted air.

And the polluted air? Clearly, over this wilderness, the source could not be local. But pollutants can travel a long way on the wings of the wind; and looking upwind from the Adirondack airshed, the researchers at last could tell where the acid that was destroying these wilderness lakes was coming from. Upwind, the air that brought the rain was coming in directly over the Ohio River Valley and the southern Great Lakes region—the industrial heartland of America. This was a region that had long been troubled by air pollution—a pollution that was, because of the burning of high-sulfur coal, particularly high in the sulfur dioxides and nitrous oxides that would, when dissolved in water, form sulfuric and nitric acids.

That was the conclusion the acid-rain researchers reached. As good scientists should, they published them. These publications soon reached the eyes of the coal-using industries that were accused in their pages of killing the Adirondack lakes. And all hell proceeded to break loose.

"It's impossible for people outside the Midwest to recognize the degree of passion—I mean real passion—which coal engenders in this part of the country," says Pete Clapham softly. Clapham, the author of two standard textbooks in ecology, is a former professor at Case Western University who now runs an environmental consulting service in Cleveland. Lately he has been doing work on acid rain for the Sierra Club. "The kind of anguished cries you hear from people when acid rain is mentioned have to be taken seriously," he goes on. "And I think we can. But that means that you have to have a slightly different viewpoint than if your only purpose is to stop acid rain.

"If you're on the consuming end of acid rain, you want to get the job done as fast as possible. If you're on the producing end, even if you want to get the job done as fast as possible, if you've seen the obstructions that take place, I think you have to recognize that you have to be—much more patient and creative."

The "obstructions" and the "anguished cries" that Pete Clapham refers to have been going on since the publication

of Likens' first work in 1972. Some of them have a rueful sort
of merit; others are just so much technical garbage, couched
in simple language that makes them seem nontechnical. And
because it is important to understand the difference between
the garbage and the meritorious, we are now going to have
to delve a little deeper into the mechanisms by which acid
rain, as it is currently perceived by most scientists, both here
and in Scandinavia, actually works.

The chain of phenomena that concludes by poisoning
lakes in the Adirondacks has its beginning in the coal-burning furnaces and power plants of Ohio and Michigan and
Kentucky and Pennsylvania. The precise details of certain
parts of that chain are not yet clear, but enough is known to
pin down the general outlines. "You start off with sulfur in
your coal, and nitrogen in your air," explains Clapham, "and
you burn the coal in the air, and you end up with a bunch of
SOx and NOx—sulfur oxides and nitrogen oxides. Nobody
really knows the chemistry by which they combine to form
sulfuric and nitric acids: the chemistry of the atmosphere is
very tricky. At the same time, however, we know that the
situation's gotten worse, much worse, since we started using
tall stacks as control methods for keeping sulfur oxides at
low levels around the plants." The tall stacks—originally put
in, ironically enough, as pollution-control devices—disgorge
the SOx and NOx high above the ground; the wind takes
them up and away. Hundreds of miles to the north and east,
they drift into the mountains of New York and New Hampshire and Maine and Vermont. Sunlight falling on them during the journey initiates the complex chemical reaction
which Clapham admits is not yet fully understood, and acid
ions are born. These ions are easily dissolved in water; raindrops condensing among them, or falling through them from
above, sweep them up like coins on a croupier's table. Acid
rain results.

Just how acid is acid rain? It varies. Some storms are more
acidic than others; the acid level may also vary from place to
place, or even from time to time, in the same storm. Generally, though, the answer to that question is, pretty strong.

Normal rainfall is slightly acidic due to picking up dissolved carbon dioxide on its way down through the atmosphere; its value on the pH scale—the sliding logarithmic curve normally used to measure acidity, on which 7 is neutral and each decrement of 1 down toward zero represents a tenfold increase in the hydrogen-ion concentration that gives an acid its bite—is usually somewhere in the neighborhood of 5.6. Acid rain goes far beyond this. It is usual for rainfall in the western Adirondacks to have acid levels of around pH4, and it is not uncommon to find levels approaching pH3.6—one hundred times as acidic as normal. A reading of pH4 indicates an acidity level about the same as that of an orange or a tomato; a reading of pH3.6 is equivalent to that of a pickle or a tumbler of vinegar. The acidity of the rain, in other words, is measurably about as high as that of the most acidic substances you would normally have around your house.

What happens when this vinegar rain falls into a lake? Nothing, in the beginning. The beds of most lakes have materials in them which can absorb acids, creating a buffer not unlike a giant antacid tablet. But eventually this buffering capacity is used up; and then, slowly at first but with mounting swiftness, the pH value of the lake water begins to decrease. When it passes pH5, the fish in the lake stop reproducing; there are no more new fish, and the old fish die off or are caught, one by one, until eventually the last one is gone and the lake is sterile. There were, at last count, 237 lakes in the western Adirondacks that had passed this biological point of no return, and hundreds more teetering on the brink.

The destructive effects of acid rain extend far beyond the mere acidification of waters. Falling on soils, the rain leaches out heavy metals; these then enter the watercourses along with the acid, and there they make their way into the food chain and quickly build up to toxic levels through biological magnification. Acidified water running through a city water system can also dissolve trace metals from the pipes, threatening the health of unwary users: for this reason and others, federal regulations limit acidity in drinking water to pH6.0

or above, ten times more acid than distilled water but still far below the acid levels now found in the Northeast's lakes and rivers.

A particularly frightening effect of acid rain is its tendency to slow the growth of the vegetation it falls upon, leading to decreased agricultural productivity and lower-than-normal tree harvests from affected forests. Since some plants—strawberries and tomatoes, for instance—seem to do very well in acid soil, and will initially increase their growth rates as soil pH is raised, damage to vegetation by acid rain has long been discounted by the coal-burning industry. Recent studies, however, leave no doubts about its reality. "Broccoli, carrots, beets, and radishes suffer yield losses of up to fifty percent when exposed to simulated acid rain," states David Gardiner of the Sierra Club's Clean Air Office in Washington, D.C. "Acid rain accelerates the erosion of protective waxes from the leaf surface, damaging the leaf and increasing the susceptibility of the plants to disease and pest attack. The formation of nitrogen-fixing nodules on the roots of legumes is inhibited seventy percent." Even acid-tolerant plants can be damaged. "The reproductive structures of plants may be particularly susceptible to injury by acidity," Gardiner maintains. "Tomato plants exposed to acid rain, for example, show a decrease in pollen germination and pollen tube growth, which results in lower quality and quantity fruit."

Not everyone agrees with this Doomsday scenario, of course. One who does not is President Reagan's Secretary of the Interior, James Watt: he believes, or so he has informed interviewers, that acid rain is a minor problem that has been built into a major one by environmental groups seeking financial contributions. "Every year there's a moneymaking scare," he told Missouri outdoor writer Charles J. Farmer, who reported the conversation to the readers of *Audubon* magazine. "This year it's acid rain." Not surprisingly, coal-company executives tend to agree with this view. Seizing on the fact that the mechanics of acid rain are complex and

unpredictable, they have attempted to downplay their part
in its cause. "A very basic issue . . . is still in disagreement,"
stated coal-industry spokesman William N. Poundstone to a
Senate committee in May 1980, "and that is whether or not
the rain is even becoming more acid." Acid rain, he maintained, could be a completely natural phenomenon. Sulfur
dioxides are emitted from growing plants, volcanoes, and
other nonhuman sources: as for nitrous oxides, "lightning
alone may be half of the NOx problem."

Poundstone and others have pointed to what they consider
serious flaws in Likens' work. To show that the acidity of the
rainfall in the Adirondacks was increasing, for instance, Likens had taken measurements at a number of stations in the
western part of the range and compared them to measurements taken in the 1950s from the same network of stations;
but in the interim, all but two of the stations in the network
had been moved. The measurements were thus of rain falling in one set of places in the 1950s, and falling in a separate
set of places, up to several miles distant from the first set, in
the 1970s. The methodology of the first set of measurements
was also different, and much cruder, than the methodology
used for the second set. Added to this are some unexplained
local variations in the data: lakes a few miles apart, similar
in size and setting, but with widely varying levels of acidity.
There are too many questions, say coal-industry spokesmen,
to allow us to regard Likens' work as anything but questionable itself. The regulators should therefore maintain a pru-
dent silence.

Are these criticisms valid? Pete Clapham doesn't think so.
"The indirect methodology which was used in the fifties,"
he points out, "will give you an error of plus or minus a factor
of two in hydrogen-ion concentration. That's too much, and
we're aware that the new approach will do much better. But
the changes in the acid levels are on the order of fifty, and a
factor of two is a reasonable experimental error when your
differences are over fifty. Or even forty, or even twenty-five,
or even *ten*. And as for the station locations—that's fine
when you're dealing with small areas, but here you're deal-

ing with a whole region, and the local differences in mete-
orology are swamped by the regional phenomena. I wouldn't
use it for a local problem, because there it does make a difference. But, Christ, you're talking about something which
has already come at least a thousand miles. What difference
does it make if your stations are two miles apart?"

And even if the Likens study is ultimately discredited—
which no one but the coal industry seems to think is likely
to happen—what about the others? Eugene Likens is not the
only scientist who has been working on acid rain: the 1979
International Conference on Acid Rain in Toronto was not
called to discuss the work of a single researcher. There is,
for beginners, Likens' colleague Carl Schofield at Cornell,
the first to actually link fish declines in the Adirondacks to
acid-rain buildups. There is Martin Pfeiffer of the New York
State Department of Environmental Conservation, and Stephen Norton of the University of Maine, and Eville Gorham
of the University of Minnesota. There are probably hundreds
of others in the United States—not to mention the Cana-
dians, who were onto acid rain well before us, and the Scan-
dinavians, who were onto it before them. Canada's top
environmental officer, John Fraser, has called acid rain "the
most serious environmental problem Canada has ever
faced"; it is unlikely that he would have said that just to
please Gene Likens. As Pete Clapham puts it, "Even with
Ronald Reagan in power, acid rain is not going to go away."

But if it is relatively easy to discredit the coal industry's
criticism of the acid-rain studies, it is much more difficult to
decide what to do about the problem the studies reveal. The
standard answer, proposed by environmental groups and by
most of the government agencies which deal with the problem, is to force the installation of so-called "stack scrubbers"
—devices which wash the sulfur-laden particulates from factory smoke by passing it through sprays of water as it rises
up the chimney. The coal-burning industries dislike this approach: they say it is too costly to install and operate the
scrubbers, and anyway, they have a wretched record in
terms of dependability. "Down-time" caused by improperly

operating scrubbers would be too great for the plants to remain economically viable.

Surprisingly enough, perhaps, Midwestern environmentalists and environmental scientists tend to agree with the coal-using industries on this point. "Scrubbers," mutters one Ohio Sierra Club activist who also happens to be an engineer specializing in water pollution controls. "Those are the things that take the stuff that dirties the air and use it to dirty the water." "All they do," complains Pete Clapham bitterly of the national environmental groups, "is push scrubbers, scrubbers, scrubbers, scrubbers, scrubbers. But that's not going to be the solution to the problem. The reason for that is that scrubbers do nothing but clean the air, and it's hard for the industry to view cleaning somebody else's air as being very important." Clapham has suggested a number of alternatives. Washing the coal—crushing it to powder and treating the powder with water or solvents to remove the sulfur prior to burning it—is one possibility. Another is so-called "fluidized-bed combustion," in which the crushed coal is mixed with crushed limestone and supported on a curtain of air in the firebox: the limestone reacts with the sulfur dioxides during the combustion process to form calcium sulfate, a solid which remains behind to be either utilized in other industrial processes or hauled off and buried. Coal gasification, which converts the coal to natural gas before burning it, is also highly efficient at removing sulfur. "The determined opposition of the Midwestern states to the implementation of a plan to reduce acid rain is going to continue," Clapham emphasizes, "until you can somehow find an alternative to scrubbers which can go onto existing plants at relatively economic costs."

In Washington, David Gardiner disagrees. "With acid rain in Ohio," he told me, "we're faced with the old problem that the least-cost alternatives are also the least effective." Coal washing removes less than fifty percent of the sulfur in coal; fluidized-bed combustion and solvent extraction are somewhat better, but they are correspondingly more expensive. None of these techniques affects nitrogen oxide levels significantly. Scrubbers do much better: they have the capacity to remove virtually all of the sulfur oxides and relatively high proportions of the nitrogen oxides as well. The coal industry claims that they cannot be made reliable, but these claims are belied by experiences in Japan, where scrubbers have been mandatory for some time and where they have shown a reliability rating of up to ninety-eight percent—far better than normal, for any type of machinery.

One thing Clapham and Gardiner do see eye to eye on is the need for the coal-burning states of the Midwest, and Ohio in particular, to stop obstructing efforts to curb acid rain. "Ohio," says Clapham, "should take a leadership role in the acid-rain question, because it stands more to gain by being a leader in solving the problems of high-sulfur coal than by obstructing into the middle of the twenty-first century." Unfortunately, he doesn't see this happening. "You know," he muses, "we can't even work out the physics of acid rain. We don't know the chemistry of it. And to figure out the sociology of it on top of that is purely impossible. And yet that's what you've got to do to solve this coal question." Gardiner is more blunt: he sees, not sociology, but practical, hardball politics. Environmentalism may have less effect, ultimately, than regionalism. "Ohio is resisting," he says, "and the New England states are ganging up on them. They're going to get it rammed down their throats."

Not, you understand, the best way to win friends and influence people. But inevitable—unless Ohio does something about the problem first.

And not only Ohio. The Adirondacks are not the only place in North America where the destruction of lakes by acid rain is occurring: reports, these days, are coming in from all over the continent. The lakes of Minnesota's Boundary Waters Canoe Area are slowly succumbing to acidification; acidified lakes have begun to turn up in the California Sierra and the Colorado Rockies. At least 140 lakes in Ontario have gone under. Wisconsin has found more than 2,500 lakes with pH readings below 6.0—not destroyed yet, but approaching the

ACID RAIN DISTRIBUTION

AVERAGE ACIDITY OF PRECIPITATION
IN pH

NORMAL RAINFALL: pH: 5.6

critical point. Readings as low as pH3.6 have been taken in lakes in New Hampshire and Vermont. Rivers and streams have also turned acid: Hubbard Brook in New Hampshire now has a pH of 4.1, Como Creek in the Rockies is down to 4.7, Twitchell Creek in the Adirondacks has been measured at 4.3. A study by the Canadian Department of Fisheries and Oceans in 1980 found nine rivers in Nova Scotia with acidity levels of pH4.7 or below, and eleven more which they considered "threatened." All in all, according to the findings of the International Conference on Acid Rain, some fifty thousand lakes and streams in the United States and Canada are either below the critical point or teetering on the brink. And some estimates are higher than that. The Ontario government, for example, has stated that it believes that 48,000 lakes in Ontario alone may "go critical" within the next two decades.

Ohio cannot be blamed for all that.

Where does the rest of the acid come from? There are a variety of sources. Part of it can be blamed on coal-burning plants elsewhere—in places like Sudbury, Ontario, or Four Corners, New Mexico. Part of it may, as the coal industry insists, come from natural sources—volcanoes, lightning, and the respiration of plants. Large portions of it must certainly be blamed on the automobile: acid rain falling in the Rockies, for instance, contains next to no sulfuric acid, but much nitric acid. That is characteristic of the emissions spectra, not of power plants, but of internal-combustion engines. Ohio does not contain all the internal-combustion engines in North America: Cleveland and Akron are not upwind from the entire continent. Scapegoating the industrial Midwest is not going to stop the acid rain that is currently falling in Pasadena. We must do better.

Whatever we do, we must do it rapidly. The acid-rain problem is getting worse, not better, and there no longer remains a great deal of time in which to solve it. Already rain in West Virginia has been measured at a pH of 1.5, or more than ten thousand times normal. Lake Tear of the Clouds, the source of the Hudson, has been acidified; so has Ontario's Lake George, perhaps the most-often-painted lake on the North American continent. Elimination of the salmon runs in several Nova Scotia rivers has been linked to acid rain. The specter of an entire continent of sulfuric-acid waters lurks in the wings, unwanted but impossible to push away.

"We don't have much time to fool around," says Canada's John Fraser bluntly. Fraser is right. We cannot go on arguing over details of the process while our waters are turning to nitric and sulfuric acid: we must act. The potential penalties for not acting are far too severe. As Stephen Norton of the University of Maine put it to *Audubon* magazine's Jon R. Luoma, "I would not like to see us run it as a long-term experiment and have it turn out that we were right."

CHAPTER **15**

The Waters of Hell

I CAME TO Gallup in a snowstorm. The ground was cold, and the thin air of the high-plateau country of western New Mexico had turned thick and white. The contours of the old Spanish-style buildings in this town of twenty thousand were muffled; through the flurrying snow, the surrounding red-rock terrain for which Gallup is famous was nothing much more than a buff-colored blur. But that was all right: I had come to look at neither the architecture nor the scenery.

I had come to look at the river.

Bundled against the chill, snowflakes clinging to my eye-lashes, I left my motel and wandered down to the Second Street Bridge near the center of town. Beneath the bridge the Rio Puerco slid by, a pale ghost dimly seen through the fluttering air. The braided, meandering stream was only a few feet wide; it looked lost in its broad, concrete-walled channel. There was nothing to indicate the scene enacted there scarcely twenty months before, when a wall of angry water four feet high had come pouring down that channel, foaming, swirling, red with suspended sediments—and palpitating with radioactivity.

If there is water in Hell, it must certainly be radioactive. No other pollutant could be as appropriate. Radioactivity is not, like a disease germ, a living thing that is drunk in with the water and then parasitizes itself on its unwilling host; nor is it, like a toxin, a molecule that reacts with other molecules in the human body to upset the delicate chemical balances of metabolism. It is more fiendish than either of these. Radioactive atoms are atoms in the process of tearing themselves apart. In so doing they emit tiny bits of charged matter known as alpha and beta particles; even smaller, uncharged subatomic fragments called neutrinos; and bursts of intense, uncontrolled energy, the gamma rays. Like millions of miniature bullets, the particles and the gamma rays penetrate nearby materials, shattering their atoms and turning them, too, radioactive—the "chain reaction" which, in an uncontrolled form, leads to the atomic bomb.

At sufficiently high levels, radioactivity can cause massive human damage. Hair falls out; skin sloughs off. Internal organs, led by the liver and the pancreas, stop functioning. Death can occur within days. At lower levels, the damage is less obvious, but it is there. Under the constant bombardment of subatomic particles, organs go subtly haywire, altering bodily functions, tinkering with hormone balances. Genes are torn apart, causing cell mutations. The count of white cells in the blood typically climbs, either because of alterations in the liver or because the bone marrow, the blood's red-cell factory, is malfunctioning. Cancers appear. The level of radiation necessary to induce a cancer has never been satisfactorily determined, but it is not high, and some scientists have wondered aloud if any level at all is completely safe.

Though water itself can be made radioactive through contact with another radioactive substance, most radioactivity in water is carried in dissolved or suspended compounds, and these often have chemical properties that multiply the problems associated with their radioactivity. Plutonium, for example, a product of nuclear reactors, is not only radioactively but chemically carcinogenic, so much so that as little as one thirty-millionth of an ounce has been found to cause cancer. It is also highly toxic in small amounts. Strontium 90 mimics the action of calcium when ingested; the body deposits it in the bones, where it remains actively irradiating the surrounding tissue for the rest of the individual's life. Similarly, cesium 137 is picked up and used by the body as if it were potassium; since the metabolic uses of potassium cover the entire body, ingestion of cesium 137 is equivalent to putting a miniature radiation factory into every living cell.

Most parts of the world are subject to trace amounts of natural radiation, called "background radiation," at all times. The amount of this background varies from place to place; it is particularly high around Gallup because of the presence of large quantities of uranium ore. But it was not background radiation that the Rio Puerco carried that July day in 1979. It was radiation of a much more concentrated form, caused not by the mere presence of the uranium ore but by the mining of it. Upstream from Gallup some sixteen miles, near the town of Church Rock on the Navajo Indian reservation, a tailings dam had failed at a mine operated by the United Nuclear Corporation—a nuclear-power giant with corporate headquarters at Falls Church, Virginia. Eleven hundred tons of solid tailings, and 100 million gallons of fiercely radioactive water, had cascaded into a tributary of the Puerco.

Uranium mining is not a particularly efficient operation. Uranium does not typically occur in lodes, but in low concentrations scattered more or less uniformly through a parent rock, usually sandstone. To obtain the uranium, the parent rock must be quarried, crushed in a mill, and treated with a chemical solution to leach the uranium from it. The uranium is taken away to be refined into nuclear warheads or fuel pellets for nuclear reactors. The crushed rock—mountains of crushed rock—is left behind as tailings.

The tailings are worthless. They are also hazardous; besides containing the highly acidic remnants of the chemical leachate, they still shimmer with up to eighty-five percent of the radioactivity originally removed from the mine. In days past, before the onset of nuclear enlightenment, the tailings from uranium mines were often blithely passed out by the miners as road gravels, construction fill, or even material for making bricks or artificial stone to use in building houses; but those days, generally, are past. United Nuclear is an enlightened company. At the Church Rock mine the tailings had been carefully piled and sealed off behind dikes, or "tailings dams," so that rainwater leaching through them could be contained. The carefully built, continuously monitored dams were objects of pride to the company, which was convinced that it was dealing with wastes in a state-of-the-art manner. It was one of those "state-of-the-art" dams, however, that gave way that July day in 1979, catapulting Church Rock, Gallup, and points downstream suddenly and frighteningly into the nuclear age.

A few blocks from the Second Street Bridge, in a small yellow building on a Gallup side street, I found New Mexico environmental officer Bob Triviso surrounded by the clutter typical of an understaffed and overneeded office. Triviso remembered the day of the Church Rock spill very well, and was glad to talk about it. "When we first reported in to work that morning," he recalled, stroking his small black beard, "we had a call from our central office in Santa Fe, alerting us to the fact that the dam had broken and released the tailings. So we ran down to the Rio Puerco to see what was going on. And the first thing we noticed was that the level of the water running through there was extremely high. Normally, I would say you'd have, oh, a foot of water running through there, maybe ten feet wide, twenty feet wide in some areas, but that day, when we got there, it was running bank to bank and roughly four feet deep. Our central office asked us to take some samples, which we did, right there off the Second Street Bridge. I think we must have filled maybe four or five gallon containers. Some of the radiation specialists from out of our Grants office arrived later, and I took them down to the state line—the Arizona/New Mexico line —where they took some more samples. There and at various other points along the stream."

What those samples turned up was sobering. As the crest of water from the tailings spill roared through town, it carried levels of radioactive elements such as thorium and radium at up to six thousand times the "normal" amounts. Other heavy metals—selenium, arsenic, sulfur—also spiked to abnormally high concentrations. The river's acidity, as New Mexico environmental writer Allan Richards was later to remark, reached a pH value "equivalent to that inside a car battery."

The radioactive levels were also, of course, very high. Those first samples taken by Triviso off the Second Street Bridge were churning with radioactivity, and although the levels dropped dramatically in the next few hours as the crest of the flood flushed on through, some remained: studies a month later showed radiation levels as high as 10 picocuries/gram, more than double what would be considered "natural background" even in uranium-rich New Mexico.

There were immediate concerns that these high levels of radioactivity would leach through to the groundwater; warnings were issued, signs were posted, and a well-monitoring program was set up as a cooperative venture between the New Mexico Environmental Improvement Department and the federal Public Health Service. Unfortunately, however, this monitoring program was seriously flawed. Some of the flaws were due to what Triviso calls "politicking": there were, he says, "all types of agencies that started getting involved. You had EPA, you had NRC—they had the EID involved—and it seemed like everybody was coming up with reports instead of having one unified effort. And I think that added a lot of the confusion as to how this should be handled." Some of the flaws were in administration, and some were in the design of the program, which had the testers taking samples from every well within a hundred feet of the river, ignoring the fact that most of those wells reached down more than 1,500 feet to tap deep aquifers and thus could not be expected to be affected by radiation infiltrating from the river. The biggest flaw, though, was not something that could have been remedied by either better administration or better design. No matter how carefully the data were collected and tabulated, they would remain scientifically questionable. The difficulty was not inaccurate measurements: the difficulty was that there were no baseline data to compare those measurements to.

"The big problem," comments Don Payne, "is that when they started their mining operations no one thought to set up sampling programs to define the background. So you can look at it now and tell where it stands in relation to the drinking-water standards, but you don't know what it was before." Payne works for the U.S. Public Health Service in Gallup: he was involved in the monitoring program after the Church Rock spill along with Bob Triviso and others. He considers the results of that program "frustrating." "They've been running up there since the midsixties," he says, "and the effluent pump for the mine is radioactive. They've only recently begun treating the effluent to remove U-226 and the gross alpha particles. We don't know how much of that has gotten into the water already. There may also be natural levels of radiation in the river, we don't know. And nobody has any perc data, so we don't know how fast water from the river is percolating into the surrounding aquifers. There is just no baseline to work from. Trouble is, we've been oblivious to the problem for years."

And not only in Gallup. We've been oblivious to the problem everywhere. The Church Rock spill is the largest known accident in the United States involving the release of radioactivity into water supplies, but it is not the only one. Though the nuclear industry likes to point to its laudable human-safety record—there has never been a death traceable to the operation of a commercial nuclear reactor in the United States—the fact is that spills involving potentially dangerous amounts of radioactivity are distressingly common at all stages of the nuclear-power process. They are common at mines: the Church Rock spill was not an isolated occurrence, but one of at least fifteen known tailings accidents at uranium mines in the Rocky Mountains since 1959. They are common at fuel-processing facilities. They are common at waste-storage sites, where even the best available technology does not seem to be able to prevent the leakage of liquid radioactive wastes into surrounding streams and aquifers. They are least common at the operating power plants themselves, but even in the plants there have been more accidents than their operators would care to admit. At Monticello, Minnesota, for example, two thousand gallons of radioactive water poured into the Mississippi River from a Northern States Power Company nuclear plant when a worker forgot to shut off a hose. A leak at Consolidated Edison's Indian Point Plant No. 2, a few miles above New York City on the Hudson River, caused a spill of 120,000 gallons; it was, fortunately, contained within the plant. And at Harrisburg, Pennsylvania, they are still trying to figure out what to do with the 600,000 gallons of water that pooled in a reactor-containment building after the near-disaster at Three Mile Island in 1978. "The containment building was not designed to contain water," worries plant director Gale Hovey, admitting that there is some concern that "we could leak this highly radioactive water into the environment."

Problems with radioactive water have been reported from all over the nation. In Idaho, for instance, wastes injected into deep wells at the federal government's Idaho National Engineering Laboratory near Twin Falls have migrated over one thousand feet into the Snake River Aquifer. In South Dakota, tailings piled at Edgemont have leached radioactivity into the Cheyenne River. In Colorado, measurements of up to two thousand times the "normal" amounts of radioactive elements have been found in the water supplies of communities taking their water from Great Western Reservoir, the result of weapons manufacture and storage at the Army's Rocky Flats Ordnance Depot. In Kentucky, investigators at the Maxey Flats Dump on the Ohio River above Louisville have traced leakage of radioactive wastes for several hundred feet toward a nearby aquifer, even though the dump ranks as one of the best-designed and -maintained low-level-waste-disposal sites in the country. And in the state of Washington, where the federal government's Hanford plant near Richland is one of the largest and oldest nuclear-research facilities in the world (it made the plutonium for the Nagasaki bomb that ended World War II), 115,000 gallons of high-level wastes leaked into the Columbia River over the course of one two-month period, earning the continent's second-largest river the sobriquet "most radioactive river in the world"—a title it held until the accident at Church Rock.

Perhaps the most frightening tales come from upstate New York, in the region around the Niagara River. Here at Model City, a tiny town halfway between Niagara Falls and Lake Ontario, eight thousand tons of highly radioactive waste left over from World War II's Manhattan Project—responsible for the birth of the atom bomb—are slowly migrating toward Lake Ontario in open ditches; while at nearby Tonawanda, a suburb of Buffalo, sleuthing by a task force from the New York State Assembly discovered that more than 37 million gallons of wastes from the same project were flushed down shallow wells in the mid-1940s. This method of disposal was chosen deliberately, according to a source involved in the project, because it would be impossible to trace. It is. No one knows today where it has gone, or what aquifers it might have entered.

Radioactive water is not a small problem. And it will get larger. There are seventy operating reactors today. More than twice that many are scheduled to be operating by the turn of the century. Every one will produce wastes that will remain dangerous for a quarter of a million years. The problems we are currently having with radioactive wastes in our water supply have all come down upon us in less than forty.

Things are calm again in Gallup, New Mexico. The Rio Puerco—the "Perky," as they call it locally—is back in its bed; that bed has been stripped clean from the mine to below Gallup by United Nuclear crews with shovels and fifty-five-gallon drums, and the water's radioactivity is back down to "acceptable" levels, whatever that may mean. A well at the Church Rock school had to be closed due to extremely high levels of gross alpha particles, but Don

Payne thinks that it was a case of natural radioactivity in the aquifer rather than having anything to do with the spill. "It was a new well, and they were pumping it into the system," he says. "Luckily, it was being diluted. The day we received the report on it we closed it down." The crisis is over, and attention has wandered. The reporters have all gone away. And Don Payne is mad.

"The mill-tailings spill," he says, watching the snowflakes filter down outside his office window, "was a relatively minor occurrence when you look at the long-term exposures people are getting. There are natural radioactivity levels in these people's water, and it's being compounded. There's forty thousand gallons a day being lost into a Gallup sandstone aquifer at that mine right now, just loaded with radioactivity and heavy metals. The tailings pond was supposed to be built for total retention, but the bottom wasn't sealed. UNC is trying to drill wells to intercept the seepage and pump it back, but that doesn't strike me as a terrific way to deal with waste."

Across the room, Payne's colleague Mark Mattson speaks up. "They're talking now about doing what they call 'in situ' mining," he says. "That's where they inject chemicals directly into the ground and leach out the uranium without mining it. That could certainly have some effects on the groundwater. I'm not excited about it at all. We wouldn't have the radon gas from the mills, of course. But I think I'd rather have the radon gas."

Down at the EID, Bob Triviso nods in agreement when I repeat Payne's and Mattson's words. "You know," he says, "from the spill itself there was a lot of contamination, high contamination at the outset. But for all practical purposes, it just flushed on down. It's gone. They called that a crisis, but I'm not so sure. I think the *real* crisis is what's happening now."

CHAPTER **16**

Salt

WATER POLLUTION IS a complex and many-faceted problem.

Human and animal wastes pour into our rivers and leak from septic tanks into shallow aquifers. Byproducts of industrial processes contaminate streams and groundwater supplies with toxic compounds, both natural and man-made. The rain is acid. Pesticides and herbicides used on farms and commercial forest lands drift into watercourses from sprayplanes or leach into the ground from treated fields. Nuclear-power and weapons-manufacturing plants contribute radioactivity; nuclear plants and other electrical-generation facilities using steam-driven turbines also contribute enough waste heat to the waters they sit beside that pollution-control experts have begun to speak of the phenomenon of "thermal pollution"—a rise in the temperature of a body of water that causes a change in its ecology, either rendering it sterile or, more commonly, creating conditions ideal for the growth of unwanted aquatic organisms such as blue-green algae or disease bacteria.

Our very human fear of death, and our horror of the ravages of cancer, have kept public attention centered largely on the toxic and/or carcinogenic pollutants, principally industrial discharges and the outfalls from municipal sewage plants. This, in turn, has fostered a common perception of pollutants as things in the water that are either filthy or exotic; and most, to be sure, are. But there is one extremely widespread and serious pollutant which is neither. It is a pollutant which is clean, a pollutant which is tasty, a pollutant which we keep in containers on our tables and sprinkle over our food each day. It is, of course, salt—a substance which seems totally innocent, but one whose potential problems are so severe that heading them off may prove to be one of the biggest pollution-control challenges we will ever face.

Salt pollution causes damages in many ways. Water polluted by salt is functionally no different from sea water: undrinkably bitter, disruptive of the metabolisms of freshwater organisms such as humans, animals, and crop plants, and terribly destructive to metals. As one authority has written,

> Excessive salinity has pronounced damaging effects on virtually all water uses. . . . In agriculture, salinity kills crops, decreases yields, forces change to less profitable crops, promotes excessive water use, and increases capital and operating costs. In home and industrial uses, salinity decreases potability, corrodes plumbing, appliances, and equipment, increases treatment costs, and at high concentrations or prolonged exposure (depending upon an individual's cardiovascular salt-tolerance level) can be a hazard to human health.*

These are not small problems. Nor are they isolated: salt pollution is a problem in at least eighteen states, and current estimates indicate that salinity-related problems will have cost the United States between $1 billion and $1.5 billion by the year 2000.

The Romans, when they conquered ancient Carthage, sowed the Carthaginian fields with salt so that they could

---

* George Pring, *Environmental Defense Fund v. Douglas M. Costle: Reply Brief*, U.S. Court of Appeals Docket No. 79-2432, June 30, 1980, p. 7.

never grow crops again. We do likewise, but with one important difference: the fields we sow with salt are our own.

Chemists define a salt as an acid in which the hydrogen molecules have been replaced by those of another metal (hydrogen being classed, chemically, as one of the metallic elements). Thus table salt, known chemically as sodium chloride (NaCl) is hydrochloric acid (HCl) with the hydrogen replaced by sodium; magnesium sulfate (MgSO$_4$) is sulfuric acid (H$_2$SO$_4$) with the hydrogen replaced by magnesium; and so forth. There are numerous salts, and they come in a bewildering variety of chemical guises—toxic and nontoxic, colored and colorless, acid, basic or normal—but the ones we are concerned with here are a relative few: those which are both readily soluble in water and stable enough to be commonly found in nature. In addition to table salt, these include principally the salts of potassium, magnesium, and calcium. In small doses, none of these is harmful; in fact, most are beneficial, and some are necessary. But the farms of America's irrigated regions are not getting them in small doses.

"Take a look at that Pepsi-Cola can on the shelf behind you," says George Pring, leaning back in the swivel chair in his office at the University of Denver School of Law. I turn, and there sits the can, staring at me—rusted, broken, and covered with a thick layer of what appears to be chemical corrosion. Ugly! Pring smiles. "That came out of an irrigation ditch in the Imperial Valley," he explains. "Lovely, isn't it? That's all salt. Not just your basic chloride of sodium, but the others too—the potassiums, the calciums, the whole spectrum of salts, all of which are incredibly destructive to wildlife, and to plants, and all of which take a very profound toll on domestic pipes, and machinery, and whatnot. It's not a killer pollutant in the literal sense—but it's one of the most vicious economic pollutants you can run into. The current estimate is that we're causing over fifty million dollars in damages every year, just in the United States portion of the Colorado Basin. Not to mention what we send over the bor-

der into Mexico." And also not to mention legal work. That's
how Pring got into it—legal work. An attorney specializing
in Western environmental law, he spent seven years with
the Environmental Defense Fund before coming to teach at
the University of Denver. A great deal of that time was spent
in what he now refers to as "the salinity case"—EDF's suit
against the federal government for knowingly continuing
policies that led to drastically increased salt pollution in the
Colorado River.

Having some salt in a river is perfectly normal, especially
in arid regions. Rivers dissolve salt from the stone and earth
of their beds; the rivers run into lakes, which evaporate,
concentrating the dissolved salts in smaller amounts of
water. In extreme cases, the lakes disappear altogether, leaving their salts deposited in the dry soil of their former beds.
Rains leach these salts into the earth, creating lodes of saline
groundwater. Sedimentary rocks formed from the sands and
silts of ancient seas incorporate the salts from the seas into
their structure, and as these are eroded by rivers the rivers
pick up the salts in great quantities. The number of Salt
Creeks, Salt Rivers, Bitter Licks, Salt Washes, and so forth
that are scattered across the American landscape suggest
how great those quantities can be.

The problem is particularly acute in the Colorado Basin.
Here, under skies that seldom rain, the rivers course over a
countryside consisting of thousands upon thousands of
square miles of sandstones, limestones, shales, and other
sedimentary rocks, all laid down when a wide, shallow sea
covered the area millions of years ago. The sea was very
salty, and the salts were trapped in the sediments that
formed the rocks. As today's rivers cut down through those
rocks, they dissolve the salts from them. In the dry air, evaporation rates are high; water from the rivers is continually
escaping to the skies, leaving behind its salt load to be carried by the water that remains. Thus, smaller and smaller
volumes of water carry greater and greater volumes of salt,
and natural salinity levels are very high. Human activities
have compounded these. There are fifty milligrams of salt

per liter of water in the headwaters of the Colorado. In pre-irrigation times, this amount underwent an eightfold increase between the headwaters and the Gulf of California, to approximately four hundred milligrams per liter. Today the increase is more than seventeenfold, to almost nine hundred milligrams per liter—on good days. There are times when it spikes up to the neighborhood of four thousand.

"Salinity," says Pring, in his best courtroom manner, "is increased by either of two phenomena: loading or concentrating. That is to say, increased runoff will do it, an industry or a municipality expanding, a new agriculture going in—there's going to be loosening of the soil, there's going to be more chemical salt ions in the river, loading the amount of salinity in the river. The converse also does the same thing. The more new industry you have in the upper basin taking purer upstream water out and subsequently not returning it —things like power plants turning water to steam—then your basic volume of salts are carried in an even smaller quantity of water, and that ups the concentration."

This looks like a Catch-22 situation, and it is. If you put the water you've used back into the stream, you are dumping extra salts in along with it, and that increases salinity problems downstream; but if you don't put the water back, then you're reducing the amount of water available to carry the baseload of salt, and that also increases salinity problems downstream. "You know," muses Pring, "the problem of salinity just keeps going round and round chasing its own tail. If you are, as a farmer, getting relatively saline water coming onto your crops, then of course the longer time it takes to travel across your field, the more evaporation, and settling, and deposition of the salts you're going to get. Which is bad. So you want to move it across your field very fast. Wonderful. You move it across that way, you use five times more water than you need, in order to get the pressure up to flush it through fast. You waste four fifths of the water. You have four times as much water going back into the system, polluted with surface contact, and so the guy next downstream gets saltier water than he did before.

"Salinity breeds inefficiency. There's a whole circle of problems: as the quality of the water gets worse, our misuses of the quantity becomes even greater." And in the Colorado Basin, with its water already in short supply, misuses of the quantity simply cannot be afforded.

The Colorado is not the only place that is having trouble with salinity: everywhere that irrigation is practiced, the salinity loads in the rivers are increasing. There are salt problems in the Rio Grande Valley, where salinity has built up in the reservoir behind Falcon Dam due to a large-scale irrigation works in the Mexican states of Coahuila, Tamaulipas and Nuevo León. There are salt problems in Utah and in Nevada. There are severe salt problems in the San Joaquin Valley of California, where many years of irrigation have left the San Joaquin River itself too salty to be used on crops, leaving San Joaquin farmers no choice but to import water from the north, at great expense, through the Central Valley Project. (The salt load in the San Joaquin currently threatens even that. Water from the northern-California rivers is transported to the Central Valley Project via the Sacramento–San Joaquin Delta. The San Joaquin has become salty enough that the mix of waters in the delta is now often of questionable quality for agricultural use.)

Groundwater irrigators, of course, are free from the problems caused by salinity buildups in the rivers. But groundwater irrigators have their own problems with salinity. Many aquifers contain saline waters in their lower levels, so that water pumped from them becomes progressively saltier as it is used up. There are also aquifers which contain nothing but saltwater: these are often side by side with freshwater aquifers, so that withdrawing the freshwater causes the saltwater to move in. In Kansas, a major saltwater lode underlies two major freshwater sources, the Ogallala and the Dakota aquifers, separated from them by less than two feet of rock. The saltwater is under pressure; wells punched into it cause it to push upward, contaminating the freshwater aquifers above. It is a problem that has become more acute as the demand for water has increased; already, several portions of the Dakota have been rendered unusable by wells that have accidentally been drilled too deep. Seacoast irrigators (and seacoast cities) have a similar problem. There, withdrawal of water from freshwater aquifers often causes the sea to move in. Numerous once-fresh wells on both the Atlantic and Pacific coasts are now bringing up seawater: the problem is particularly acute in Florida, southern California, and parts of Texas, New Jersey, and Long Island.

Salt pollution is a serious problem, and a number of serious attempts have been made to deal with it.

Since salt buildups are particularly common in poorly drained soils, one solution is to improve drainage. Hundreds of thousands of perforated drainage tiles have been buried in cultivated fields in irrigated regions of the United States in an attempt to move waste water off faster: there are at least seventeen thousand miles of these tiles in the Imperial Valley alone. In the San Joaquin Valley, government engineers are hard at work on a massive ditch called the San Luis Drain, designed to parallel the river and to intercept most of the saline runoff waters that would normally fall into it, an approach which may have some value, although it is difficult to see how replacing a natural drain with an artificial one can ultimately be considered much of an advance. To slow the movement of seawater into coastal aquifers, attempts are being made to inject freshwater into wells in a line paralleling the freshwater/saltwater interface, artificially repressuring that portion of the aquifer so that the flow of freshwater is once again outward; the technique works, but it also, of course, uses a great deal of water itself. In some areas, the threat of salt pollution is being met straightforwardly by the installation of desalinization plants. So far, the biggest of these is a reverse-osmosis plant being constructed at Yuma, Arizona, by the U.S. Bureau of Reclamation: when and if this plant becomes operational (that time, as I write, has not yet come), it will suck up the entire volume of the salty Colorado, take the salt out of it, and pour it back into its bed to flow fresh and sweet into Mexico.

To Pring, all such technological solutions seem to miss the

point. It is, he says, "a sort of whole American bass-ackwards notion that to cure pollution you have to have created it, instead of preventing it in the first place." What is needed is not after-the-fact cleanup; what is needed is before-the-fact controls. Salt, he says, is "an absolutely marvelous pollutant —I say marvelous in a negative sense, because the level of salt in the water turns out to be an almost perfect barometer of growth and development. The more growth and development, the higher the salt content. The higher the salt content, the less growth and development. It's a fascinating closed circle. But the point is, to control salinity you have to put land-use controls into effect." You can't simply develop haphazardly; you must, somehow, enforce types and patterns of development that will prevent salinity buildups from occurring. Allowing salt to pour in and hoping you can take it out later is no longer a viable strategy. That was the reasoning behind the Salinity Suit. EDF lost that suit, but Pring intends to keep fighting for the principle.

Is Pring right, or are those who push the drain tiles and the desalinization plants right? My own view is that both are. The problem is of such a scale that neither approach to it will work by itself. We cannot ignore the technological approaches: the time is too late, and the salt loads in many of our major irrigation streams have already increased too far. Land-use controls will prevent further salt pollution, but they cannot clean up what is already there. That can be done only by aggressively pursuing desalinization and soil-drainage projects, and there is no question in my mind that these should go forward.

At the same time, however, there is no question that land-use controls must be instituted, if only to stop practices like those exposed in 1961 in Arizona's Welton-Mohawk Valley: there farmers were found to be pulling extra water from the Colorado, using it to irrigate their crops, and replacing it with brine drawn from former irrigation wells that had turned salty. The salinity index of the Colorado in downstream Mexico jumped from measurements in parts per million to measurements in parts per thousand, and a major international incident was narrowly averted by a series of meetings between legislators from the two countries. That is the kind of thing that happens when upstream developments ignore downstream needs, and that is the kind of thing that land-use controls can and must be invoked to prevent.

In parts of California's Imperial Valley, if you ask for a glass of water in a restaurant it will be brought to you with a slice of lemon floating in it. That is the cosmetic approach. It is necessary; the water would not be palatable without it. But it is not sufficient. The answer to salt pollution is not salty lemonade. It is unsalty water.

...IV

CHAPTER **17**

Losing Control

IT SEEMED SO simple, once.

We built our cities on the banks of rivers, and took water out of the rivers. We built them on the shores of lakes, and took water out of the lakes. If there were no lakes or rivers, we dug wells, or we laid pipelines to places where there *were* lakes or rivers. To ensure drinkability and palatability, we added chlorine and we passed the water through filters. Water supply was a straightforward business. Design, build; operate, maintain; expand as necessary. We thought it would go on that way forever.

It didn't.

Today, we cannot count on taking water out of rivers and lakes: those that are not fouled beyond use are already being taken by someone else. We cannot lay pipelines: there are too few sources left for the pipelines to tap. We cannot dig wells, because the water in the ground either is disappearing at altogether too rapid a clip or is too full of unidentifiable compounds with frightening polysyllabic names for us to safely drink it. Treatment remains helpful: but for treatment to work we must know both what we are treating for and how to treat for it, and often we know neither. Our demands for water grow greater and greater, but there is less and less water available to meet those demands. Supplying water to our cities and industries and farms has become a complex, frustrating, and often insurmountably difficult task. We are —to put it bluntly—losing control.

"This division is about ten years old," says Arnold Schiffman pointedly, "and I'm the eighth guy in the job. None of my predecessors were fired, and one is dead." A small, nattily dressed man with a direct, rapid-fire manner of speaking, Schiffman is the director of the Water Resources Division of the New Jersey Department of Environmental Protection. It is a totally unenviable position. New Jersey holds the dubious distinction of having, on a state-by-state average, the most critical water-supply problems in the nation. The rivers often run as heavily to sewage as they do to water; the groundwater contains a virtual pharmacopoeia of exotic chemicals. Politically, the system is hopelessly tangled, with a hodgepodge patchwork of some 618 water companies serving fewer than 570 municipalities. New Jersey's rainfall is fifty percent higher than the national average; the state is bounded by two major rivers, the Delaware and the Hudson, and sits on top of what is universally conceded to be the best network of aquifers on the East Coast. None of this does any good. The water-supply situation is a disaster.

"We are," complains Schiffman, "riding a water-resources roller coaster." He paces back and forth across his Trenton office, a bundle of energy looking for an outlet. Groundwater pollution is "ubiquitous." Pace. "We've closed hundreds of wells in the last five years. And that's just through our regular routines: if you'd go out and look, you'd find a lot more. If you were to name a contaminant, I could find it in the groundwater someplace. Out here in the Pine Barrens, we've got an aquifer that holds seventeen trillion gallons and recharges at a million gallons a day. You can also take a dump truck out there filled with toxic wastes and open the valve and by the time you've closed it again the stuff is all gone. The sand just sucks it up. These things are a legacy we're just beginning to find. On most of them there are no federal or state standards, but we can't fail to act just because we

don't have any numbers. I don't want to wait until there are
bodies in the streets."

Well closures at this time, Schiffman estimates, represent
a loss of "nine or ten million gallons a day" to the state water
budget. In a state where water demands routinely exceed
safe yield by more than sixty million gallons a day, that is a
significant loss. Surface-water supplies can do little to make
it up: the surface supplies themselves are drastically over-
stressed. "Our reservoir systems are basically inadequate—
they've got a collective deficit higher than the safe yield of
the entire Newark system. Most of them are at the tops of
their watersheds, so they're very small. The quality is excel-
lent, but there's not enough of it. Most of the water companies just use river intakes. The Passaic, for instance, is a main
source. There are sixty sewage-treatment plants on the Passaic, so the people on the river are drinking sewage. The
sewage-treatment plants are biological, and they don't work
if it gets too cold. Then the ammonia level goes way up, and
you can't chlorinate the water. We lost forty million gallons
a day that way in the middle of last winter's drought." This
was at a time when the state's water deficit was already running over 100 million gallons per day, and New York City,
itself suffering from drought conditions, was making plans to
pump twenty million gallons a day into eastern New Jersey
through a temporary pipeline laid across the George Washington Bridge.

How does the future look? Will it be any better? Schiffman
shakes off the question. "I'm not working on the future," he
says emphatically. "I'm working on the past. Let's get the
stuff built that we need now, and then worry about the future. Look at this." He snatches up a bound report from
cluttered table in the back of the room and begins reading
aloud from it. It sounds like a description of New Jersey's
current water problems: overdrafted reservoirs, serious pollution, political snarls. After a paragraph or so, he stops and
points to the date on the binding. It says "1958." Almost a
quarter of a century later, there has been no significant
change.

"After this report," Schiffman states, "they floated a cou-

ple of bond issues and built two new reservoirs, Spruce Run
and Round Valley. But they never connected them into the
system. They have a seventy percent overcapacity, and no
way to move the water. There's a $345-million bond issue
for new reservoirs and connecting pipelines on this November's ballot. But if we build all these goddamn pipelines,
who's going to pay for the electrical costs? It costs fifty thousand dollars a month to bring water from rural reservoirs to
urban areas. Who's going to come up with that money?
Who's going to pay for water treatment? We don't even have
the funds to operate the plants to treat the sewage we're
drinking. We were getting some money to build treatment
plants from the EPA, but the Reagan Administration is cutting it back. They're talking about zero funding in 1982.
Without those bucks, we're in trouble." He pauses, shaking
his head grimly. "We saw the light at the end of the tunnel,"
he continues finally, "and somebody collapsed the tunnel."

Schiffman's tale of woe is, unfortunately, not at all unusual. New Jersey is an extreme case, but it is not alone:
hardly a single spot in the nation can be said to have a truly
trouble-free water supply. In southern Florida, the fragile
wetland known as the East Everglades, which serves as the
recharge area for the Biscayne Aquifer—the source of
Miami's drinking water—is filling up with houses and pavement, reducing infiltration rates and leading to severe overpumping and saltwater intrusions into the Miami water
system. In Wisconsin, Michigan, Illinois, and Indiana, the
shores of Lake Michigan sport a gigantic bathtub ring: sending the Chicago River's flow backward through the Chicago
Sanitary and Ship Canal into the Des Plaines River has
served its primary purpose admirably, flushing Chicago's
wastes down the Mississippi, using Lake Michigan water as
the carrier, but it has also partially drained the lake. In the
last few decades, the water level in the 22,000-square-mile
lake has fallen by more than five feet. In Nebraska, where
agriculture depends on the disappearing waters of the Ogallala, a state water official is asked point-blank if there is any

other source of water available to support that agricultural economy after the aquifer has been emptied. His sad but straightforward reply: "In a word, no."

Everywhere there are problems. Everywhere.

I live in a small, country corner of the state of Oregon, in a city with a population of less than sixteen thousand. Ten miles away lies another little city, the county seat, with perhaps forty thousand people in it; there is nothing else even remotely approaching that size for more than a hundred miles in any direction. A scattering of villages with populations of under three thousand each dot the valley around the two little cities. A major river, one of the Pacific slope's largest, flows through our valley; the rainfall in the valley is more than twenty inches a year, and in the surrounding lake- and stream- and spring-filled mountains it exceeds sixty inches. There is little heavy industry. If there is anyplace in the nation where difficulties with water supply should be escapable, it should be this valley. Water should not be a problem—not here, not now.

And yet it is. Even here in our wet little out-of-the-way valley, water-supply problems are intense. More than twenty-five percent of the land within my city is under a building moratorium because the water pressure in the mains is inadequate to serve any new houses. One nearby small town has seen its well water turn brown, saline, and undrinkable; it is now petitioning to be joined to the water system of the county seat. Residents of another small town had to drink bottled water for a decade because their water system could not adequately treat the river to make it drinkable, a situation which was finally solved—at great expense —just last month. Now the residents can drink their tap water, but there is some question about flushing their toilets; their sewage plant, according to the city manager, is "about to fall into the river." The river is used as a water source by at least one downstream city. Pollutants from the light industries in the county seat regularly pour into one of the river's principal tributaries; these, together with agricultural runoff, have so dirtied the tributary that it must be posted against swimming by the county health department. Thirty miles to the west, over the line into the next county, a leaking chemical dump threatens another of the river's side branches—this one entering the mainstream just above a one-hundred-mile stretch that is world-famous for its fishing and white-water rafting.

The problems are, I repeat, everywhere. There is no escape.

In Denver, George Pring talks about the future of the Colorado Basin. The outlook is grim. Thirteen million acre-feet of water—about 4,000,000,000,000,000 gallons—runs down the Colorado each average year. That water is completely apportioned under the terms of the Colorado River Compact, an agreement signed in 1922, after intense negotiations, by six of the seven Colorado Basin states (the seventh state, Arizona, came on board in the mid-1940s). Every drop is already spoken for; there is—on paper, anyway—no water left for any new use anywhere in the basin. And still the demands for it keep coming.

"The upper portion of the Colorado River Basin," Pring points out, "is where the largest percentage of our next two decades of real growth in energy development is projected to take place. The upper-basin states—Colorado, Wyoming, Utah, and New Mexico—are very rich in energy minerals. Coal, uranium, oil shale—the development of these is going to magnify many times over the effects to water. Energy development takes a lot of water. And yet it's a water-short area, with a highly water-polluting series of industries. Where's the water going to come from? You're going to see some very real problems. Right now, if you talk to state of Colorado officials, their expressed concern is to hurry up and build enough dams up here to stake their claim to the water that they now have protected only on paper. Basically, their position is, we can't rely on the Colorado River Compact. We've got to build a lot of useless reservoirs twenty years ahead of their time to stake our claim, to show that we're entitled to this water, even though we don't need it yet, even though it just *sits* here.

"You know, the water-supply problems of the Colorado Basin are very profound, not only because of the actual numbers being used by the customers, but by the way the Colorado River Compact was drawn. When the compact was negotiated, they relied on water measurements from a very short range of years, and estimated that the basin would probably produce an average of sixteen million acre-feet a year. Unfortunately, the years they looked at came in what we now, in retrospect, see was an extreme of the cycle. Dendrochronologists—tree-ring people—have now gone back to the late Paleozoic, in a federal study, and they put out the figure that it's probably 13.2 that's a reliable, long-term, this-century-next-century type of average. Well, the water that got divided up was calculated at fourteen and above. So, first of all, they divided up more water than was going to be there. According to the compact, the upper-basin states are entitled to something over five million acre-feet a year, and the lower-basin states the rest, out of the fourteen million, but it's not fourteen, it's thirteen, and where do you drop that extra million acre-feet off? And the other problem is, it doesn't matter what that figure is, because at a certain point you run into such severe quality problems—you're reducing flow, you're increasing salinity—that nobody downstream can *use* any of that water. And so the idea that the upper-basin states have 5.4, 5.6, whatever it is the compact says, to play with is just absurd."

But don't the basin states themselves realize this? Haven't they stopped to consider where the water is coming from? Pring nods. "They have, but everybody figures they'll get in first, and it's everybody *else's* project that's the joke, and will be the one the door slams on. They've all been playing this very tender little pas de deux together, and hoping no one comes in on the federal level, or the judicial level, and spoils it. You know, it's sort of like a whole series of politicians playing a game of musical chairs, and each one telling himself, 'There's no way that the music is going to end while I'm standing where there is no chair.' "

And so it goes, everywhere. The Fryingpan-Arkansas Project is built on the headwaters of the Arkansas River, and downstream the John Martin Reservoir dries up. Montana farmers go to the state legislature for laws keeping energy development out of the Yellowstone Basin; otherwise there will not be enough water in the river for their irrigation systems to keep the crops growing. New York City insists on drawing its whole entitlement out of the Delaware in a drought year, and a saltwater slug from Chesapeake Bay moves up the river in response to the lowered pressures and threatens the intakes for the Philadelphia water system. In a scene bordering on farce, the attorney general for the state of Idaho threatens irately to sue the state of Washington for attempting to make it rain by seeding clouds—clouds that might otherwise blow on over and rain in Idaho.

Everywhere the problems: everywhere the pas de deux, the musical chairs.

In Cleveland, the Cuyahoga River is supposed to be a symbol of the way things can be done properly if people put their minds to it. Not long ago, it was one of the two or three filthiest rivers in America. Greaseballs eighteen inches and more in diameter floated on its surface; oil swirled across it, not in slicks, but in thick films. The thick brown water oozed and stank. One memorable day in 1969, the Cuyahoga achieved a sort of dubious immortality by literally catching fire. In the section of Cleveland known as the Flats, where most of the city's steel mills are located, the filth on the water's surface went massively up in flames, destroying two railway bridges and threatening general destruction. Alarms rang, and the fireboat *Anthony J. Celebrezze* had to rush upstream from its berth in the shadow of downtown Cleveland's Terminal Tower and put out the river.

Today that couldn't happen. The greaseballs are gone; the constant film of oil has been reduced to an occasional slick. The smooth brown river, still opaque but no longer stinking, flows gracefully through the city and into Lake Erie; fish and waterfowl have begun to return, and at least one restaurant has opened a riverbank terrace. Recovery is proceeding splendidly. Or is it?

Some Clevelanders aren't so sure.

It is a windy Sunday in March 1981, and I am in the back seat of ecologist Pete Clapham's car, weaving about the Flats through a maze of huge factories and tiny macadam roads, trying to get a glimpse of the Cuyahoga. Beside Pete in the front seat, Ed Fritz keeps up a running stream of directions and commentary. A civil engineer, environmentalist, and practicing leprechaun, Ed has been active in Cleveland water politics, inside and outside both industry and government, for more than a quarter of a century. He and Pete, old friends, are obviously enjoying themselves. The river is mostly hiding.

"I wish," says Ed, twisting around in the seat to address me, "that people would stop talking about the time the river caught fire. The fire was really irrelevant. The things that burn in a river are not the primary problem; it's the oil that's emulsified in the water, not the oil that's floating on top, that you want to worry about. That and the whole chemical soup the river carries. And that isn't much better now than it was before the fire." The car noses into another blind alley. "The steel industry," Ed continues, "has spent a great deal on pollution control, not all of it wisely—mostly because they're the steel industry, and they never do anything wisely. And the city has a new treatment plant. Trouble is, it was all designed by people from World Headquarters." That phrase, "people from World Headquarters," is an Ed Fritz trademark; it means people too important to ignore and not knowledgeable enough to figure out how to get the job done right.

Pete finally finds the river—at its mouth. He pulls the car to a stop, and we all pile out, watching the water swirl down its final straight, riprapped channel and into Lake Erie. "You know," muses Ed, "treating sewage is a good idea. But we've fouled it up. We've lost track of our original goal of pollution control in the drive for contracts, and we've grossly over-built, to the point where we can't operate what we've got. We've got these complicated, overdesigned computerized plants, and they keep breaking down, and nobody knows how to fix them, so they don't run. The United States has higher sewage-control standards than Canada, but they live up to theirs. We don't.

"And even if we did, we still wouldn't be solving half the problem. We'd be controlling the point sources—but most of what goes into a river doesn't come from point sources. It's nonpoint runoff from parking lots and streets, where it's picked up oil droppings, and little pieces of asbestos from brake drums, and gasoline, and God knows what else. If you've ever driven more than a couple of blocks in a city snow, you know that the slush that builds up inside your fender is just as filthy as it can be. Well, all that ends up in the river, and we still don't know how to even begin to control it." He breaks off, gesturing down the river and out into the lake. Near the horizon is a small orange box; the mouth of the still-filthy river points directly at it. "That," says Ed, "is the principal intake for the city of Cleveland's water supply. Now don't you feel comfortable?"

But if, as Ed insists, our control of pollution isn't working, it isn't alone. Our control of water shortages isn't working, either. The Central Arizona Project proves that.

As the Cuyahoga is supposed to be an example of what can be done in the field of pollution control, the Central Arizona Project (CAP) is supposed to be an example of what can be done in the field of raw-water supply. It is, its boomers tells us, the answer to the water-supply problems of Phoenix, and Tempe, and Tucson, and half of the rest of Arizona. When it is completed—presumably in the fall of 1985—a switch will be thrown, and water from the Colorado River will start its journey from the pool behind Havasupai Dam on the California/Arizona border, up the bank, under the Buckskin Mountains, and across the deserts of central Arizona. Three hundred and seven miles away, and two thousand feet up, some of the water will reach Tucson; the rest will have been left behind at Phoenix and Tempe and Mesa and other Arizona communities and farming regions. One million two hundred thousand acre-feet of water each year—ninety tons a second—will make the journey, traveling through the

world's largest precast-concrete pipe, pipe so big that a nor-
mal-sized pickup parked beside a section of it looks as
though it were something carved on the head of a pin. It will
cost $3 billion, but it will be worth it. Arizona, the boomers
say, will be able to cease worrying about water.

It isn't going to be quite that easy.

In the courtyard at Pima College, Doug Shakel—an outspoken opponent of the CAP—sits cross-legged on the grass
and ticks off the big pipeline's many problems. There are, to
begin with, going to be considerable amounts of extra costs.
Pumping costs for Tucson water now run about $15 an acre-
foot: the cost of CAP water, delivered at the end of the canal,
will be more than three times that. A non-CAP reservoir will
have to be built to store the water deliveries so that they can
be fed into the city's system at controlled rates, and the reservoir's price will have to be amortized into the water bill
along with the extra raw-water costs. Tucson's water rates
promise to go sky-high.

There are many other problems besides the straight dollar
costs. Colorado River water, for instance, is up to twice as
saline as the well water Tucson is now drinking. Coupled
with the economic factor, that means that Tucson residents
will be paying through their noses for water that they may
have to hold their noses to drink. CAP pumps will consume
more electricity than the entire city of Phoenix, and the construction of the project's Orme Dam at the junction of the
Salt and Verde Rivers east of Phoenix will not only flood out
the homeland of the Yavapai Indians but destroy the world's
only known desert bald eagle nesting site. The Indians of
the San Xavier Reservation southwest of Tucson are suing
the city over rights to the water once it finally gets there. The
list of drawbacks—economic, environmental, quality-re-
lated, energy-related, legal—goes on and on.

"I still think there's a chance it won't get built to Tucson,"
Shakel says. "My feeling is, it will get to Phoenix—the structure on to Tucson will have begun the initial phases—and
then someone will say, 'God, look at the *problems* they've
got with that in Phoenix. Do we really want to pay that

price?' And someone down here will lead a crusade, and keep Tucson from buying that water. I think when the price is finally driven home, they'll say, 'We can't afford this nonsense.'"

And even if Shakel is wrong—even if all the objections are overcome and the pipeline does get built to Tucson—there will still be a problem. It doesn't really matter whether the city can afford all those various costs, economic and otherwise, or not. There won't be enough water anyway.

Frank Brooks of Tucson Water is, unlike Doug Shakel, a strong backer of the CAP. Like most Arizona water officials, Brooks has been happy to see the big pipe built, and is looking forward to its completion. At the same time, however, he remains firmly convinced of one point: no matter what its more ardent partisans may claim, the CAP is no savior. It will help, but not as much as may be believed. "The CAP," Brooks states, "is a diminishing resource. Just the fact that the pipeline is coming in doesn't mean it will be full at all times, forever after. As a mater of fact, present estimates are that by about 2020 or so the flow in the Colorado River will be used so much that our allotment from there will have to be reduced by half. And it may seem easy to ignore a problem that's forty years away. But the problem with ignoring it is that in the life of a city, forty years passes awfully fast."

Does this mean that the stringent conservation program that Tucson has had to impose will continue after the CAP water arrives? Brooks nods. "It has to," he says simply.

Three billion dollars in federal money. Massive amounts of resources and energy. Severe environmental disruption. And no solution.

Somehow, sometime, we are going to have to start looking at things differently. Somehow, we are going to have to understand that we are up against a new kind of water-supply problem—a problem for which the old solutions no longer work.

We started with a simple situation: water demand here, water supply there. We went and got the water. The demand was small, the supply large: the systems for getting the water could be small-scale. Everything was very reasonable.

The demand grew. The systems for getting the water grew also. It was a logical response: everything was still reasonable.

The demand grew further, and further, and further. The systems grew along with it. And everything still seemed so reasonable about this that it was a long time before anyone noticed the flaw: there were three parts to the water equation, not just two. It was not just water demand and water systems that were involved, but water supply as well. And while the demand and the systems could grow indefinitely, the supply could not: in fact, the supply was shrinking. Someday, inevitably, if growth continued, there would come a time when the two growing portions would overwhelm the shrinking one. At that time, the situation would undergo a metamorphosis: supply would replace demand as the governing factor. Instead of saying, Here is the demand, where is the supply? we would have to start saying, Here is the supply, how much demand can we serve with it?

Sometime in the last forty years, unnoticed, that point was passed. We paid no attention, but continued as always—building systems to match the demand instead of the supply. And in the ensuing muddle, the water situation got away from us. We are losing control; and the more we follow the old, outmoded ways, the more control we will continue to lose.

A water system, no matter how big, fancy, well planned, and technologically advanced it may be, is valuable only when it has water in it.

CHAPTER **18**

The Arkansas-Traveler Response

IN THE OLD story-song, "The Arkansas Traveler," a man on horseback riding through an Arkansas rainstorm comes upon an old man sitting on his cabin porch and playing the fiddle. Behind him, the rain is leaking through hundreds of holes in the cabin roof. The traveler reins in his horse. "See here, old man," he shouts importantly, "why don't you fix your roof?"

"Cain't fix it now, stranger," hollers the old man, still sawing away on the fiddle. "Hit's a-raining too hard."

"Well, then," says the traveler reasonably, "why don't you wait till it stops and *then* fix it?"

The fiddler ponders this a moment. "Don't leak then," he replies at last.

For far too many years now, our response to water problems has been burdened by precisely this Arkansas-Traveler kind of reasoning. During a water-supply crisis—a drought, or a toxicants spill, or a sewer explosion—we become very concerned. Commissions are appointed, studies are initiated, plans are drawn up. For a time, we may actually practice proper control measures. Always, however, the crisis

222

eventually passes: the sewer is repaired, the spill is cleaned up, the weather turns wet again. The studies and the commissions peter out; the plans are put on the shelf, and the old habits trickle back.

This is a totally understandable, very human reaction. But it is a reaction we can no longer afford.

In the mid-1960s, the Northeast was hit by a major drought. Wells and reservoirs dried up; rivers ran low. People and governments wrangled over nonexistent supplies. New York City was particularly hard hit. Lawn sprinkling, car washing, street washing, and all other unnecessary uses of water were prohibited. Decorative fountains were turned off (all except one at Tiffany's, in which the water had been replaced by clear gin). At the ongoing New York World's Fair, officials refused to allow the state of Oklahoma to fill a 5,500-gallon pond in its exhibit, forcing exhibit officials to import water from back home on the "dry" Great Plains. A pumping station on the Hudson River at Chelsea, built during a similar drought in the 1940s but never used, was remembered, and City Water Commissioner Armand D'Angelo put his foot down: that pumping station would never be brought on line, he stated emphatically, because "that water is not very good water at all." A few dry months later he changed his mind. The pumping station was quietly activated, and for the first time in several generations New Yorkers drank the Hudson.

In Albany, state officials did what state officials always do in times of stress: they authorized a study. A study group, named pointedly the Temporary State Commission on the Water Supply Problems of Southeastern New York, was put together under the executive directorship of a SUNY College of Environmental Science and Forestry professor named Robert D. Hennigan. Hennigan and his young, energetic staff plunged enthusiastically into their work, and soon came up with a set of recommendations. The basic problem, they said, was not the drought, but the fact that the New York City water system was woefully inefficient and underdesigned. Even under drought conditions, there was enough runoff in the Northeast to supply its population many times over; but it had to be distributed to the places where the people were, and, once there, it had to be used efficiently. These two requirements, distribution and efficiency, were interrelated, and neither was being met. The commission staff issued a report calling for a modest increase in facilities tied to an aggressive conservation program, a combination which could carry the city and the region well into the next century with complete confidence. The report was sent up to Albany, couched as a set of specific, carefully-drawn legislative proposals. It quickly disappeared into the first stages of the legislative machinery.

It never came out the other side.

Bob Hennigan is an articulate, wry-humored man with a shock of silver hair and the kind of quietly controlled power that can fill a room simply by coming into it. Tracked down in his Syracuse office, he greets me warmly, motions me to a straight-backed chair, and launches into a capsule description of New York City's water problems—pulling no punches. The city, he announces, is "psychologically bankrupt as well as financially bankrupt." The city government's attitude toward the rest of the state is "very cavalier—they don't give a damn about the people downstream from their reservoirs." The commission's good-faith work has been poorly received: "We issued eighteen reports, and finally came out with some recommendations, and everybody screamed and hollered. The main recommendation was for conservation, and people didn't like that. We also called for a reservoir in the Adirondacks, at a place called Goulie Number One. Everybody raised perfect hell about that, and the legislature passed a law prohibiting dams above a certain point on the Hudson, and that took care of Goulie Number One, but it didn't do a thing for the New York water problem. So we backed off, and called for a reservoir lower down, at Hinkley. That got the support of the conservation groups, but the people of New York City didn't know we'd done them a favor, and all they did was scream and holler. And then it started to rain. . . ." The rain did it. The commission was shelved along with its recommendations, and the next drought, fifteen years later, caught the city as unprepared as ever.

It is that way virtually everywhere.

Across the continent from New York, Dwayne Georgeson —himself a target of environmentalists for failing, they say, to push conservation hard enough—sits in his office at the Los Angeles Department of Water and Power and decries the foot-dragging of Californians on all forms of water-problem solutions, including, in very large measure, conservation. It is the familiar complaint: action during a drought, backsliding later. "People tend to remember," he says, "especially the news media, that during the drought in 1977 Marin County conserved sixty percent, and San Francisco conserved forty percent—the city of Sacramento conserved twenty percent—but what they fail to report is that in the years *since* the drought, water consumption has gone back to pre-drought levels. During the drought, the Department of Water Resources was proudly publishing monthly conservation levels throughout California communities, thirty-five cities. And sometime in 1978 they stopped publishing the reports, because the trend throughout California was uniform. All communities—including Marin County, San Francisco, Monterey, Sacramento—were going back to pre-drought levels."

I ask if Los Angeles has maintained a conservation program since the drought. He nods affirmatively, but adds that it doesn't seem to be doing much good. For instance, the city had a speakers' bureau in 1977 that took the conservation message to more than two thousand different civic groups. "That's still going on," he remarks, "but it's focused in a somewhat different direction, because with the drought behind us—we just went through the three wettest consecutive years in the city's history—the civic groups are not turned on by a conservation speaker."

We can no longer afford this Arkansas-Traveler response to water management. We must do better.

The residential water meter is a basic tool of water management. With a water meter on each house, you can tell precisely where your city water supply is going, pinpointing leaks and outlining areas in need of particularly high levels of service. You can charge customers for each gallon they use, thus rewarding water conservers and penalizing wasters; you can make people conscious of their own use patterns, helping them to manage their water use more efficiently. The water savings can be immense: when Independence, California, installed water meters in 1979, per-capita water use immediately dropped by approximately seventy-five percent. In this day of increasing water shortages, it is absurd not to have meters in every home.

And yet we do not. There are many cities in the nation where large numbers of customers are unmetered. There are no meters in most of dry Denver. Sacramento, which has one of the highest per-capita water-use figures of any city in the nation, is unmetered. Worst of all, perhaps, New York City is unmetered. Water rates for New York City buildings are levied by means of a formula the Arkansas Traveler would recognize immediately: prices are determined largely by the width of street frontage the building occupies.

This does very little for conservation efforts.

"Most people in the city," says New York water-department spokesman John Cunningham, "don't really realize that they pay for their water. They presume it's free. It's hidden in their rent bill, so there's no incentive to conserve." This is one reason why New York City water consumption has climbed twenty-five percent since 1966, while the city was actually losing twelve percent of its population.

Water meters for New York were a prime recommendation of Bob Hennigan's study group at Syracuse. Universal metering, they wrote in their final report,

> could reduce water consumption by 240 million gallons or more a day once the metering program is completed. Metering is a technical precondition to other conservation measures such as leakage control and water pricing, and an essential management tool in controlling unaccounted

for water and in establishing equitable rate schedules. . . .
Universal metering would be able to reduce consumption
at a cost one-third of supplying the same amount of water
with a new project. If the possible environmental impacts
of a new project are included, the cost disparity would be
even greater.

The words fell on deaf ears. John Cunningham states that
although his department supports water meters in concept,
"universal metering in the city is not currently in operation,
nor are there any plans to do so in the immediate future."
And in Syracuse, water activist Sam Sage dismisses metering's chances with a wave of his hand. "That," he says, "has
gotten nowhere, and it didn't really even create a lot of
thought."

We needed that thought. We still do. We must think about
our water systems between crises as well as during them:
that is the only way to keep the crises from happening. Water
meters are the best tool we have for getting people to think
about water, and they are therefore indispensable. If we are
going to make a serious effort to avoid the water-supply disasters that are lurking in our future, the Denvers and the
Sacramentos and the New Yorks are going to have to be
metered along with the rest of us. The old fiddler on that
Arkansas front porch is never going to fix his roof if he
doesn't even know where it is leaking.

And if Doug Paine is right, we may not have very long to
find those leaks before the disasters start intensifying.

Paine is a meteorologist, a member of the Atmospheric
Sciences Unit of the College of Agriculture and Life Sciences at Cornell University. In the winter of 1981, while
drought stalked the East Coast, he issued a pair of papers
that sent waves of consternation through the ranks of the
already jittery Northeastern water managers: the Northeast,
he suggested, was in for more of the same for at least the
next six years. Basing his work on an exhaustive computer
analysis of temperature, precipitation, and sunspot trends

over the last forty years, Paine concluded that "unusual periods of extreme cold . . . will be the rule rather than the exception during the first half of the 1980's, specifically over the interior Northeast. . . . (These) unusually cold winters in the East could also be associated with sizeable precipitation deficits like those incurred during 1980."

Paine's work suggested that water deficits by 1986 in the Northeast could run almost twice the size of the water deficits incurred during the drought of the 1960s in the same region. In areas of New York where normal four-year precipitation runs around 140 inches, the model suggested that rain totals during the first four years of the 1980s could dip as low as 100 inches. The most frightening thing about the reports, though, was not their specific predictions: it was the chance those predictions had of being correct. The model had already predicted the 1980–81 winter weather with uncanny precision, right down to the low temperatures in January and the record February rains.

"The point of all this," Paine wrote me in May 1981, "is that even full reservoirs and more than the normal rainfall for the next two months will not change the decade-long water picture in our estimation. Conservation plus attempting to adjust our water usage cycles to be more in tune with natural cycles and anomalies in the 1980's would seem to be well reasoned advice.

"Nature seems to be challenging our ability to think deeply about this situation, not just in superficial terms."

The following chapter suggests some paths along which this deeper thinking must go.

CHAPTER **19**

The Better Way

WHAT SHOULD WE do to get our water system under control? There are three things—all of them important.

First, we need a genuine, rapid, and realistic assessment of our national water situation. We need to know how much we actually have—locality by locality, region by region, and for the nation as a whole. We need to know where there are surpluses, and where there are deficiencies. We need, in short, a determination of the country's safe yield—not expressed as a single national figure, but as an interlocking matrix of figures which takes into account the fact that what one city uses another must forgo. There have been stabs at this sort of thing before, but they have been halfhearted stabs, waylaid by a lack of national commitment to the problem. In the late 1970s, the Water Resources Council was making a fair start at overcoming this: they were rewarded, if that is the term, by being disbanded by the Reagan Administration. We can no longer afford to be like the ancient monarchs who slew the messengers who brought them bad tidings. We must do better.

Hand in hand with this assessment of the nation's ability to supply water must go a similar assessment of the nation's need for water. Again, this must be not a single national figure, but an interlocking matrix of local figures. Single-figure national projections have strictly limited usefulness, because they fail to pinpoint where specific needs are located; and unrelated local-need figures too often turn out to be meaningless exercises in wishful thinking. Needs are comparative, not absolute. Any local boomer knows that his area is going to grow forever—just ask one. Water planning can no longer be based on the way we hope things will be: it must be based on the way things are. If Detroit grows twice as fast as the rest of Michigan, the rest of Michigan cannot grow twice as fast as Detroit.

Finally, we need to develop a serious plan to match water supplies with water needs—and, once it is developed, we need to implement it. The two cannot be separated: we must not act without planning, but neither should we plan without acting. There has been entirely too much of that already.

The plan needs to be built on four basic principles. These are:

- Local needs should be met, insofar as possible, from local supplies.
- Water supplies should not be allowed to shrink.
- Water should be used appropriately and efficiently.
- Both ends of the tap are important.

Let us look at these four principles more closely, one at a time.

• *Local needs should be met, insofar as possible, from local supplies.* This means, obviously, that local water supplies need to be developed and used in an orderly manner before we turn to distant ones—that development should proceed outward, step by step, making the most of all resources available at each stage before proceeding to the next. It also means, less obviously, that some attempt should be made to hold local needs down to a level that can be met by using local supplies. Heavily water-dependent industries (such as breweries) don't belong in water-poor states (such as Colorado). Melons and other water-dependent crops should not be grown in the nonexistent rains of Yuma. Probably some efforts should be made to reverse the current population trends that have seen us flooding into the Sun Belt cities of Arizona and southern California as if there were enough water there to support the entire nation. There isn't. If local demands are to be met by local supplies, then local demands are going to have to stay within reasonably close balance with what local supplies can support. For years, our approach has been to solve water-distribution problems by taking the water to where the people were. We have now reached a time when it makes far more sense to reverse this —to take the people to where the water is. This should be done, as much as possible, by using the carrot of encouragement instead of the stick of regulations. But it should be done.

• *Water supplies should not be allowed to shrink.* In an era when we are running out of water, we should not wantonly destroy the water we have. This point seems obvious enough, and yet we fail to act on it. We continue to pour pollutants into our streams and aquifers, rendering them unusable: we continue to pour salt into the Colorado, and to drawn down our seacoast wells until the sea runs into them. We use the excuse that changing our ways would "cost too much," but it will cost us far more not to change them. In Louisville, county health official Bruce Lane asks a rhetorical question: Is it worth it to write off an aquifer so that people can dump their trash on a short-term basis? The short-term, expedient answer to that might be yes; but the long-term answer is no. We must begin to think long-term. (Isn't it odd how we can support billions of dollars' worth of technological solutions, such as reservoirs and pipelines, to expand our long-term water supply—but when it comes to keeping our current supply from shrinking, everything is "too expensive"?)

• *Water should be used appropriately and efficiently.* I prefer these concepts to the concept of conservation, similar though they are in many ways. The term "conservation," unfortunately, has come to carry some quite severe negative connotations. It is synonymous, in many people's minds, with doing without. Conservation is tightening our belts and weathering the crisis: it is what they were doing in Marin County, California, during the great 1977 drought, when restaurants began charging for water and lawns dried up from lack of sprinkling, when citizens were implored to "shower with a friend" and the walls of toilet stalls carried the cheery poetic advice "If it's yellow,/Let it mellow;/If it's brown,/ Flush it down." If that's the way saving water works, people tend to think, then no, thanks: if it's going to hurt, count me out.

But it doesn't have to hurt. We can save enormous amounts of water just by eliminating inappropriate and inefficient uses, without suffering any hardships in the least.

Most homes, for example, contain extremely inefficient water devices. It takes five gallons of water to flush a standard toilet; the job could be just as easily done with three, and some new toilet designs require less than two. (The Clivus Multrum composting toilet, a Swedish development now available in some parts of this country, uses no water at all.) Since the toilet accounts for approximately forty-five percent of the water used inside the average home, the savings available here are enormous. Low-flow shower heads use about fifteen percent less water than regular heads, with no discernible effect on the cleanliness of the body under the shower. Leaking faucets and toilet seals, according to one estimate, lose approximately twenty-five to thirty percent of all water that flows through the American home; an aggressive program of leak repairs can keep that water in the system for use instead of pouring it through the sewage plant and back into the river totally untouched. When all these things are added up, it becomes apparent that anywhere from forty to seventy percent of our in-residence water "use" isn't used at all. Making mechanical changes to eliminate this waste will result in significant water savings without any effect on water-use habits whatsoever.

Outside the home, the water-saving possibilities continue.

The greatest use of water, at the average residence, is not plumbing; it is that vast expanse of water-hungry green grass that surrounds the home like a medieval moat. Lawns, like many other things about American society, are a holdover from our English roots. In rainy England they make sense; in sunny Arizona, they are totally inappropriate. There are native plants that can be used for landscaping with far less water; the effect will be different from a green lawn, but not necessarily less attractive. It's a matter not of going without, but of getting used to something different. When we converted to automobiles, we had to do without the horse and buggy. Few people today would consider that a hardship.

Industrial and agricultural water uses are also subject to reduction without hardship, simply by eliminating what is inappropriate and inefficient. In many cases, the problems are identical to those in the home, and can be attacked in an identical manner. Toilets and washbasins in factories are subject to the same leakage and designed with the same degree of water overkill as those in home bathrooms; irrigation equipment often delivers far more water than the plants it supports can use. Decorative plantings outside factory offices can be changed to native vegetation—just as lawns can —and farms can stop growing wet-climate crops in dry climates. Drip irrigation, where water is supplied in measured quantities directly to a plant's roots via buried pipelines, can save fifty to sixty percent over conventional irrigation methods; plant productivity goes up, and weeds—deprived of water—go down. Israel, which uses drip irrigation almost exclusively, has proved it to be both water- and cost-effective. It is past time to employ it extensively here.

Along with these measures, there are huge possibilities open to both agriculture and industry in the area of water recycling. Industrial-process cooling water does not have to be dumped: it can be saved, allowed to cool, and used again and again. Water used to clean vats and tanks for reuse can itself be reused to a moderate degree; for example, the water from the final rinse of one vat can be saved and used for the first-stage cleaning of the next vat. On farms, irrigation runoff can be collected at the bottom of the field, pumped back to the top, and used again, as long as its salt content is not unacceptably high. Or runoff from one field can be led to another field at a lower elevation and used there as initial water.

None of these water-saving changes requires any sacrifice of us beyond getting off our backsides long enough to put in the new machinery. We have everything to gain and nothing to lose. It is nonsensical not to pursue them because of a vague feeling that conservation has to hurt.

• *Both ends of the tap are important.* This last proposition is perhaps the most crucial of all. If we are to solve our water problems rather than compound them with ill-conceived "solutions" that amount to more of the same, only bigger, then we must recognize that the water problems of any one area are not, in the final analysis, separable from the problems of the nation as a whole. Reduction of water deficiencies in one area must not be allowed to increase water deficiencies elsewhere. There is no longer a superabundance anywhere. The taps of New York City can be connected to the Delaware River only so long as doing so does not make the taps of Philadelphia run dry.

The case of Los Angeles is highly instructive here. In many ways, the water habits of Los Angeles are, or should be, a model for the nation. The city has an active conservation program: 618,000 residence retrofit kits containing toilet dams and low-flow shower heads have been distributed by the water department since 1976, an active leak-detection unit patrols the streets, and the department—as Dwayne Georgeson explains—sends speakers to civic groups to preach the conservation message at every opportunity. Many cities today are fighting the imposition of water meters; Los Angeles has had universal metering since 1901. The city's per-capita-use figures are among the lowest in the state— less than San Francisco, less than San Diego, half that of meterless Sacramento. Angelenos comprise fifteen percent of the population of California, but use only 1.5 percent of the state's delivered water. By any reasonable measure, Los Angeles should be held up as a model.

And yet it is not. In fact, precisely the opposite has happened: it is scorned, reviled, and feared as a water-guzzling monster. Sierra Club Legal Defense Fund attorney Buck Parker probably summed up the general attitude very well when he told me that, in his opinion, "two thirds of the environmental problems west of the hundredth meridian have to do with water and Los Angeles." What is the reason for this? Why should a city so careful to conserve be so detested?

Part of the reason, surely, has to do with the symbolic, rather than the actual, Los Angeles. To most Americans, Los Angeles is not just the city proper, but the whole smog-ridden sprawl from the Tehachapi Mountains south to San Diego. That's not just fifteen percent of California's population, it's fifty percent, and the amount of the state's water deliveries it uses is closer to one fourth than one fiftieth. It is a national symbol of bigness gone wrong, and there is an automatic assumption that this wrongness applies to water as well as everything else. But that is not the major reason behind the fear of Los Angeles' water policies. The main reason is not symbol but actuality. Los Angeles is grabby.

Los Angeles may use less water than other parts of the state, but the water that it does use is taken with little or no regard to what needs may exist at the other end of the pipeline. This has been going on since the beginning. When the Owens Valley aqueduct was first built in the early twentieth century, the rights and the desires of the residents of Owens Valley were largely ignored. The residents showed their displeasure by blowing up the aqueduct, but it was repaired, and the desertification of Owens Valley went forward. Now the process is being repeated at Mono Lake. The city is not just importing Mono Basin water—it is importing it with no concern for what happens to the Mono Basin as a result, and is heavy-handedly dismissing all attempts to find solutions. An interagency task force of state and federal officials produced a plan in early 1980 to save the lake and still provide

Los Angeles with all the water it needed. It was a carefully drawn plan, a long time in the making. Los Angeles officials publicly opposed it, privately denounced it ("That's bullshit," one of them remarked scornfully when I brought it up)—and went on draining Mono Lake. It is this sort of thing that has caused Los Angeles its trouble. The solutions to the water-supply problems of the Los Angeles Basin must not themselves create water-supply problems in other parts of the world. Both ends of the tap are important, and the water needs of the intake must not be ignored or overwhelmed by the water needs of the faucet.

Cities can no longer plan for just themselves. We have a common problem, and it is going to require common solutions.

Are such solutions possible? I may be overly optimistic, but I think they are. Though the course I have outlined appears complex and difficult, it may not be quite so complex and difficult as it seems at first glance. The key is this: much of the machinery necessary to steer this course is already in place. We need not spend precious time creating new agencies or gathering new knowledge or training new experts or designing new methodologies. The agencies, the knowledge, the experts and the methodologies all exist: all we need to do is point them in the right direction.

We have, for example, in our local water companies, and our state water-resources boards, and our federal Bureau of Reclamation and Army Corps of Engineers, a very great deal of expertise in dealing with water transport and evaluating water use. Our water experts in these agencies currently are in the habit of making demand projections and designing projects to fit them, but there is no reason that this has to continue: projects can be designed to fit supply as well as they can be designed to fit demand. It's merely a matter of telling the designers what we want, and then holding them to it.

We have the Weather Bureau and the federal and state Geologic Surveys to tell us where water is found, and how much of it is there, and how fast it is renewing itself—the "national safe-yield survey" that has been spoken of. Most of the information for this survey already exists in the files of these agencies; all that is really needed is a directed, concerted effort to put it all together.

We have public-health agencies on every level of government—state, federal, and local. These agencies have a centralized data bank at the federal Center for Disease Control in Atlanta, Georgia, as well as localized state and county filing systems. We have the clean-water offices in the EPA and its various state equivalents—New York's Department of Environmental Protection, Oregon's Department of Environmental Quality, New Mexico's Environmental Improvement Division, and so forth. Here is the expertise for the national effort that must be made to keep water supplies from shrinking. A separate army of bureaucrats is not needed; all that is necessary is to pay some attention to the soldiers we have already put in the field.

The one thing that we do *not* have is coordination; but even that is not so far distant as it might seem. A revived Water Resources Council, specifically vested with powers of policy coordination and insulated from both the pork-barrel politics of Congress and the ideological yo-yo of changing administrations, could go a long way toward remedying this lack. In the past, the council issued voluminous reports and uttered advice which often seemed pompous because it was quite without any grounding in enforcement. But it could be much better. All we need is the will to make it so—that plus the courage to truly centralize our policy-making on the vital issue of water, and the wisdom to tell the difference between the centralized making of policy and the decentralized means for determining the best way to carry it out.

In the meantime, while we wait for the Millennium to arrive, there are a few things that each of us can do to help preserve our water and our options. Here is a small list, broadly adapted from the California Department of Water Resources' pamphlet *Save Water*, with additions from several other sources:

1. Use water completely. Don't run your dishwasher or washing machine without a full load. If you are hand-washing dishes, do more than one meal at once; when you send the kids to wash for dinner, fill the basin and let them all wash at the same time. Consider reusing cooking water: the pot that boiled the potatoes can also cook the peas, with quite interesting savory results.

2. Eliminate unnecessary uses of water. Use a compost pile instead of a garbage disposal. Sweep your sidewalk instead of washing it. Don't use your toilet for a wastebasket or an ashtray; you don't need to flush five gallons of water down the drain to carry away half an ounce of cigarette ashes or one square of toilet tissue with a lipstick blob in the middle of it.

3. Don't let water run unnecessarily: Turn it off. Turn it off while you shave, or while you brush your teeth. Turn it off while you soap the car you're washing, or soap your body under the shower. Don't run water out of the tap to cool it for drinking: keep a jug of cold water in the refrigerator instead. If you must run the hot water until it gets hot, run it into a container and use it to water your plants. When you fill the tub, don't fill it so far that when you climb in the top two inches of bath water will cascade through the overflow drain and slosh merrily away to the sewage plant without having ever been used at all.

4. Plan your outdoor watering. Don't water in the bright sun, or in the wind; you'll lose half the water to evaporation. Set the sprinkler so that it hits what needs to be watered without hitting the sidewalk, the car, and the side of the doghouse as well. Consider a soaker instead of a sprinkler for ornamental plantings. Though it seems like an odd thing to do, water during summer rains; that's the time during the hot months when evaporation is at its absolute minimum and when every drop counts the most. Make sure you don't overwater; know the difference between a green lawn and a swamp.

5. *Think about water while you plan your landscaping and your vegetable garden.* Use native plants as much as possible—they know how to get along on the rainfall your area gets. Group plants with similar water appetites in the same place to facilitate watering. Plan around established shrubs and trees; their deep root systems allow them to get by with less irrigation than new plantings. Garden on a slope so that runoff from watering at the top will trickle down and water the bottom. Weed assiduously—eliminate competitors for your plants' water ration. Mulch the soil to prevent evaporation of soil water.

6. *Look for leaks—and repair them.* A leaking faucet that drips only once in five seconds will still pour more than a gallon a day down the drain. Most such leaks are completely preventable, using tools found in virtually every home and techniques that can be easily learned from books or by cautious experimentation in a few minutes' time. Leak detecting can be harder than leak repairing, but here are two tricks that may help. To detect leaks in a toilet tank, place a little food coloring in the tank; if the color appears in the bowl before a flush has taken place, a leak is present. And to check the house as a whole, use your water meter as a detector. Turn off all faucets and water-using appliances, check the meter, wait half an hour, and check it again; if there has been a change in the reading, there is a leak somewhere in your house. (Needless to say, this second technique works only in towns with meters.)

7. *Install water-saving devices.* When replacing water-using appliances such as washing machines, dishwashers, toilets, and shower heads, be certain that the replacement uses as small an amount of water to do the job as possible. With existing devices, install retrofit water-saving kits: toilet dams, flow constrictors in shower heads, aerators on kitchen and bathroom faucets. Don't stick a brick into your toilet tank —bricks disintegrate—but consider placing in the tank a plastic gallon jug with the top cut off, weighted with a few stones to keep it in place.

8. *Finally, save other things as a way of saving water.* This is not something one would automatically think of, perhaps; but since every manufactured item you purchase uses water—often great amounts of it—in the manufacturing process, conservation of other items is also conservation of water. Use one tank less of gasoline per month and you've lowered your annual personal water consumption by 2,400 gallons. Keep your living-room carpet an extra year and save fifty thousand gallons for that year. Lower the thermostat on your electric heating system from seventy to sixty-eight and save the nine hundred gallons per kilowatt-hour that would normally go into the production of the extra electricity.

Be aware of the water cost of what you do. Often simple awareness is the greatest single factor in bringing about change.

Water planning is often an extremely discouraging business. In a field full of complex interchanges and balances and adjustments, simple solutions are ultimately counterproductive, but simple solutions often seem to be the only ones that will sell. City administrators tend to see the answers to water problems in terms of more and bigger pipes instead of supply–demand balances; they see sewage disposal as a problem of getting rid of something, not as a factor in regional water-system planning. Consumers are notoriously conservative, slow to change, and hard to educate: when the water rates go up they scream, and when the water tastes funny they write nasty letters to the water company, but otherwise their concern with water is limited to turning on taps and flushing toilets and setting sprinklers, and if not forced to change they will continue to do it in the same pattern until Doomsday. Even a drought cannot necessarily force conservation. When my city's treatment plant was knocked out by a flood a few years ago, only a trickle of water remained in the reservoir. The city government appealed to people not to use it, so that there would be some reserve left if it was necessary to fight fires. This request was ignored.

Finally, city water crews had to go around and turn off everyone's water at the mains in front of their houses—and even then some people went out and turned it right back on as soon as the trucks rounded the next corner. With such attitudes to fight, it is easy to sympathize with water planners who give up the fight for wise use and limit their planning to figuring out ways they can go out and grab more. Such an approach certainly seems often enough as though it were the only one that would sell.

But it isn't. City administrators may be prone to straight-line thinking, and consumers may be inherently conservative, but neither group is blind. Water problems *can* be solved imaginatively and creatively: robbing the next valley over is not the only solution to water shortages. If anyone doubts, all they have to do is look at Tucson, Arizona.

By all normal standards, Tucson's water situation should be disaster—and, indeed, the problems are huge. We have spoken of those problems elsewhere in this book. There is little rain in Tucson, far too little for its population. The balmy, year-round sunshine sucks water out of everything in sight with grim efficiency: the annual evaporation rate is greater than the recharge rate of the local aquifers. Water is being mined to supply the community, and like all mined materials it represents a finite supply. The Central Arizona Project, if it is more than a dream on the wind (there are many people in Tucson who believe that the great pipes should never and will never arrive), will still leave the city drastically short. Tucson should, logically, be nothing to point to except as a horrible example.

And yet there is promise too in Tucson's water situation—great promise, perhaps more promise than in any other American community. Tucson is proof that a policy of appropriate and efficient use—what is usually called "conservation"—actually works.

The story begins a few years ago, with the election in the city of a conservation-minded city council. The council decided to do something about the water problem. They studied the issue for a long time—held hearings, commissioned reports, ran surveys, and generally covered all the bases. Then they proclaimed a new rate structure for the community. The new rates were inverted, which meant that the more water you used the more you would pay per gallon—a conservation incentive which also had the advantage of providing a form of "lifeline" rate for people on limited incomes as long as they kept their water use down. To simplify bookkeeping, the water department suggested that the new rates be imposed at the beginning of a new fiscal year—June 1. The council agreed. The necessary papers were signed, and the city council closed down for the summer, with many of its members out of town on vacation.

That was a mistake. As Pima College's Doug Shakel puts it, "It turns out that there was one thing that everybody had overlooked, and that is that Tucson water consumption goes along level until about the middle of May, and then we start getting 95-, 98-, 100-degree days, and water consumption goes way-y-y up. So come June first, and people whose water bills the preceding month had been fifteen dollars, or eighteen dollars, were getting bills for $85, or $110, or $150— and people said, *My Gawd!* And the city council was out of town."

At that point, to use Shakel's indelicate but totally appropriate phrase, the shit hit the fan.

A recall movement was started against four of the absent city council members. Momentum for the recall built over the summer, and by the time the council was back in session in the fall they were feeling pretty shaky. As nearly their last official action before the recall election took place, they repealed the new rate structure.

Despite this effort at calming the troubled waters, the recall was successful. Four new members of the city council were elected, chosen from among the leaders of the recall effort. The new council studied the water-rates issue for six weeks or so, announced publicly that it had been mistaken —and reinstated the inverted rates.

At about this same time, the Tucson water department, up against the need for significant capital improvements to meet current demand levels, decided to try to avoid them by shifting the demand levels around a bit. It wasn't supposed to be a conservation program, in the beginning. Water use, in any community, tends to peak from about four to about eight in the evening, as people come home from work and turn on their sprinklers. Tucson decided to try to smooth that peak out by asking people to water at other times instead, spreading the use more evenly around the clock. They called it "Beat the Peak." City residents, shaken by the events of the water-rates recall, latched onto Beat the Peak as a conservation program. Instead of merely shifting in time, consumption went down by nearly one fourth.

It has stayed down ever since.

"The main thing that's hard to figure out about it," says Tucson Water's Frank Brooks, "is why it works so well. It's never worked anywhere else in the country. When you raise water rates, something happens, and people get very conscious of water—that summer. But by the next year after the raised rates, usage patterns go right back to what they always were in the past. That has not happened here, and it's been about five years.

"When we conceived the plan, we assumed that there would be some conservation, but that was not the focus. But many people have actually changed their lifestyle in the last four years. It's a permanent change at this point. There are literally hundreds of people who have taken out their grass lawns, that take all the water, and have put in desert-type lawns. And once you've done that, you're relatively committed—you're not going to take it back out, and put in grass again, unless you want to spend a lot of money."

By investing in their desert landscaping—the kind of thing they have begun to call "Tucson lawns" up in Phoenix— Tucson residents have made a monetary investment in the water future of their community, and that makes it easier for them to want to protect it. But the really intriguing—and hopeful—thing about Beat the Peak is not that people have changed their lawns, but that they have changed their habits and attitudes at the same time. "You know," muses Brooks, "in the past, people grew grass because it was sort of the thing to do. And if you didn't mow your lawn, and keep it nice and watered, you were sort of looked down upon as tearing the neighborhood down. In other words, the peer-group pressure was that you kept the place looking nice with grass. Well, with all this turnaround, we've turned the ethic around, too. Now if you have a beautiful lawn—let's say you really go all out, you've got clover, and you've got bluegrass, both of which shouldn't grow in this climate, and use huge amounts of water—if you have a lawn like that, you are looked upon as socially unaware, and sort of a nut. So there's been a peer-group-pressure kind of situation to make a change."

How did Tucson accomplish its miracle? The actual mechanics have been deceptively simple: they are all things that have been tried elsewhere. The inverted rate structure. A rotating watering schedule. The distribution of forty thousand toilet dams and low-flow shower heads. Things that have never worked for anyone else, either singly or together, for more than a few months. Why do they work here?

Brooks isn't sure, but he thinks it has something to do with awareness. The program has been very public, very open, very high-visibility, and this has helped it enormously. "The biggest thing is just to *think* about it," he explains. "To be aware that you left the hose running. And because we talk about water saving so much, people have an awareness of what they're doing. You don't have to strain to save any water, to change your habits—it's just that you think about what you're doing, and you use less. Because a large amount of water—in the past, and even now—has been wasted. Some guy is watering the lawn on a Saturday afternoon while he watches the baseball game, and all of a sudden he thinks, 'Hell, I've let that water run two hours over there.' And he goes and moves it. But he's watered it about five times more than he needs to. And—that's the kind of awareness that makes a difference."

What's true for Tucson is true for the rest of the nation as well. If we could develop that kind of awareness in everyone, our water difficulties might be just about over. Much earlier in this book, I pointed out that the lawns of Arizona lay at the bottom of our national water problem. Tucson has shown us that the lawns of Arizona can also be the solution.

And if the solution doesn't lie in Tucson, perhaps it lies in Boulder, Colorado. Here an innovative little company named PureCycle is quietly building a thriving regional business for itself, based on the radical idea that in a water-poor area like the eastern slope of the Front Range, houses shouldn't use any water at all.

Or at least any new water. PureCycle families are like any others: they must drink, cook, wash dishes, wash clothes, and flush wastes down toilets. All these tasks take water. In a conventional house, this water comes from an outside source, flows out of the faucet, and swirls away down the drain. It does the same in a PureCycle house, but with one difference: the drain is the outside source.

At the PureCycle plant, a low gold-colored building perched on a small rise on Boulder's eastern edge, sales manager Mark Palmer proudly demonstrated the company's revolutionary approach to water supply. A PureCycle installation is a device for total water recycling. Wastewater is subjected to a five-stage process which removes virtually all conceivable contaminants. A bacterial digester removes fecal material and other solid organic wastes; a membrane the company refers to as an "ultrafilter," capable of removing anything down to fifty Angstrom units in size (including all bacteria and even most viruses), takes out the remaining solid matter. Activated-carbon and ion-exchange units eliminate dissolved chemicals, including any of the frightening organics and heavy metals (pesticides, solvents, rat poisons or what have you) that may creep in. A final burst of intense ultraviolet light kills anything living that might have managed to survive through the previous four stages. The result is water that far exceeds federal and state drinking-water standards; in fact, most PureCycle customers are drinking better water than their neighbors on conventional systems.

All this is housed in a small shed next to the customer's residence which looks, to the casual viewer, as if it might hold garden tools. It retails for about the price of a septic-tank installation, and is serviced monthly for a fee equivalent to that charged most city water and sewer customers.

I asked Palmer if there was any chance that the treatment machinery could malfunction and allow something besides pure water to come out of the faucets connected to it. He shook his head. "There are sensors at every stage of the process," he explained, "measuring conductivity, turbidity, and UV transparency. These are connected to a microprocessor. Any time the parameters aren't met, the water is automatically shunted back to the sewage-side storage tank until the instruments give a positive reading." The computer has several remedial measures up its sleeve: back-flushing filters, regenerating ion-exchange resins, modulating ultraviolet light. As a last resort, it has the ability to shut the whole system down and automatically dial a repair crew over the customer's home phone line. The crew is able to come prepared: the computer pinpoints the problem, prints out the offending instrument reading, and even provides a precise readout on how much water remains in the freshwater side of the system, so that the repairmen will be able to schedule their call before the customer runs out.

The plant itself, of course, gets its water from a PureCycle system. I tasted some drawn into a plastic cup from the water cooler in the lobby. My notes record that it tasted "like water, with overtones of plastic cup." It was slightly better than the Denver city water I had been drinking that morning in my hotel.

All water on earth is recycled water: the hydrologic cycle sees to that. In the past, we have concentrated on getting more water by expanding the amount of this naturally recycled water we use. But we have just about reached the limits of that approach; perhaps, as the PureCycle experience suggests, the time has come to try a different tack. There are, after all, two ways to make more of something.

You can make it in more places.

Or you can make it faster.

CHAPTER **20**

"Two Threads Woven Intrinsically Together"

THE TROUBLE WITH humans, Buckminster Fuller once complained, is that we don't understand wealth.

Wealth is not properly a measure of what we have managed to accumulate, but a measure of how long and at what rate we can continue to accumulate it. "Wealth has nothing to do with yesterday," Fuller stated, "but only with forward days. How many forward days, for how many lives are we now technically organized to cope? The numerical answer is the present state of our true wealth." He spoke bitterly of the "geometrical compounding of inevitable expenditures" that arises from this misunderstanding of wealth: "For instance, we are saying now that we can't afford to do anything about pollution, but after the costs of not doing something about pollution have multiplied manifold beyond what it would cost us to correct it now, we will spend manifold what it would cost us now to correct it. . . . We have no difficulty discovering troubles but we fail to demonstrate intelligent search for the means of coping with the troubles. This is primarily due to our misconditioned reflex which says that 'we can't' afford to do the intelligent things."

By Fuller's measure—and it is surely the correct one—the water wealth our ancestors began with on this continent has now been reduced to the near-edge of poverty. How many "forward days" remain in the shrinking aquifers of the High Plains? For how many lives are we "technically organized to cope" by using the chemical-laden waters of Long Island, the sewage of the Passaic, the saline and overburdened Colorado? It is not comfortable to have to think of these things, but it is necessary. When we were water-wealthy, we could afford to regard water as an inalienable birthright to be used any which way we wanted, anywhere we were, anytime we got the urge. We can no longer—to use Bob Hennigan's word—be so cavalier. If we are going to survive the death of the Ogallala and the salination of the Colorado and the collapsing of Florida and the dissolving of New Jersey—if we are going to survive at all—then we must begin looking at water supply differently, and handling water supply differently.

There is no other way.

It is imperative to remember this: water and life are inseparable. From the first stirrings of self-reproducing molecules in the warm seas over what is now Australia some four billion years ago, to the complex and marvelously coordinated community of specialized cells that is a human or an oak tree or a dandelion or a dragonfly, water has been life's ever-present companion. Life is totally dependent upon water for its existence. In fact, life *is* mostly water: water comprises from one half to nine tenths of the weight of every living creature on earth. Each living cell is at heart nothing more than an extremely complex array of chemicals held in solution in a tiny droplet of this simple, marvelous, and universal liquid. As the naturalist David Cavagnaro has written, "Water and life are two threads woven intrinsically together. . . . They are responsible, in their peculiar relationship, for everything we are and all that we do, every one of us, including also the pine, the columbine, the chipmunk, and the bee." And when this relationship is properly understood, it becomes obvious that Fuller is right. It is no longer permissible to say that we "cannot afford" to make any changes in the way we handle water.

Given the current state of our water resources, given the absolute importance of water to our future, we cannot afford *not* to.

Here in my Oregon valley, it is raining. The rain pounds on the roof, lashes the windows, makes rivers of the sidewalks. Leaves from the oak at the corner of the lot float in the gutters like galleons. I sit by the window, coffee cup in hand, watching the rain leap from the sky; I walk in it, feel it soak my denim pants, soak my jacket, drip from my hat brim, run down my nose. Six hundredths of an inch of rain per day falling on one square foot of land equals five ounces of water; five ounces per square foot equals seventeen hundred gallons per acre, equals one million gallons per square mile, equals four *trillion* gallons per United States of America. Six hundredths of an inch per day also equals twenty-one and one half inches per year—roughly the U.S. average. We receive, as a nation—free and clear, no strings attached—four trillion gallons of brand-new, freshly recycled water each and every day of our collective lives.

Four trillion gallons of water per day! That is 167 billion gallons per hour, 2.8 billion gallons per minute, 46 million gallons per second. One gallon every five seconds for each and every citizen of the United States. Four trillion gallons: gone like the wind. How have we done it? Where have we gone wrong? What manner of people are we, to come so close to the limits of a resource so seemingly limitless?

The rain stops; the clouds clear. It has been a cold rain: snow mantles the surrounding mountains, powders the summits, dips toward the town like the skirts of an ill-made bed. That mountain snow is one of the great miracles of our planetary existence. It will store tremendous amounts of water through the winter, releasing it slowly into the streams and the aquifers, extending the land's supply from the wet season far into the dry—as it has been doing for the last several billion years, as it will continue to do for several billion more. Without snow, life would never have crawled up out of the seas. I climb the hill behind my house, dropping into the wooded canyon beyond to the edge of the boulder-choked stream at its base; I sit by the stream, watching it, absorbing the sound and the vigor of its flow, keeping time to its endless, ever-changing music. Flowing water has always been a symbol, from the Preacher of Ecclesiastes to the country-Western star who implores you to Cry Her a River. "Lead me beside the still waters," prays the Psalmist (not so still, these!). Every drop of water that ever existed still exists. Water is not destroyed, only used; the same molecules that washed the feet of dinosaurs pour today out of New York City drinking fountains. We cannot destroy it, either; but we can make it unusable, and that amounts to the same thing. Or we can demand it where it is not.

The stream flows away down the hill. It always has. How long is always? How much longer will it be—until it is all gone?

ACKNOWLEDGMENTS

I owe this book to Max Gartenberg. It was he who conceived the idea; he who first suggested scope, content, and format; he who found a publisher; and he who, by means of adroitly timed letters containing a hunch here, a clipping there, a musing comment or word of encouragement, kept the project going from conception to completed volume. Max created the book; I merely did the research and writing, on the whole a much simpler task.

Special thanks are also due to my brother Jack and his wife, Ruth Spangler, for housing me and doing a great deal of my research legwork in Louisville, Kentucky; to Bryan Frink and Lithia Travel Service for handling my rather complicated travel itinerary; to Judith Kunofsky and David Hastings of the Sierra Club in San Francisco for suggesting contacts in water-conservation matters around the nation; and to Merlin McDaniel for supplying a considerable amount of my research materials, suggesting directions and interpretations, preparing the maps, and reading the manuscript prior to publication. Others who helped include (city by city):

FLAGSTAFF, ARIZONA: My good friends Dave and Hwei-Yun Gore for hosting me for a much-needed weekend of rest in the midst of my research, as well as providing much of the material on which the chapter on desalinization was based (and the Grand Canyon in the snow was marvelous!).

PHOENIX, ARIZONA: Randy Weiss of the Arizona Department of Water Resources.

TUCSON, ARIZONA: Doug Shakel of the Sierra Club; and Frank Brooks of the Tucson Water Utility.

252   Acknowledgments

Los Angeles, California: Dwayne Georgeson of the Los Angeles Department of Water and Power; Tom Cassidy of the Mono Lake Committee; Bob Chun of the California Department of Water Resources; and my old friend Dirk Benedict, a.k.a. Lieutenant Starbuck (for a lunch in Hollywood when spirits were at their lowest ebb).

San Francisco, California: Dan Sullivan and Buck and Fran Parker of the Sierra Club.

Denver and Boulder, Colorado: George Pring of the University of Denver Law School; Judith Breister of the Environmental Defense Fund; and Mark Palmer of the PureCycle Corporation.

Washington, D.C.: Greg Skillman and Joe Rutledge of Congressman Jim Weaver's office; David Gardiner and Jim Elder of the Sierra Club; Brent Blackwelder of the Environmental Policy Center; and Larry Williams and Dave Burmaster of the Council on Environmental Quality.

Dodge City, Kansas: Ralph Thomas of the United States Department of Agriculture; and Harry Ziekle, Director of Utilities for the City of Dodge.

Garden City, Kansas: Mike Dealy of the Southwest Kansas Groundwater Management District No. 3.

Wichita, Kansas: John Gries of the Department of Geology, Wichita State University.

Louisville, Kentucky: Jim Detjen of the *Louisville Courier-Journal* (for graciously sharing his notes, his knowledge, and himself); Margaret and Michael Loeb of the Sierra Club (for arranging and hosting a meeting of area water officials and activists); Steve Hubbs of the Louisville Water Department; Tom Westerland of the Jefferson County Air Pollution Control District; Bruce Lane of the Jefferson County Health Department; and citizen activists Jackie Dunn, John Gray, Winnie Heppler, and Jean Barnes.

Lincoln, Nebraska: Michael Jess of the Nebraska State Department of Water Resources.

Gallup, New Mexico: Don Payne and Mark Mattson of the U.S. Public Health Service; and Bob Triviso of the New Mexico Environmental Improvement Division.

Ithaca, New York: Doug Paine of the College of Agriculture and Life Sciences, Cornell University.

New York City: Bob Oskam (for sharing his apartment for three days); Andrea Sklarew of the New York office of the Environmental Protection Agency; and John Cunningham of the Water Division of the New York City Department of Environmental Protection.

SYRACUSE, NEW YORK: Sam Sage of the Sierra Club; and Bob Hennigan of the SUNY College of Environmental Science and Forestry.

CLEVELAND, OHIO: Pete Clapham and (especially) Mr. and Mrs. Ed Fritz of the Sierra Club.

ASHLAND, OREGON: Ed Fallon, Dennis Barntz, Keith Marshall, Scott Dinges, Jim Ciamataro, and Pete Newell of the Ashland City Water Department; Dr. Rodney Badger of the Southern Oregon State College chemistry faculty, and Dr. Wayne Linn of the biology faculty; Bob Wilson of the Ashland Public Library; and the staff of the Documents Collection at the Southern Oregon State College library.

SALEM, OREGON: Ron Eber of the Sierra Club; and Harry Demeray and Ted Groszkiewicz of the Oregon Department of Environmental Quality.

PULLMAN, WASHINGTON: my sister Lillian (for many efforts at running down sources and materials); Jim Crosby of the Washington State University Hydrology Laboratory; and Jim Hudak and Gordon Fish of the Pullman Water Department.

BIBLIOGRAPHY

BOOKS

Boyle, Robert H., John Graves, and T. H. Watkins. *The Water Hustlers.* San Francisco: Sierra Club Books, 1971.

Braun, Ernest, and David Cavagnaro. *Living Water.* Palo Alto, CA: American West Publishing Company, 1971.

Brown, Michael. *Laying Waste: The Poisoning of America by Toxic Chemicals.* New York: Pantheon Books, 1981.

Buley, R. Carlyle. *The Old Northwest.* Indianapolis: Indiana Historical Society, 1950.

Carson, Rachel. *Silent Spring.* New York: Houghton Mifflin Company, 1962.

Disch, Robert, ed. *The Ecological Conscience: Values for Survival.* Englewood Cliffs, NJ: Prentice-Hall, Inc., 1970.

Hydrology Handbook. New York: American Society of Civil Engineers, 1949.

Powell, John Wesley. *Report on the Lands of the Arid Region of the United States,* 2nd ed. Washington: U.S. Government Printing Office, 1879.

Thomas, Harold E. *The Conservation of Groundwater.* New York: McGraw-Hill Book Company, 1951.

Trewartha, Glenn T., Arthur H. Robinson, and Edwin H. Hammond. *Fundamentals of Physical Geography,* 2nd ed. New York: McGraw-Hill Book Company, 1968.

Wright, Jim. *The Coming Water Famine.* New York: Coward-McCann, Inc., 1966.

MAGAZINE AND NEWSPAPER ARTICLES

"A Clean Air Primer." *Sierra*, May/June 1981.

"Acid Rain Falling in Sierra Nevada." *Medford Mail Tribune*, February 16, 1981.

Adams, Jim. "Aftershock of Sewer Blast Reverberates in City Hall," *Louisville Courier-Journal*, February 15, 1981.

Adler, Jerry. "The Browning of America," *Newsweek*, February 23, 1981.

"After Four Years, Well Water Still Contains Pesticide," *Ashland Daily Tidings*, April 29, 1981.

"Alligators Come to the Rescue as Drought Parches Florida," *Ashland Daily Tidings*, May 16, 1981.

"Arizona Looks for Solutions to the Water Crisis," *Sierra Club Population Report*, August 1981.

"Authorities Fear Groundwater Contamination from Latest Quake," *Ashland Daily Tidings*, April 29, 1981.

Baechler, Phil. "Palouse Needn't Worry About Water," *Spokesman-Review*, May 3, 1981.

Barnbaum, Bruce. "Mono Lake Disaster." *Loma Prietan*, October 1981.

Blake, Simon. "California's Peripheral Canal: A Ditch to Disaster?," *Homegrown*, March 1981.

"Brewery Denies Killing Fish," *Medford Mail Tribune*, June 3, 1981.

Briggs, Jean A. "There's No Synwater Industry to Bail Us Out," *Forbes*, March 16, 1981.

Brinkley, Joel. "Tour of Illegal Dumps Shocks EPA Group." *Louisville Courier-Journal*, February 3, 1979.

Brown, Michael. "Drums of Death." *Audubon*, July 1980.

Byer, Harold G., William Blankenship, and Robert Allen. "Groundwater Contamination by Chlorinated Hydrocarbons: Causes and Preventions," *Civil Engineering*, March 1981.

Canby, Thomas Y. "Water—Our Most Precious Resource," *National Geographic*, August 1980.

"Chemical in Groundwater." *Medford Mail Tribune*, May 11, 1981.

Christian Science Monitor News Service. "Reagan Plan Would Treat Symptoms, Not Cause of River Pollution," *Ashland Daily Tidings*, April 27, 1981.

"Church World Service Enters Decade of Water," *Service News*, May 1981.

"Cleaner, but Still Far from Sparkling, Tributary," *Business Week,* May 29, 1978.

"Confusion Reigns as Groundwater Cleanup Begins," *Engineering News Record,* October 1, 1981.

Cowley, Joe. "Conservation Urged to Protect Reservoirs," *Medford Mail Tribune,* August 6, 1981.

"Creeks Still Contaminated, 208 Water Official Says," *Medford Mail Tribune,* May 7, 1981.

Detjen, Jim. "Illegal Dumping Only One Problem in Waste Disposal," *Louisville Courier-Journal,* January 22, 1979.

———. "In the Drink . . . What You Can't See in Water May Hurt You," *Louisville Courier-Journal,* July 23, 1978.

———. "Ohio's Problems Pose Threat, Officials Say," *Louisville Courier-Journal,* July 23, 1978.

———. "Region Needs to Take More Stabs to Slay Toxic Dragon," *Louisville Courier-Journal,* February 15, 1981.

———. and Jim Adams. "EPA Tests Reveal Toxic PCB in Creek near 'Valley of Drums,' " *Louisville Courier-Journal,* March 20, 1979.

———. "The Barrels: A Problem that Just Won't Go Away," *Louisville Courier-Journal,* January 17, 1979.

"Distler May Face More Prosecution over Chemical Wastes," *Louisville Times,* December 5, 1980.

Dumanoski, Dianne. "Acid Rain," *Sierra,* May/June 1980.

"EPA Identifies Polluted Streams," *Ashland Daily Tidings,* July 30, 1981.

Egginton, Joyce, and Hank Morgan. "The Long Island Lesson," *Audubon,* July 1981.

Evans, Steve. "Toxics Found in California Rivers," *Homegrown,* March 1982.

Feder, Barnaby J. "Industry Seeks Entirely New Ideas on Conservation," *New York Times,* August 12, 1981.

Findley, Rowe. "The Bittersweet Waters of the Lower Colorado." *National Geographic,* October 1973.

Fischer, Hank. "Montana's Yellowstone River: Who Gets the Water?," *Sierra,* July/August 1978.

"Florida's Battle of the Swamp," *Time,* August 24, 1981.

"Great Western Drought of 1977." *Time,* March 7, 1977.

Green, Caroline. "Water Saver: Ex-Farmer is Sold on Drip Irrigation," *Ashland Daily Tidings,* October 13, 1981.

Griffin, Sean. "Unknown Chemical Spill Kills Fish in Bear Creek," *Ashland Daily Tidings,* April 30, 1981.

"Grim Future for the Water-Short West," *Business Week*, May 23, 1977.

Hanley, Robert, Diane Henry, and Deirdre Carmody. "Rainfall Alone Won't End the Region's Jitters over Drought," *New York Times*, February 15, 1981.

Hinds, Michael de Courcy. "A Lifetime's Supply of Recycled Water," *New York Times*, February 5, 1981.

"Home Systems that Purify Wastewater," *Business Week*, December 22, 1980.

"How to Ration Water: Marin County," *Newsweek*, March 21, 1977.

Howington, Patrick. "Could Our Sewers Blow Up Again? Yes, But . . . ," *Louisville Times*, March 6, 1981.

"Illegal Chemical Suspect in Louisville Sewer Blasts," *Ashland Daily Tidings*, February 13, 1981.

"Is This Drip Necessary?," *Time*, May 18, 1981.

Janson, Donald. "Cost of New Hookups Forces Some in Jersey Town to Use Toxic Water," *New York Times*, August 7, 1980.

Jeffery, David. "Arizona's Suburbs of the Sun," *National Geographic*, October 1977.

Johnson, Bob, and Stan MacDonald. "Official Says Hexane Leak Overwhelmed Ralston Plant," *Louisville Courier-Journal*, February 15, 1981.

"Key Environmental Goal for 1980's: Keeping Hazardous Wastes out of Groundwater," Special Issue, *Civil Engineering*, September 1981.

"Long Dry Winter," *Newsweek*, March 7, 1977.

Luoma, Jon R. "Troubled Skies, Troubled Waters," *Audubon*, November 1980.

Lysinger, Pat. "Deep Well People Fight for Water," *Oakley Graphic*, December 31, 1980.

"MX: The Air Force Targets the West," *Palm & Pine*, March 1981.

"Marin County: The Bucket Brigade," *Time*, February 14, 1977.

Matthews, Samuel W. "What's Happening to Our Climate?," *National Geographic*, November 1976.

Molotsky, Irvin. "House Unit to Issue List Tomorrow of Dumps Posing Threat to Water," *New York Times*, September 28, 1980.

Moody, Joan. "What HAVE We Done to the Rain?," *The Nature Conservancy News*, November/December 1980.

"More Mysteries and Perils in the Environment," *New York Times*, February 4, 1981.

"NYC Prepares for Water Crisis," *Willing Water*, February 1981.

Norris, Ruth. "Hit Lists at Interior?," *Audubon,* September 1981.

"Nuclear Plant Reports Leak," *Ashland Daily Tidings,* August 1, 1981.

"OSU Study Defines Changes in Store for Western Deserts," *Medford Mail Tribune,* June 7, 1981.

Oakes, Sarah, and Samuel H. Sage. "New York City's Hudson River Project," *Sierra,* March/April 1979.

"Officials Won't Name Spill Source," *Ashland Daily Tidings,* May 30, 1981.

"Ohio River May Be Dirty, but It's Cleaner Than It Used to Be, U of L Study Indicates," *Louisville Times,* January 2, 1981.

"Owens Valley: Fact and Fable of a Water War," *Aqueduct,* Spring 1977.

"Peninsula Water Allocation Controversial," *Ventana,* April 15, 1981.

"Pesticide May Halt Hunting Season," *Ashland Daily Tidings,* September 18, 1981.

Polsgrove, Carol. "In Hot Water: Uranium Mining and Water Pollution," *Sierra,* November/December 1980.

"Process Sapping Land Fertility," *Bonanza,* February 1981.

"Radioactivity Seeps Into Idaho Wells," *Ashland Daily Tidings,* May 22, 1981.

"Rationing Ends Cheap Water Myth," *American City and County,* May 1977.

Reisner, Marc P. "Colorado's Water Wars: Old Battles Renewed," *Denver Post,* November 4, 1979.

———. "When the Rockies Run Dry, There'll Be No More Water," *Washington Post,* December 23, 1979.

"Resource Management: Forests and Water are Interrelated," *Bioscience,* April 1979.

Richards, Allan. "Disaster at Church Rock: The Untold Story," *Sierra,* November/December 1980.

"Righting the Rivers," *Newsweek,* October 2, 1978.

Roberts, Walter Orr. "We're Doing Something About the Weather!," *National Geographic,* April 1972.

"Salt Lake County Considers Growth Moratorium," *Sierra Club Population Report,* August 1981.

"Samples Yield Low Levels of Toxic Wastes," *Ashland Daily Tidings,* March 7, 1981.

Seligman, Dan. "Water," *Pacific Northwest*, March/April 1981.

"Sewer Collapse and Toxic Illness in Sewer Repairmen—Ohio," *Morbidity and Mortality Weekly Report*, March 6, 1981.

Shaffer, David. "TMI Water Filter Nearly Ready, But Some Want to Block Use," *Easton Express*, March 1, 1981.

Smith, R. Jeffrey. "Administration Views on Acid Rain Assailed," *Science*, October 2, 1981.

Stevens, William K. "Rapid Population and Farm Growth May Strain Southwest's Water Supply," *New York Times*, August 12, 1981.

Stewart, Kay. "Indiana Tanker Spill Kills Fish," *Louisville Courier-Journal*, August 22, 1980.

Stoler, Peter. "Is Clean Water a Thing of the Past?," *Sierra*, March/April 1981.

Sullivan, Dan. "Club Faces Hard Choices on State Water Referendum," *The Yodeler*, March 1981.

"Suver Gets Clean Bill of Health," *Beyond Waste*, June 1981.

Trendler, Kathy. "Dangerous PCB Levels Found in Fish," *Homegrown*, March 1981.

Tuvel, Harry N. "Jersey Drought Hastens Water Supply Project," *Civil Engineering*, February 1981.

Vesilind, Priit J. "River with a Job to Do: The Ohio," *National Geographic*, February 1977.

Vitullo-Martin, Julia. "Ending the Southwest's Water Binge," *Fortune*, February 23, 1981.

Wallis, Claudia. "Bad News for the Birds," *Time*, October 5, 1981.

"Water Board Should Heed Study's Proposal," *Rocky Mountain News*, August 24, 1980.

"Water Curtailment Order Becomes Latest Calamity to Hit Florida," *Ashland Daily Tidings*, May 15, 1981.

Zeldin, Marvin A. "How Safe is the Water We Drink?," *National Wildlife*, May 1981.

Zonana, Victor F. "Quandary over Water—To Sell It or Not—Faces Utah Farmers at Power-Plant Town," *Wall Street Journal*, February 27, 1981.

BOOKLETS, PAMPHLETS, PAPERS, REPORTS, SPEECHES, ETC.

Alternative Budget Proposals for the Environment. Environmental Defense Fund *et al.*, March 18, 1981.

Arizona Groundwater Management Study Commission Final Report, June 1980.

California's Department of Water Resources. California Department of Water Resources, 1978.

California State Water Project, The. California Department of Water Resources, 1979.

California State Water Project, The: Current Activities and Future Management Plans. California Department of Water Resources, October 1980.

California Water Plan, The: Outlook in 1974. California Department of Water Resources, November 1974.

Clean Air Act, The: A Briefing Book for the Members of Congress. National Clean Air Coalition, July 1981.

Conservation: Practical Ideas for the Homemaker. Los Angeles Department of Water and Power, 1977.

Contamination of Ground Water by Toxic Organic Chemicals. U.S. Council on Environmental Quality, January 1981.

Cronk, Gene E. *Results of a Peak Management Plan for Tucson, Arizona* (draft version). Tucson Water Utility, 1981.

Delta Alternative Review Status (draft version). California Department of Water Resources, February 1977.

Delta Water Facilities. California Department of Water Resources, July 1978.

Denver Water Department Staff Review of "Water for Denver . . ." Denver Water Department, October 1980.

Department of Water and Power Long-Range Water Conservation Program. Los Angeles Department of Water and Power, March 8, 1981.

Dodge City Data. Dodge City (Kansas) Economic Development Department, May 1980.

Drinking Water and Cancer: Review of Recent Findings and Assessment of Risks. U.S. Council on Environmental Quality, December 1980.

Easy Ways to Save Water Money & Energy at Home. Potomac River & Trails Council, 1980.

Energy: Facing Up to the Problem, Getting Down to Solutions. A *National Geographic* Special Report, February 1981.

Environmental Defense Fund v. Douglas M. Costle: Reply Brief, U.S. Court of Appeals Docket No. 79-2432, June 30, 1980.

EPA's FY 82 Budget. Environmental Protection Agency, March 11, 1981.

Grandfathered Rights: What Are They and Who Needs Them? Arizona Department of Water Resources, 1981.

Groundwater Issues Welling Up: EPA Proposes Protection Strategy. Sierra Club, December 8, 1980.

High Plains Ogallala Aquifer Regional Study. High Plains Associates, 1978.

How Many More Lakes Have to Die? Canada Today, February 1981.

Industrial Water Allocation & Conservation in California. California Office of Emergency Services, January 1978.

Landscaping in the Desert. Tucson Planning Department, August 1979.

Lower Ground-Water Levels Projected in Western Kansas. United States Geological Survey, June 15, 1981.

Mono Lake Facts. The Mono Lake Committee, 1980.

Mono Lake Status—1980. Los Angeles Department of Water and Power, 1980.

Mono Lake Status Report. Los Angeles Department of Water and Power, December 1980.

Mono Lake: Paradise in Peril. The Mono Lake Committee, Fall 1979.

Morris, John R., and Clive V. Jones. *Water for Denver: An Analysis of the Alternatives.* Environmental Defense Fund, 1980.

Nation's Water Resources 1975–2000, The. U.S. Water Resources Council, December, 1978.

Neil, Thomas. *Incidents in the Early History of Pullman and the State College of Washington.* The Pullman *Herald,* 1922.

1980 Toxic Substances Task Force Report. Toxic Substances Task Force of Jefferson County (KY), September 24, 1980.

Owens Valley, The. Los Angeles Department of Water and Power, 1977.

Owens Valley Groundwater Conflict. William Kaufmann, Inc., 1978.

Protecting the Environment: What We're Doing about It. Chemical Manufacturers Association, 1979.

Pullman, Washington: The Artesian City. Pullman Chamber of Commerce, 1911.

PureCycle: A Water Recycle System. PureCycle Corporation, 1980(?).

Paine, Douglas. *A Technique Defining the Possible Emergence of a Major Drought Over the Eastern Half of the United States.* Cornell University, 1981.

————. *Projected Climate Trends into the 1980's*. Cornell University, 1981.

Pring, George W. *Agriculture and Instream Flows: How Montana Stacks Up with the Rest of the West*. Keynote Address, Conference on Water, Great Falls, Montana, October 11, 1980.

————, and Karen A. Tomb. *License to Waste: Legal Barriers to Conservation and Efficient Use of Water in the West*. Rocky Mountain Mineral Law Institute, 1979.

Report of Interagency Task Force on Mono Lake. California Department of Water Resources, December 1979.

Rio Puerco Tailing Pond Spill: Brief Status Report. U.S. Government Environmental Health Services Branch, August 20, 1979.

Save Water. California Department of Water Resources, 1979.

Saving Water in Landscape Irrigation. University of California Division of Agricultural Sciences, April 1977.

Stormy Weather: The National Wildlife Federation's 1981 Environmental Quality Index. National Wildlife Federation, March 1981.

Story of Water Supply, The: A Trip Behind Your Water Faucet. American Water Works Association, 1966.

Summary of Activities with Respect [TO] UNC Tailings Spill. U.S. Public Health Service, September 11, 1979.

Summary of Consultants' Findings for the New Jersey Statewide Water Supply Plan. New Jersey Division of Water Resources, June 1980.

Supplying Water for Tomorrow: Final Legislative and Program Recommendations. Temporary State Commission on the Water Supply Needs of Southeastern New York, February 15, 1975.

Test Results of the PureCycle Water Recycle System. PureCycle Corporation, June 19, 1979.

United Nuclear Corporation Dam Breakage and Spillage: Status Report. The Navajo Nation, August 2, 1979.

Warning: Toxic Waste. A Courier-Journal *Special Report*. *Louisville Courier-Journal*, December 1979.

Water and Power Conservation . . . A Way of Life. Los Angeles Department of Water and Power, 1977.

Water Crisis, The (*Nova* transcript). WGBH-TV, Boston, 1980.

Water for Tomorrow: Recommendations of the Commission. Temporary State Commission on the Water Supply Needs of Southeastern New York, 1974.

Water Quality/Water Rights. California Water Resources Control Board, 1981.

Ways for Communities Facing Drought to Reduce Water Usage Significantly at Minimal Cost Through Retrofits & Leak Repair. Environmental Policy Institute, 1980.

We're Running Out: A Special Section of Reprinted Articles. Wichita (KS) Eagle and Beacon, February 1979.

What Everyone Should Know About the Reclamation Reform Act of 1979. National Farmers' Union, August 24, 1979.

INDEX